PROCEEDINGS

Rock-cut Caves of Maharashtra

2nd Annual Archaeology of Maharashtra International Conference

in honour of Prof. Walter Spink, 14 & 15 January 2015

Centre of Archaeology, Centre for Extra-Mural Studies, University of Mumbai,

& INSTUCEN Trust, Mumbai

ISBN13: 978-81-932316-9-2

First Published 2020

Published by

India Study Centre Trust

Email:instucentrust@gmail.com

Conference Co-ordinators

Kurush F. Dalal & Suraj A. Pandit

Editors

Geri Malandra & Raamesh Gowri Raghavan

Typesetting

Raamesh Gowri Raghavan

Cover Design

Shashank Sawant

Table of Contents

Foreword 1

Arvind Jamkhedkar, Chairman, ICHR, New Delhi& Chancellor, Deccan College PGRI, Pune 1

Editorial 2

Geri Malandra, Malandra Consulting LLC, Durango 2

Keynote Address Ajanta and the Trajectory of Vakataka History 5

Prof Walter Spink, University of Michigan, Ann Arbor 5

Rock-cut Art and Architecture of the Cālukyas in Southern Deccan: Background, Chronology and Sculptural Disposition 20

Prof. Adiga Sundara, Director of Archaeology & Museums, Government of Karnataka (Retd.) . 20

Chronology of the Brāhmaṇical Caves at Shiur, District Nanded, Maharashtra: A Reappraisal 26

Vaishali M. Welankar 26

The Hiatus in Buddhist Cave Architecture in Maharashtra: Contesting Claims 40

Yashadatta Alone, Jawaharlal Nehru University, New Delhi 40

Newly Discovered Buddhist Rock-cut Caves of Maharashtra: An Appraisal 48

Shrikant Ganvir, Deccan College Post-Graduate and Research Institute, Pune 48

Origin and Development of Rock-cut Architecture of Vidarbha (Maharashtra) 60

Ganpatrao K. Mane, Amravati University, Amravati 60

Buddhist Rock-cut Caves: The Hinayāna— Mahāyāna Transition 70

Late M K Dhavalikar 70

Buddhist caves at Nasik: An Analytical Study 79

Manjiri Bhalerao, Tilak Maharashtra Vidyapith, Pune 79

Patterns of Patronage in the Jaina Caves of Maharashtra 89

Viraj Shah 89

संघंशरणंगच्छामि:Understanding the Role and Control of Monastery through the Inscriptions in the Buddhist Cave Temples of Maharashtra 103

Abhijit Dandekar, Deccan College Post-Graduate and Research Institute, Pune 103

Early Historic Caves of Maharashtra and Sātavāhana Patronage: A Case Study 107

Smita Haldar, University of Calcutta, Kolkata 107

Later Brāhmaṇical Caves of Maharashtra 148

Arvind Jamkhedkar, Chairman, ICHR, New Delhi & Chancellor, Deccan College PGRI, Pune 148

Mahāyāna Buddhism and Esoteric Practices: Kanheri A Case Study 155

Suraj A Pandit, Sathaye College, Mumbai 155

From Caves to Forts: Transformation witnessed at Daulatabad 162

Tejas Garge, Director of Archaeology & Museums, Government of Maharashtra 162

The "*Ajantacarita*": The Legacy and Future of Walter Spink 176

Geri Malandra, Malandra Consulting LLC, Durango 176

Foreword

Arvind Jamkhedkar, Chairman, ICHR, New Delhi & Chancellor, Deccan College PGRI, Pune

The Rock-cut caves of India have been an object of curiosity and study for European travellers for more than three centuries, but the studies were put on a rational and systematic footing by the joint efforts of James Fergusson and James Burgess. The net result of their inquiry was put before the world of scholars in the form of their joint publication 'Cave Temples of India' in 1888, though the initial writings of Fergusson go as far back as 1840, which were presented in the form of research papers read before learned gatherings. The results of the study have stood the test of time, as the chronological framework that was arrived at remains more or less unaffected. Though this was mainly a study of rock-cut caves as a form of architecture, Fergusson developed a methodology the aid of which made the study more precise. The ethnography, historical and religious traditions, and the historical chronology were also taken into consideration. The section of their work on the Buddhist Caves of Western India thus became a great help towards understanding the one thousand years of Buddhist architecture in India as a whole, as the counterparts in other parts of India had perished long back because of use of timber and bricks, which was the most common material used for construction in Early and Early Medieval times, in India.

There are a fairly good number of cave sites in the Deccan, like Karhāḍ, Kanheri, Junnar and Nasik that deserved a detailed study, which in turn would have refined the chronology established by Fergusson and Burgess, but Ajanta offered a special challenge because of the richness and variety of architecture and sculpture and the unique paintings that embellished the walls of the Vihāras there. The group of caves, of both the phases together, also covered a span of more than seven hundred years and the sculpture of the second phase was very much akin to that of the Gupta period. Professor Spink studied the thirty caves at the site with new tools of inquiry to discern the relative chronology of the caves of the two phases, and the chronology within individual caves. He thus was able to practically give a complete history of each of the caves at Ajanta. His endeavours thus established what is generally known as the 'Shorter Chronology' at Ajanta. His comparative studies of the rock-cut and dry masonry architecture of the Deccan enabled him to revise its chronology and the interrelationship between the Vākāṭaka, Cālukya and the Rāṣṭrakūṭa phases of architecture.

Professor Spink's work mainly on the rock-cut architecture of the Deccan and specifically that on Ajanta, has been a subject of debate, but it has also simultaneously inspired a number of young scholars to take up afresh work on a number of other individual sites like Junnar, Kanheri, Dharashiv, Nasik and Pitalkhora, especially regarding related problems like the Late Hinayāna caves and the architecture and sculpture of the Vākaṭakas of the Nandivardhana branch in eastern Vidarbha.

In view of the above, it was thought worthwhile by the Centre for Archaeology, Centre for Extra-Mural Studies, University of Mumbai to hold an International Conference on the subject, with a view also to felicitate Professor Spink, as he on the verge completing the publication of a series of volumes on Ajanta.

Editorial

Geri Malandra, Malandra Consulting LLC, Durango

In January 2015, the Centre for Archaeology, Centre for Extra-Mural Studies, University of Mumbai convened a remarkable seminar on the rock-cut caves of Maharashtra. As intended, this gathering felicitated the enormous scope and impact of dear Walter Spink's life work on Ajanta -- "one of the greatest creative achievements of the world." But it did much more. Like Professor Spink's scholarship which is ongoing, the papers published here demonstrate the range and excitement of current rock-cut cave studies. Our material may be ancient, but today's scholars continue to discover new material and provide new interpretations.

As Dr. Jamkhedkar explains in his Foreword, since the 1880s, this work has depended on scrupulously detailed field observations, comparison with known religious and historical documents, ethnography, and more. While the basic sequence of rock-cut cave development was discovered by Fergusson and Burgess, Dr. Spink and others have provided countless corrections and amplifications to the basic question "when did the caves develop?" What he found challenged traditional Euro-centric and Ganges-centric history and assumptions about the pace of ancient site development.

Of course, "when?" is just one part of the puzzle. Dr. Spink has also pioneered the use of finely detailed field observation combined with deep reading of epigraphs and historical texts, to work out "who" constructed the Ajanta caves, and "why?" For many of the rock-cut sites beyond Ajanta, knowledge of historical and religious background is essential. But he has validated the unique role of archaeology and art history to connect and explain not just monuments, but cycles of economics, politics, and religion.

Ultimately, these papers demonstrate that the sites themselves are often the most compelling "texts" about themselves. These studies can greatly amplify and deepen our knowledge of the history and culture, continuity and innovation in ancient Maharashtra. In the "Spink tradition," the scholars at the seminar challenged many aspects of rock-cut studies:

- Reappraising chronologies: Prof. Alone questioned what the concept of "hiatus" meant at Ajanta; Dr. Bhalerao re-analyzed Nasik's developmental sequence and meaning; Dr. Jamkhedkar refuted previous assumptions about the sequence of the later Brahmanical caves.
- Sectarian transitions and implications for timelines: Dr. Dhavalikar reappraised assumptions and data about Ajanta's Hinayana/Mahayana transition, refuting Schlingloff's conclusions about dates and sequence.
- Patronage and use of caves: Dr. Shah described in detail the patterns of patronage of the Jain caves; Prof. Dandekar used inscriptional evidence to query what Buddhist people – not just the rulers/patrons actually did; Prof. Haldar outlined a comprehensive compilation of patterns of Satavahana-period donations; Dr. Pandit used archaeological, art historical, and textual evidence to decode how Kanheri used by Mahayana and esoteric Buddhist sects.
- Technological innovation and continuity, regional distinctiveness and interaction: Prof. Sundara clarified the sequence and antecedents of Calukya sites and sculpture; Dr. Mane demonstrated the very ancient megalithic antecedents of Vidarbha's rock-cut tradition; Dr. Garge shed light on the roots of Daulatabad fort's excavation in much earlier rock-cut techniques.
- More recent discoveries: Dr. Welankar reappraised the sequence of Brahmanical caves at Shiur; Prof. Ganvir illustrated how there is more to know but documenting the many rock cut caves discovered over the past six decades.

The seminar conveners assembled a unique group of scholars whose papers cover an extraordinary range of topics tracing Maharashtra's rock-cut tradition and techniques, from prehistoric megalithic culture to its latest expression in the great Daulatabad fort complex.

2nd Annual Archaeology of Maharashtra International Conference

This volume, published by the India Study Centre Trust, certainly does great honor to Dr. Spink's legacy. At the same time, it also provides a most valuable, detailed portrait – one that cannot be found in one place elsewhere – of the discoveries, studies, and meaning of rock-cut sites across the state.

14 January 2015

10.00am	Welcome Address	Mugdha D. Karnik, Director, CEMS
10.30am	Introductory Address	Arvind P Jamkhedkar
11.30am	Keynote Address	Walter Spink
2.30pm	Adiga Sundara	Chronology of Brāhmaṇical Caves in Karnataka vis-à-vis Maharashtra
3.00pm	Vaishali Welankar	Chronology of Brāhmaṇical Caves in Maharashtra
3.30pm	Yashadatta Alone	Chronology of Late Buddhist Caves in Maharashtra
4.30pm	M.S. Nagaraju	The Early Buddhist Caves of Maharashtra and their Architecture
5.00pm	Shrikant Ganvir	The Early Caves in Vidarbha
5.30pm	Ganpatrao K. Mane	Brāhmaṇical Caves of Vidarbha
6:00pm	Geri Malandra	Session 4: Tête-à-Tête with Prof Spink

15 January 2015

10.00am	M K Dhavalikar	Early Mahāyāna Caves in Maharashtra
10.30am	Manjiri Bhalerao	The Caves at Nasik
11.00am	D. Daylen	Early Buddhist Caves in the Āndhradēśa
11.45pm	Leela Wood	Royal Themes in Ajanta Paintings
12.15pm	Shrikant Pradhan	The Painting Styles of Ajanta and Nāgārjunakoṇḍa
12.45pm	Anura Manatunga	Art: From Ajanta to Sigiriya
2.30pm	Viraj Shah	Jaina Patronage/Patronage of Jaina Caves in Maharashtra
3.00pm	Jayaram Poduval	Patronage of Brāhmaṇical Caves in Maharashtra
3.30pm	Abhijit Dandekar	From Patronage to Patronisation: Sanghaṃ Śaraṇaṃ Gacchāmi
4:00pm	Smita Haldar	Sātavāhana Patronage of Buddhist Caves
4:45pm	Arvind P Jamkhedkar	Late Brāhmaṇical Caves
5:15pm	Suraj A Pandit	Late Buddhist Caves
6:15pm	Tejas Garge	From Caves to Forts
6:30pm	Valedictory Address	Geri Malandra
7:30pm	Comments	M K Dhavalikar
7:45	Vote of Thanks	Kurush F Dalal

Keynote Address
Ajanta and the Trajectory of Vakataka History

Prof Walter Spink, University of Michigan, Ann Arbor

In circa 462, very shortly after the Vākāṭaka Hariśēna had become emperor, a host of eager workers, coming from many different parts of what is now called Maharashtra, and armed with little more than their chisels and their hammers, arrived at Ajanta's deep ravine (Fig. 1). Their goal—or rather the goal of their rich and courtly patrons—was to renew the famous old Buddhist site—to bring it up to date (Fig. 2). Working for less than two decades—really for more like a total of fourteen years—they struggled to develop a gathering of caves that, in terms of quality and quantity, to say nothing of speed, turned out to be—even if it was never finished—one of the greatest creative achievements of the world.

This great project, which was certainly allowed, and supported by the new emperor himself, probably owes its inception to two powerful courtiers. One was Hariśēna's Prime Minister, Varāhadēva, donor of Cave 16 (Fig 3). The other was the local king of the Ajanta region, Upēndragupta, who sponsored the adjacent Cave 17, as well as the splendid caitya hall, Cave 19 and the adjacent Cave 20. Not surprisingly, they chose to put their caves at the very centre of the ravine—reflecting their own central importance--where they could dominate the now rapidly growing community of caves from the start.

The Prime Minister, quite appropriately, also created the great Elephant Gate, by which all visitors, in those old days, entered the site, first paying homage to the beautiful Nāgarāja that you must honour and reverence as you climb up through the steep passageway, tunnelled through the black basaltic rock, to the impressive cave above. Varāhadēva's ministerial excavation now has an impressive Buddha inside; but at first both this cave and the adjacent Cave 17 were planned as nothing more than simple viharas—mere dormitories for the monks—as in the earlier Hinayana Cave 12. These first Vākāṭaka viharas were considerably simpler

conceptions than what they became a half-decade later (about 468). At that point it was decided to add a shrine at the rear, where Buddha himself would take up residence as a living presence. It was only then—when the cave became conceived as a shrine, not as a mere dormitory, that Varāhadēva, in his inscription, describes it as adorned with "beautiful picture galleries, statues of the nymphs of Indra and the like", and "clothed in the radiance of Indra's crown".[1] Such splendid decoration was obviously added for the Buddha—and of course for the eager patrons—rather than for the simple monks.

Varāhadēva, who, as prime minister surely had much to do besides making this great cave, describes himself "as extremely devoted to the Buddha, regarding the sacred law as his (only) companion". And given his high position as Prime Minister, we can be sure that he had access to the imperial exchequer. He even declares that it was Varāhadēva himself, and not his emperor Hariśēna, who "governed the country righteously, shining with the rays of his fame, religious merit and virtue".

But if Varāhadēva was the staid and solid bureaucrat, the local king, Upēndragupta, was quite different, spending his seemingly abundant resources to "adorn the world with stupas and viharas", "causing the joy of supplicants" by giving them lavish gifts , and "expending abundant wealth" to create offerings for the Buddha "which cannot even be imagined by little souled men."[2] (Figs. 4, 5). However, his exuberant lavishness may have been misspent, for he was soon going to have to face political realities for which he was ill-prepared. It would have been better to put his lavish funds into securing his region's safety—by amassing guns and tanks, rather than ordering halls filled with beautiful paintings, and covering the earth with stupas and viharas!

The problem that soon arose to disturb the productive peace of the site's opening years, was to

---

[1] From the Cave 16 inscription. Mirashi's translation of 1963 is reproduced in W. Spink, *Ajanta: History and Development*, Volume 1 (2005), 412-415.
[2] From the Cave 17 inscription. Mirashi's translation of 1963 is reproduced in W. *Spink, Ajanta: History and Development*, Volume 1 (2005), 414-418.

come from the large and powerful adjacent territory, where the neighbours, at least in the eyes of the other more devoted Vākāṭaka patrons had a reputation for aggression. These were the Aśmakas, ruling over the adjacent Aurangabad region. Like Upēndragupta and the residents of Riśika, they were also feudatories of Hariśēna; but ominous ones!!

Figure 1: Ajanta: Site from Viewpoint.

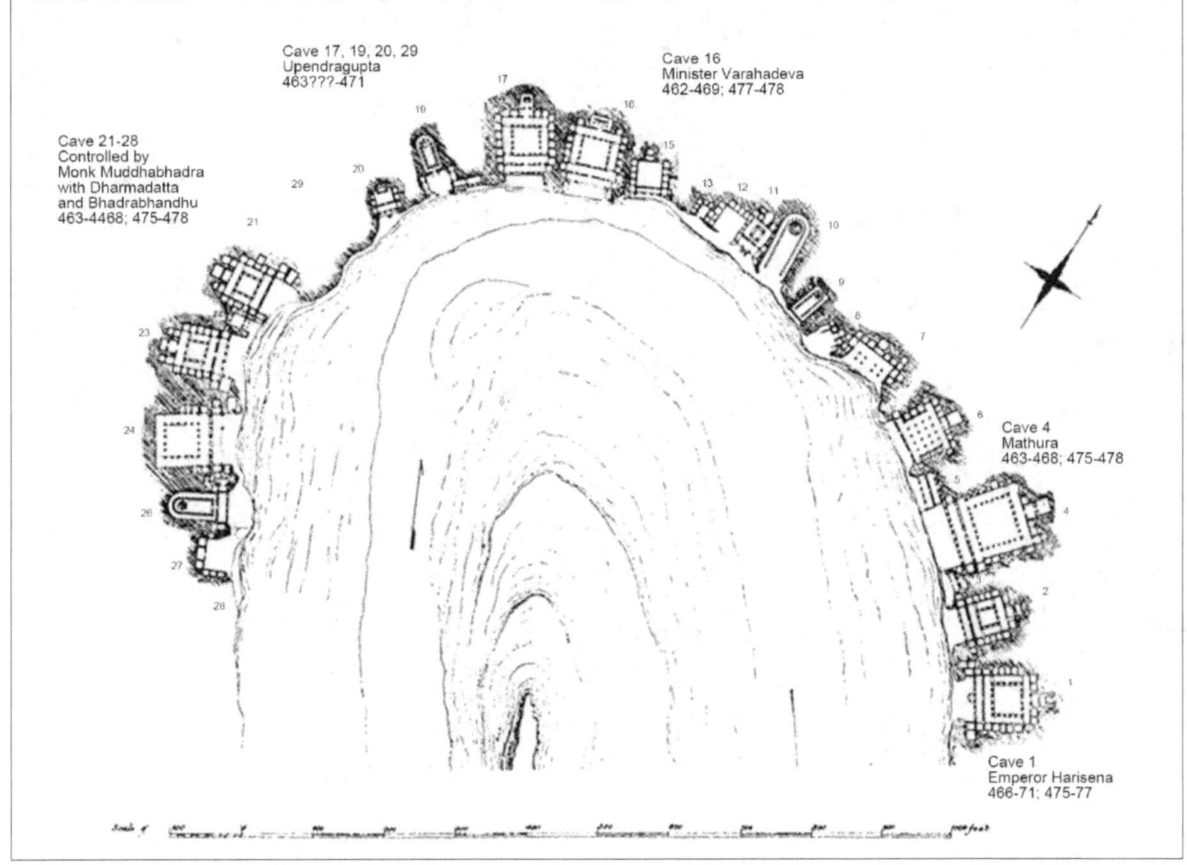

Figure 2: Ajanta: Site plan with patrons.

Figure 3: Ajanta: Cave 16 Interior from front right 462-478.

Figure 4: Ajanta: Cave 19 Façade 462-471; intrusions at sides.

The Aśmakas had also been involved with the new developments at Ajanta from the start, guided by the powerful monk, Buddhabhadra. (Fig 6). If we ask where the money for his expansive undertakings came from, Buddhabhadra suggests the source in his dedicatory inscription for Cave 26: he proudly claims that he has been the friend of the minister of

Figure 5: Ajanta: Cave 19 Yakṣa at left of arch c. 467.

Aśmaka "through many successive births"[3]. They had been recycled together through their earlier lives!! With this significant and necessary support, Buddhabhadra took over the whole western extremity of the site as the Aśmaka's own, creating the great Cave 26, a caitya hall with four attached wings, that in its size and ambitiousness immediately outdid the offerings of the local king.

Indeed, this whole magnificent Cave 26 complex is suggestive of the Aśmaka's ominous power—power that ultimately would be used to destroy the empire. But at the start, for the first half-dozen years (462-468), peace reigned over the region and the site. In fact, in this happy context, the whole ravine began to rapidly fill up from the start. It is clear, of course, that the site could not have flourished, as it so clearly did in these early years, without peace in the various realms that comprised Hariśēna's inheritance— western Vidarbha, Anūpa (lying to the northwest, Riśika (the Ajanta region) and Aśmaka (the region around present-day Aurangabad).

So, for the first half decade of Ajanta's urgent development—up until about 468, with more than a dozen rich and eager patrons involved, the site's rapid development went happily and peacefully. Obviously, everyone –patrons, planners, artists and excavators—in these early days, were vigorously aiming to outdo both their rivals and, indeed, themselves.

Figure 6: Ajanta: Aśmaka complex at western end of site

---

[3]From the Cave 26 inscription. Chhabra's translation of 1955 is reproduced in W. Spink, *Ajanta: History and Development,* Volume 1 (2005), 419-420.

But this could not last. In 468, with little or no warning, Upēndragupta, the local king, suddenly expelled the powerful Aśmakas from the site, while their great caitya hall complex was still very much in process. The fact that Upēndragupta did not even allow the Aśmakas time to finish the shrine Buddha images that were already underway, and the fact that he stopped work on all caves except for the four "royal caves"—his own Caves 17, 19, and 20, and the emperor's Cave 1—suggests the level of his concern[4]. The "abundant wealth" that he had been using so lavishly "to cover the world with stupas and viharas", now obviously—even if too late! —had to be used for arming his endangered territory.

Although Upēndragupta had co-opted many of the most experienced and skilled workmen at the site to continue developing his "almost measureless" halls, "which could not even be imagined by little-souled men", he was obviously worried about the Aśmaka's plans. As time went on, signs of haste appear in the work of decorating the caves, and finally, as the

Aśmaka threat mounted, he ordered all of his donations to be finished in a rather sudden rush (Fig 7). Or he just suddenly abandoned certain developments, like his new (and second) chaitya hall—Cave 29—that he had just started up on the hill above. Nonetheless, even as his concerns increased, Upēndragupta gave very special attention to his beautiful caitya hall, Cave 19, the intended ceremonial centre of the site, carefully attending to its splendid design and the beauty of its rich overlay of brilliantly conceived and sacred features.

However, even though he was so urgently attempting to get his hall fully completed, he did not have time to properly complete what was obviously going to be the lengthiest and most richly laudatory dedication at the site. A very spacious panel had been prepared for it, over the door of the hall. However, it seems likely that the Brahmins in the capital had not had time to compose it or for the local engravers to get it appropriately incised, before 472, when the powerful Aśmakas, seeking revenge for their earlier

Figure 7: Ajanta: Cave 26 Mara's attack, upper left 477-478.

---

[4]Upēndragupta did allow the donors of the images in Caves 6L, 7, 11, and 15 to rush their shrine images (but nothing else) to completion in early 469. Al so Buddhabhadra continued hurried work on his Cave 16 throughout 469, but made no attempt to continue it later, until at least 476 or 477, when the site was under Aśmaka control.

expulsion, now returned in force. Besides rapidly taking up work again on their own complex, perhaps to further establish their new authority, they now allowed the various other donors at the site—but with the notable (and expected) exception of Upēndragupta—to continue work on their own caves once again.

It is clear that the Aśmakas, although still feudatories of their overlord, Hariśēna, were now effectively in control of the site. And it is equally clear that Upēndragupta, who had just summarily rushed his caves to completion, had now himself been expelled from it. Indeed, the first thing that the Aśmakas had done, in taking over control of Ajanta, was to lock the doors (as it were) of Upēndragupta's splendid caitya hall, disallowing any worship there at all! In fact, this is why it shows no evidence at all of the grime from the oil lamps which would have been used in worship—so it is remarkably clean today! And another thing that the Aśmakas did was to heedlessly and insultingly cut a path right through two of Cave 19's court cells, to make a convenient access to the own great cave complex beyond to the west.

Even though the Aśmaka's self-seeking interests would soon be manifest, under their strong new authority Ajanta now flourished as never before. The technical skills and the high standards that the planners of Upēndragupta's caves, and even more perhaps of Hariśēna's 'imperial Cave 1, had developed, were now widely available to all, while the growing fame of the site must have attracted increasing numbers of workmen, eager for work and

for recognition. For we are now, at Ajanta, moving toward the very apogee of India's "Golden Age" during the rule of the great emperor Hariśēna. This apogee, defined, as it were, by the very moment of Ajanta's final and greatest flourishing in 477, was fragile, however. For after 477—that is, after Hariśēna, who had held everything together, disappeared from the scene—Central India was about to enter a long and deep dark age.

The qualities of art and culture in the Golden Age, as it moved toward this fragile apogee, is expressed best of all in the beautiful Cave 1, which probably benefited from the fact that it was not started until about six years after the site's inauguration. (Fig 8) This may have been because Hariśēna was a Hindu rather than a Buddhist. And although religious attitudes in those days were very ecumenical, that may still have already caused some delay to his own personal involvement.

In fact, this delay meant that he now had to locate his cave at the extreme eastern end of the site, because by then all of the other areas of the scarp had been taken, so rapidly did Ajanta fill up. And just to get back deep enough in the cliff to excavate the large porch and hall, the planners had to lay out a huge courtyard. This may have seemed desirable for ceremonial purposes, but it also collected debris over many centuries, and this debris built up so deeply inside the cave that it gradually reached a depth of four or five feet, even deep in the rear aisle of the cave. The legs of the great bodhisattvas in the rear aisle have been lost up to thigh level because of

Figure 8: Ajanta: Cave 1 Façade 466-477.

Figure 9: Ajanta: Cave 1 rear aisle from left 466-477.

this deadly contact with deepening debris (Fig 9).

As the most splendid and at the same time dignified vihara in India, Cave 1, in every way proclaims its imperial origins. It is the only vihara at the site with a lavishly decorated façade—it various motifs—depictions of the hunt, of battle, and of erotic dalliance—all prerogatives, indeed the duties, of kingship (Fig. 10). And this same appropriate royal focus is revealed in the hall's splendid wall paintings in the interior—again all tellingly focused on the theme of kingship. Even in the *Jātaka* tales where serpents are the central figures, the serpents are shown are serpent kings.

And in their beauty and variety—at least a dozen different artists worked on the beautiful murals—

Figure 10: Ajanta: Cave 1 façade, detail of hunt c.469.

Figure 11: Ajanta: Cave 1 interior ceiling detail c. 476.

Figure 12: Ajanta: Cave 1 interior, view to front left.

these murals, and the startlingly splendid ceiling, were all apparently being rushed to get the decoration of the cave completed in time for the expected dedication ceremonies. (Fig 11) For this reason, all can be dated to 476 and 477, although there are a few unfinished scenes that are still incomplete. In any case, these splendid murals, filling the hall with edifying stories of kings, were flourishing just as time was running out. (Fig 12) Unfortunately, however, although they represent the highpoint of the painted decoration at the site, they were underway too late to have any very significant impact on other caves, for after Hariśēna's sudden death in 477, no other murals of this type were ever done. (Fig 13) The site had already started its dramatic decline, fomented by the powerful Aśmaka feudatories.

Figure 13: Ajanta: Cave 1 interior, right rear wall, Vajrapāṇi.

But if we can credit Daṇḍin's assertion that "numerous retainers and spies in various disguises" sent by the Aśmakas were now working nefariously at the Vākāṭaka court, while the great Hariśēna was still ruling and holding his vast empire together, we can perhaps lay the blame for the great emperor's sudden death (he was in his early fifties at the time)

at the Aśmaka's door. Daṇḍin tells us little about this, except to describe the vigour of Hariśēna's rule and to blame his mysterious death as "owing to the want of religious merit on the part of his subjects". But Hariśēna's death certainly was not due to natural causes and a slow decline—diabetes or tuberculosis or cancer—for if this had been the case, he could have rushed his great Cave 1, unfinished or not, to a hasty dedication. It was only then that he could obtain the merit from his pious donation, merit that he could not receive as long as the ceremonies had not been performed. My own belief, necessarily cautious, is that he was assassinated—perhaps by poison or the knife—by the Aśmakas who had infiltrated his court.

But even as dark intrigues had been going on at the Vākāṭaka court, Ajanta, as if unaware of the dangers developing at the heart of the empire, was flourishing. The world, while Hariśēna was still alive, was one of a radiant optimism that is reflected in every form. And this, all believed, was surely going to go on into a continually happy future, supported by the strength of the great empire that Hariśēna had put together. When the Prime Minister Varāhadēva, inscribed his great Cave 16 in 477, with Hariśēna at the height of his power, he publicly described Hariśēna's political might, whether achieved by inheritance, or marriage arrangements, or war, or intrigue[5]. He announced, for all to see, at the very entrance to the site, that the emperor "controlled" or "stood over" "Kuntala, Avanti, Kalinga, Kosala, Trikuṭa, Lata, Andhra and even Aparānta"[6]. The latter name, damaged in the record, has been reconstructed by Dr. S. Gokhale.[7] And to these later holdings we must of course add the regions that Hariśēna inherited when he succeeded his father Dēvasēna in about 460. These latter important central areas were western Vidarbha, Anūpa (lying to the northwest), Riśika (the Ajanta region) and Aśmaka—the region around present-day Aurangabad. It was by extending his area of control outward, from this original base that by the end of his reign, Hariśēna had extended his original base in Central India from the western to the eastern sea (Fig 14).

But in the following year—478—when the news of

---

[5] It should be noted that since these holdings included eastern provinces previously held by the so-called "Main Branch" of the Vakataka house. Since they had been taken over by Hariśēna by the time that Varāhadēva's inscription was written (477), there is no justification to the common assertion that the so-called "Main Branch" continued into the early decades of the sixth century.

[6] H. Bakker prefers "stood over", but this has the same general meaning as the more common suggestion: "controlled" for the term missing in the record.

[7] S. Gokhale, 1992, 269-278

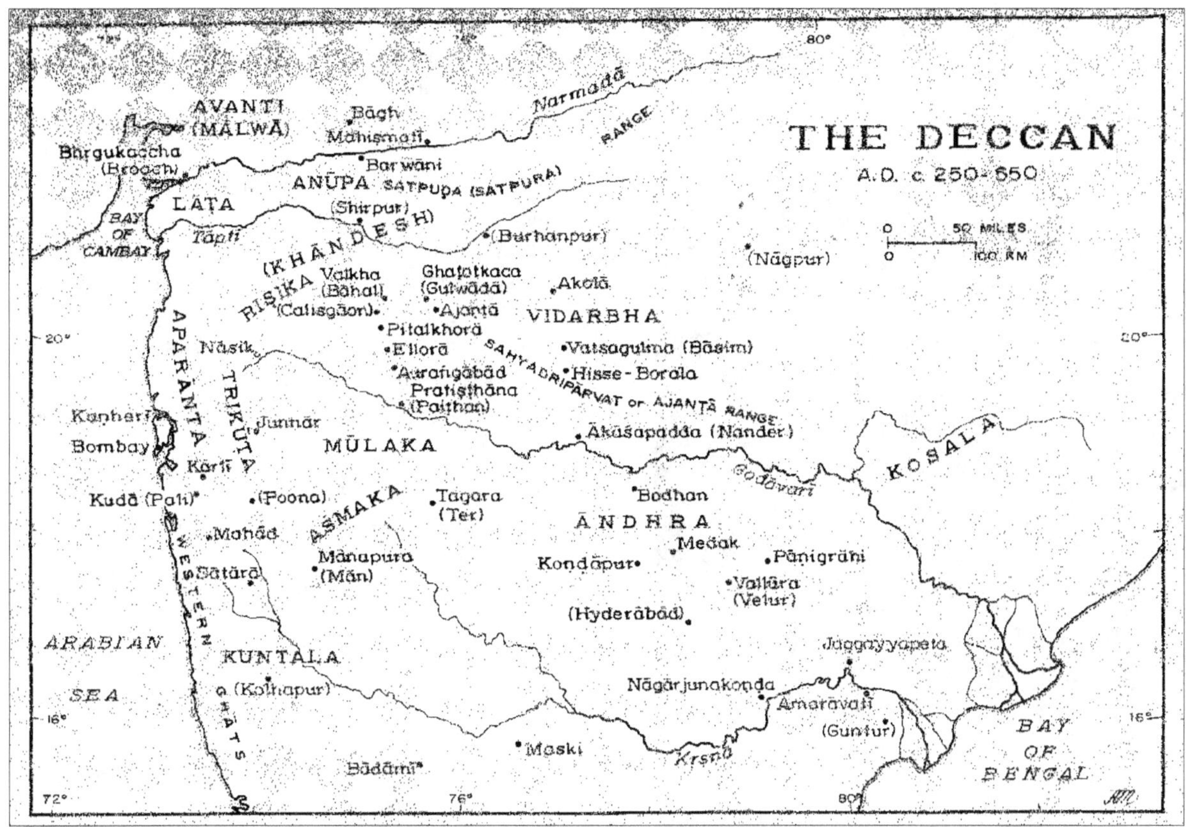

Figure 14: Map of the Deccan (from Weiner)

the great emperor's sudden death reached the site, the exuberance of Ajanta's last happy days, suddenly turn to chaos, as fears that the aggressive Aśmakas, who had in effect taken over the site, were surely intending to take over the empire too from Hariśēna's weak successor, Sarvasēna III. Indeed, it was only too soon that most of the many feudatory powers that Hariśēna had added to his empire now became part of the Aśmaka's military and political coalition. And finally, when Sarvasēna III, in the troubled context of the early 480s, saw the border of his kingdom invaded, he hastily mobilized his own forces to engage the coalition in battle. But being outnumbered and outmanoeuvred, he "became mincemeat" (Ryder) on the field of battle[8]. Or, as Kale translates it more soberly: "he fell a prey to those princes—as he was totally averse to the science of politics"[9].

But by 478, reacting to the harsh realities of Hariśēna 's passing, Ajanta was already in collapse. All of the previously powerful and established Vākāṭaka courtiers had by now, suddenly, gone into a frenzy, aiming to rush their shrines and most especially their Buddha images to completion. For it is clear that only if the shrine image was dedicated could the donor receive the spiritual benefit from his donation. No matter how much elaborate work of excavation and decoration had been done in a cave, if the shrine image did not get completed and dedicated, the cave was dead.

So, in 478, starting immediately after the emperor's death was known, all of the Vākāṭaka patrons, who had been working along on their caves at a slower pace, making sure that the work was being well done, suddenly dropped everything else, and told the workers to get the shrine images completed.

Cave 4 can serve as a typical example of how attitudes and indeed the images that reveal them changed from the happy and confident context of 477, while Hariśēna was still so powerfully ruling, to the desperate context of religious concern as the world was so suddenly falling apart in 478, after the emperor's unexpected tragic death.

In 477, the carving of Cave 4's powerful Buddha image was just nearing completion, and now, for the first time, six powerful images—the Six Buddhas of the past—were being made to complement the image of Śākyamuni in the shrine (Fig 15).

---

[8] A. Ryder, The Tale of the Ten Princes, 1927, 215. Ryder's translation is, in general, less precise than Kale's.

[9] M R Kale, Daṇḍin's Daśakumāracarita: in Spink, *Ajanta: History and Development,* Volume I, 405

Figure 15: Ajanta: Cave 4 shrine antechamber Buddhas 477-478

A richly decorated shrine doorway was also planned, with traditional representations of loving couples and exuberant floral decorations. But suddenly all these long honoured exuberant forms were replaced with Buddhas, Buddhas, Buddhas, to complement the image in the shrine. At the same time, the Buddha image itself was now being hurriedly painted, in 478, in preparation for the consecration ceremonies that were essential if the image was going to be brought to life and if the patron, who would have paid for it all exclusively himself, was going to get the credit—the spiritual benefit. As for the six wonderful standing Buddhas in the shrine antechamber, only the two that flank the shrine doorway were rushed to completion. The other four remain as instructive examples of work in progress. Even the shrine was not properly finished; its walls did not even get plastered, so say nothing of being painted. But the important thing for the patron was that, despite this necessary rush, the image was brought to life, before the patron himself fled from the site, after ordering a hasty dedicatory inscription cut roughly into the image's base.

Although only seven shrines or shrine images had been finished in all of the years prior to 478[10], But now, suddenly, no less than twelve (both new and old) were rushed to completion, like that in Cave 4, in a few months in 478, so great was the concern of the patrons about Ajanta's (and perhaps their own) uncertain but ominous future[11]. And even the Aśmaka caves were now shutting down, as both workers and the previously lavish funds were sent off in preparation now not for worship but for war. And by cruel chance this was very moment that the great Cave 26 was being finished, and that the sculptors had just reached new heights in their work (Fig 16).

This is the moment, in 477 and 478 that Buddhabhadra's artists had created the amazing Dying Buddha and the equally impressive Temptation of the Buddha, and about to start other ambulatory images of equal splendour, had not the sounds of war, or the preparations for war, put a stop to the completion of their dreams.

The earlier –Hinayana—caves at the site, excavated some 2000 years before, were clearly community offerings—inscribed on the front of the cave, "the gift of the façade by Katahadi"; and inside, "the gift of a wall", and so forth. But in the site's Vākāṭaka phase, every cave was a private offering. If you could finish it—or at least get the shrine Buddha done and dedicated—you alone would get the spiritual benefit; and if you could not finish it yourself, it seems likely that no one else would or could do it for you.[12] So this was another reason for the rush in 478. By the end of that frenetic year all of the original patrons, even in the Aśmaka caves, were gone, leaving their unfinished caves behind.

Now suddenly, the old rules—that kept the caves as such exclusive, personal, dedications--were gone, and the earlier administrative controls on the site no longer applied. Now, finally, in 479 and 480—while the site was still surviving, even if the world was changing for the worse, a host of new and "intrusive" donors—the monks still living in the caves (where else could they go?) and the local villagers, took over the site, to make their own offerings, using the many hungry painters and

---

[10]The shrine images in 6L, 7, 11, 15 were all being rushed toward completion in early 469. Upēndragupta's shrine images in Caves 17, 19, and 20 were all rushed to completion and dedication in 471

[11]The shrine images in the following caves were rushed to completion and dedication in 478:
Caves 2, 4, 8?, 16, 21, 22, 26, 27?, 26 Right Wing, 26 Left Wing; furthermore the earlier shrine images in Caves 7, 11, 15 were re-worked in 478. The shrine images in Aurangabad Cave 3 and 4A were completed by the Aśmakas in about 480.

[12] Apparently, once you had dedicated the shrine image and gained the merit, you could then share the benefits widely: typically for one's "mother and father", and even for "the whole world". "May this Hall, out of affection.....cause the attainment of well-being by good people as long as the sun dispels darkness by its rays! (verse 29, Cave 17 inscription)

Figure 16: Ajanta: Cave 26, interior: left with Parinirvana 477-478.

sculptors still in the area; and making the merit for themselves.

Neither the local villagers nor the monks had ever the right to make any offerings in the caves before, and now they were making up for it with their helter-skelter votive offerings. (Fig 17) Now they could put their new Buddha images anywhere, inside or outside the caves. But there was one proviso. Such new votive offerings could only be put in or on caves that were already dedicated—that were, therefore, alive. Indeed, every cave at Ajanta with a dedicated shrine image, has numerous intrusions in it. But if a particular cave was lacking an image (and was obviously not sanctified), no one would add their intrusive image to it, no matter how much space was available. Because such caves were dead!

This is why the emperor Hariśēna's Cave 1—even though it is the most splendid vihara in India—is dead. Despite its importance and its beauty, it attracted no intrusions. Nor would we expect that it would have them. And it is lacking something else that proves that it is ritually dead. Look at the ceiling of the shrine antechamber. It has not a trace of the grime that in any actively used cave darkened the ceilings and walls and images. Nor was a garland ever hung from the hook (now missing) at the centre;

so it shows none of the damage caused by constantly putting up and taking down garlands, as so clearly happened in Cave 2, with was very much alive. Nor does Cave 1 have a praśasti—an inscription praising both the donor and his offering. Because, as seems clear, Hariśēna's death was both sudden and unexpected, and there was no time for the Brahmins in the court to compose the dedicatory inscription or to hold the requisite ceremonies. In fact, Cave 1, the most beautiful vihara in India, was never brought to life! The handsome image is just a piece of stone.

The greatest patron who fled from Ajanta in the turbulence of 478 was none other than Hariśēna's pious prime minister, Varāhadēva. In 478 he too had to rush to get his new and revolutionary Cave 16 Buddha image done in time. But now he also had another task. With the great Vākāṭaka empire now in dire jeopardy, it fell to him, as Daṇḍin tells us, to take Sarvasēna's queen and her two young children, to the supposed safety of Mahiṣmati (in Anūpa), where Sarvasēna's brother was the Vākāṭaka viceroy, who they assumed (as it turned out, only too wrongly) would protect them. And since the old Prime Minister Varāhadēva died on the way of a "raging fever", their real protector, according to Daṇḍin, turned out to an adventurous Gupta prince from Magadha, named Viśruta. This wily young

Figure 17: Ajanta: Cave 26, interior, right wall; intrusions 479-480

hero, Viśruta, rapidly came to act as regent to the young Vākāṭaka heir, and at the same time, was engaged to marry the young granddaughter, just when the story, fulsomely describing Viśruta's many virtues, abruptly ends.

Since Daṇḍin only hints at Viśruta's future, this leaves scholars to figure out from other sources that the wily and noble Viśruta was in fact Subandhu, the famous founder (many scholars think) of what later is known as the Early Kalacūri dynasty. Indeed, was it not the case that that dynasty—the Early Kalacūri-- was originally built upon the proud but eroding foundation that Viśruta/Subandhu's close connections with the declining Vākāṭaka house supplied. It was he, of course, who in his Barwani inscription of 486, gave funds to support the long-established sangha at Bagh and "to repair the rent and broken portions of the vihara"[13]. At both of these closely contemporary Ajanta caves work broke off, as we can well understand, when the stability of the soon to be doomed empire was shattered by Hariśēna's untimely death at the end of 477[14]. Already in 478, when at Ajanta the frantic Vākāṭaka patrons were rushing to complete their shrine images, do the required rituals, and receive the eternal credit for their offering, for Central India was now entering a dark age, both politically and culturally. From the last two decades of the fifth century into the start of the sixth, few great deeds were done or monuments built, while Central India was slowly recovering from tragic loss of the great emperor Hariśēna. But beyond that is a period of remarkable renewal, when many of the monuments that we traditionally call post-Gupta—but properly

---

[13] Spink Walter, Ajanta: History and Development, Volume 7 Bagh, Dandin, Cells and Cell Doorways, BRILL, p. 34

[14] It is significant that whereas Ajanta goes into turmoil, with its Period of Disruption, at the time of Harisena's death, Bagh suffers no such trauma at this time. Although no further work was done in the Bagh caves about 477, reflecting the general disturbance of the times, it appears that the caves remained in use by the still active sangha right up to (and presumably somewhat beyond) the accession of Maharaja Subandhu just before he offered further support to the sangha in 486. See discussion in W. Spink, "Dandin, Ajanta, Bagh, and the Historicity of the Visrutacarita", W. Spink, *Ajanta: History and Development*, Volume 7, BRILL.

call post-Vākāṭaka were made.

Generally honouring Shiva that than the Buddha now, the impressive "post-Vākāṭaka" monuments can generally be assigned to the Early Kalacūri dynasty, established in the early 480s by Maharaja Subandhu of Mahiṣmati, the proper inheritor of the last fragments of the once proud Vākāṭaka house.[15] Beginning in about the second decade of the sixth century, Central India, and especially the rocky cliffs of Maharashtra, are rich with splendid rock-cut monuments—Kanheri, Jogeshvari, Mandapeshvar, Elephanta, the early caves at Ellora, the later caves at Aurangabad, and many others. (Fig 18) These are monuments that we now should properly recognize not as Post-Gupta, as has often been the case, but as Post-Vākāṭaka—honouring their connection with a rich and startling past (Fig 19).

Figure 18: Elephanta: Great Cave, north, Dancing Śiva, c 540.

---

[15] See discussion in W. Spink, "Dandin, Ajanta, Bagh, and the Historicity of the Visrutacarita", W. Spink, *Ajanta: History and Development*, Volume 7, BRILL.

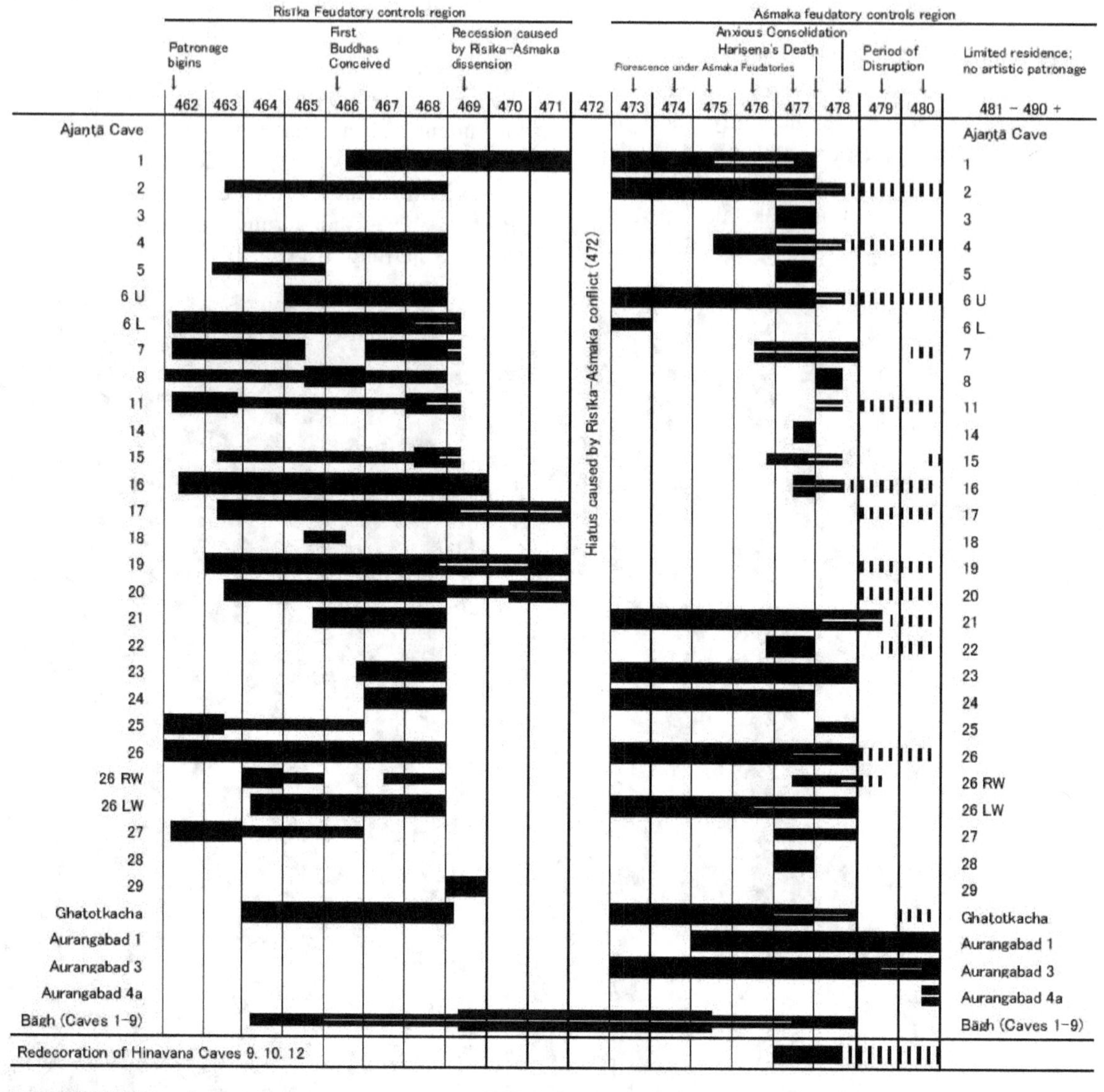

Figure 19: Time Chart: Ajanta and Vakataka Site.

Rock-cut Art and Architecture of the Cālukyas in Southern Deccan: Background, Chronology and Sculptural Disposition

Prof. Adiga Sundara, Director of Archaeology & Museums, Government of Karnataka (Retd.)

Abstract

The establishment in c.543 CE and the expansion of the Cālukya kingdom over the entire Western Deccan from the Kaveri to the Narmada and of its branches in Vēngi (Rajahmundry dt) in Eastern Deccan and in Western India, provided ample scope for the southward diffusion of especially the cave architecture tradition of the North Deccan. Consequently, under the direct patronage of the powerful Cālukya kings particularly Mangalēśa (c. 578-612 CE), a regent on behalf of Pulakēśi II (c.612-642 CE), rock-cut cave temples, four in Badami and two in Aihole, were excavated in the pleasant colourful sandstone hill ranges. Of them, the Viṣṇu layana (Cave III) in the former excavated by Mangalēśa, and consecrated in 578 CE, is the most magnificent.

Since the time of Fergusson and James Burgess (1880), these monuments are well-known and studied extensively by Henry Cousens, Ananda Coomaraswamy, Percy Brown, K. V. Soundara Rajan, George Michell and John Fritz, J.C. Harle, etc.

After briefly reviewing these well-known cave temples, an attempt is made to analyse in relation to a few relevant inscriptions, their salient features in terms of the rock material, architecture, sculpture as well as painting. As a result, certain modifications and additions in the architecture, new sculptural forms such as Para Vasudēva, Mahānaṭa (generally described as Naṭarāja), stylistic features and cultural significance could be traced. All these seem to constitute a variant tradition in the development of the rock-cut cave temple architecture in the lower Deccan.

Preliminary remarks

The establishment in c. 543 CE and the expansion of the Cālukya kingdom over the entire Western Deccan from the Narmada to the Kaveri with its supreme capital in Badami at a small distance from two other celebrated places: Pattadakal-Mahakuta, traditionally holy and Aihole the centre of a strong merchant guild that came to be known as '*Ayyāvōle Ainūrvaru*' in the entire South, and of its collateral branches in Vēngi (Rajahmundry dt. Andhra Pradesh) and in Gujarat, provided ample scope for the interaction of different art traditions of especially the cave architecture in the Deccan. Consequently, under the direct patronage of the powerful Cālukya kings, particularly Mangalēśa (c.578-610 CE), a Regent on behalf of minor Pulakēśi II (c.612-642 CE) and wealthy merchants rock-cut cave temples four in Badami and two in Aihole were founded in the pleasant colourful sandstone precipices of the hill ranges. Of them, the "*Layano Mahāviṣṇugṛha*" (Vaishnava Cave III) in the former in which was consecrated "*Viṣṇu pratimā*" in Saka 500 (578 CE) (Padigar S.V, 2010), is the most magnificent.

Since the time of James Burgess (1874), Fergusson (1899) the splendid monuments of these places are studied and made extensively well-known in their varied ramifications by Henry Cousens (1926), Ananda Coomaraswamy (1927), Percy Brown (1965, 5th ed), K. V. Soundara Rajan (1981), J.C. Harle (1994 -2nd ed),George Michel (2014), etc. For, in the upper Deccan the foundation of the rock at cave temple architecture as known now begun from around the Common Era as at Ajanta, Karle, Bhaja and the tradition, was continued up to the 9th century in the region. With the rise of the Cālukya power in Badami region from around the mid-6th century, a variant tradition in the development of the rock-cut cave temple architecture in the lower Deccan was developed. Here is an attempt made to examine the probable source of inspiration for excavating similar cave temples in the lower Deccan in a favourable and encouraging environment: natural, political and cultural; and their regional distinctive features against a chronological framework.

The Background

In Ajanta, chronologically the Buddhist cave temples are classified into two groups: 9, 10, 12, 13, and 15A of 1st century BCE—2nd century CE and the remaining, of fourth to sixth centuries; but according to Walter Spink who studied on the spot all the temples over decades, 440—480 CE. In Ellora, Hindu, Buddhist, and Jaina cave temples are respectively assigned between the end of the Vākāṭaka rule and the early-mid Rāṣṭrakūṭa, the latter part of seven century CE and the early-mid Rāṣṭrakūṭa. It was during this period that the Cālukya Mangalēśa-Pulakēśi II, had conquered the Upper Deccan ruled by the Kalacūris. It is but natural that the temple building activity therefore in Ellora now under their rule had acted as a catalytic agent for the uprising Cālukya in similar activities in their capital. The consequential, religious and architectural is analytically examined here below.

In the Badami region, the impact of the Buddhist art tradition on the architectural enterprise of the Ellora seems to be practically negligible. For, all the rock-cut temples of both Badami and Aihole areas are exclusively of the Hindu Puranic tradition and to a lesser extent of the Jaina. With regard to the Buddhist, but for a sculpture of Avalōkitēśvara Padmapāṇi with *aṣṭa bhayas* of the Mahāyāna sect, in a natural cavern located between the cave temples II and III in Badami; a natural cave partially shaped into a simple two-storied *caityālaya* and another loose sculpture of Buddha with similar characteristic features, not from a rock-cut cave temple which otherwise would have been now in existence in whatever condition, there is hardly any Buddhist monument worthy of notice. Further, there is scarcely any inscription of the Badami Cālukya period mentioning any grant to a Buddhist establishment or temple, though Cālukya Vijayāditya (696-733) is mentioned as giving equal treatment to Buddhists also along with the Bhāgavatas, the Jainas (Padigar, S. V. 2010.201).There were no doubt Buddhist monks as e.g. Piṇḍivadi Mahendrarar, the disciple of Ananda Sthavira referred to in a two-line inscription located in the storied caityālaya (ibid.261).

This is in utter contrast to the state of Jainism of which there are two cave temples one nearby the Buddhist cavern in Badami and a structural temple of architectural merit in Aihole got built by no less a distinguished person than Ravikīrti, the court poet. In Pattadakal, beside the Jaina Nārāyaṇa temple of the latter part of 8th cent, there were two pre-

Cālukya brick structural Jaina monuments one having a graceful Tīrthaṃkara image in khaḍgāsana in round relief stylistically of circa early 6h cent. CE now displayed in the site Museum in the place.

This situation of Buddhism, therefore, was not due to the dominance of the Hindu sects which the royalty followed over the so-called heterodox religious sects, Jainism and Buddhism. Apparently, therefore, the Buddhist population in the region was too meagre and insignificant to exercise and exert influence on society and royalty. The small community of average merit had to be satisfied with by rendering natural cavern/cave into simple shrines for worship. In the region of Vēngi ruled by the Eastern Branch of the Cālukya established by Pulakēśi II with Kubja Viṣṇuvardhana, his brother, as potentate has a similar story to tell in this regard. In Bhairavakonda, Guntapalle, there are Śaiva Rock cut temples datable to circa 8th cent. It appears therefore that during this period the vigorous Buddhist activities in Ellora resulting in the creation of as many as 14 cave temples and vihāras of the latter part of the 7th cent. almost exclusively was neither inspiring nor desirable in the lower Deccan. Instead, the equally vigorous Hindu and Jaina activities conspicuously expressed in the rock-cut temples 17, 18,21 of more or less the same period reasonably seem to have a stimulating effect on the rock-cut cave architecture of the Badami-Aihole region now as a strong political-economic-cultural power extending over the Deccan. Jainism was continuously in the good books of the society and the royalty even from before. Under the preceding Kadambas of an orthodox Brahmana community very well-versed in Vedic tradition, it had a distinguished rather unparalleled status (Sundara,2000. 35-46). Thus, the strong tradition of cave architecture could extend over the lower Deccan but to a certain extent necessary with regionally distinctive cultural ethos particularly in the domain of sculptural art, a concomitant part of the architecture: rock-cut or structural.

Chronological considerations

Generally, it is argued that the rock-cut cave III excavated by Mangalēśa was the first in the series and the Jaina rock-cut cave at the topmost, the last. This point of view looks apparently reasonable in view of the fact that the kingdom had grown strong and mighty politically and economically in as much as Kīrtivarma I and Mangalēśa, the parama Bhāgavatas. could patronise the excavation of magnificent cave temple III. And in view of the fact that Vikramāditya I (c. 654–71) practically embraced Śaiva faith by undergoing "*Śiva maṇḍala dīkṣā*". Probably during his time, the Śaiva cave was caused to be excavated. There is also a view that the cave temples were got excavated one after another in the order they are. In particular, K.V. Soundara Rajan (34-36) has discussed this point arriving at similar observation but inkling to think that the cave temple II with *liṅga pīṭha* essentially Śaiva could be the earliest. But I think that the locations of the cave temples I and IV and the original approach from the ground level to the former are not seriously considered in relation to their chronology. Considering these factors, I have re-examined the chronological issue.

As mentioned above, there are four cave temples: the Śaiva (two?), the Vaishnava, and the Jaina at the lower, middle and upper levels, respectively on the steep side of the South Hill having the commanding view of the large lake below locally known as Agastya tirtha in Badami. On the eastern side of the large lake is a natural cave fairly large. On the dressed back wall of the cave is sculpted a large image in bas-relief of a seated king-like person with royal attributes and flanked by royal attendants with fly-whisk. Curiously, on the pedestal are the symbols of *śankha* and *cakra*. In Aihole, within the village is a Śaiva cave temple excavated in huge boulder like a small hillock. Further in the north-eastern outskirts of the locality is a hillock with a stepped pathway from the village side on the hill to the top. In the middle zone of the path by its side is the natural cave which is partially converted and dressed into a two-storied Buddhist caityālaya, mentioned above. On the top of the on the rocky plateau is a structural Jaina temple (locally known as Megudi i.e. temple on the top), "Jinēndra Bhavana" as known from a praśasti composed by Ravikīrti an eminent poet in the court of Pulakēśi II. It was got constructed by the poet around 634 CE. Besides, on the hillock are more than 20 Protohistoric Early Iron Age Megalithic porthole chambers in various states of dilapidation. Further, down below on the north-eastern side was the extension of the megalithic site but with passage chambers in the revenue limits of Kyaddigeri and Chilapur. Besides the site on the north-eastern edge of the hillock is the Jaina rock-cut cave temple.

Of these cave temples, as mentioned above, only one i.e. Cave temple III in Badami has a dated inscription i.e. Śaka varṣa 500 (578 CE). To me the Śaiva cave temples here and probably at Aihole, it appears from the point of view the certain singular sculptures and their characteristic style rather different from the typical Cālukya style, may be dated to circa early sixth century probably belonging to the reign periods of Raṇarāga and Pulakēśi I. The Jaina cave in Badami in view of its being located relatively at the highest level; of the distinctive style of the image of Vardhamāna Tīrthaṃkara in the *garbhagṛha* of the very modest ground plan originally comprising a narrow oblong *mukha maṇḍapa*, a vestibule also narrow and a *garbhagṛha* as well as the pillars of the facade having a lion-headed base (unlike the Pallava *siṃha staṃbha* in which the seated lion in full is the base), and of the absence of *sabhā maṇḍapa* seem to indicate that the temple in all probability is the prototype of the others nearby and therefore, the earliest in the series in the locality i.e. early part of 6th century of the Banavasi Kadamba rule who as pointed above had a special reverential attitude towards Jainism throughout their rule. The Vaishnava (Śaiva) Cave temple II is in sequence the last in the series probably of the early seventh century.

The Śaiva cave temple in Aihole has a label inscription of chronological significance reading "Raṇa Vi(krāntan)" engraved on the frontal side of the plinth of the right-side aisle. This is an honorific title of Mangalēśa. In this temple are subsequently added by excavation aisles on sides of the pillar-less *sabhā maṇḍapa* open to the front open space. On the back wall of the right aisle is a colossal sculpture of Śiva as Mahānaṭa accompanied with Gaṇēśa and unusually Saptamātṛka-s in varied dancing postures, a portrayal of a rare type. The aisle on the left is partially excavated and unfinished. In the *sabhā maṇḍapa* are a few wall sculptures on the sides of the front entrance and of the entrance at the back into the vestibule. The sculptures are rather uncommon and distinct in style in the domain of the Early Cālukya art such as the Gangāvataraṇa with Ganga, Yamuna and Sarasvati in feminine form in the sky above Bhagīratha in penance, a rare feature to be noticed only here, Ardhanārīśvara and Harihara (the straight prongs of the triśūla noteworthy an early type similar to an iron triśūla found in the Early Iron Age Megaliths as at Jewargi. Meadows Taylor, 1941. At the back of the *sabhā maṇḍapa*, is a vestibule actually an incipient antarāla decorated with the sculptures of Mahiṣa Mardini (presence of a bell as an attribute in one of the hands is noteworthy in the sculpture not found in any of the sculptures of the goddess found in large numbers in the Cālukya art of the region) on the left side wall and Bhū-Varāha on the right, probably later additions. The *antarāla* opens to the *garbhagṛha* having at the centre a monolithic Śivaliṅga on a plain simple *pīṭha* carved in situ. In view of the characteristic iconographic features of sculptures and of the original plan of the temple it may be assigned to mid-6th and the subsequent additions made are of the mid seventh century. The Jaina cave temple that seems to follow the ground plan of the Śaiva cave in view of its characteristic geometrical designs on the ceiling (reminding similar designs of the panels of the Jaina stupa datable to circa first century BCE—second century CE from the excavated 'Kankali Tila' ancient site in Mathura), of the pillar-less *sabhā maṇḍapa* and of the depiction of the Samavasaraṇa scene in the aisle on the right side of the maṇḍapa may be of the early-mid 7th century.

Further, the location of the cave temples in Badami; it may be seen that in front of the Śaiva cave there is enough space in the ground for people to assemble and to have a panoramic view of the Śaiva cave temple. This facility is entirely absent to the other cave temples in the row since the lake below is up to the foot of the steep hill range. If the Śaiva cave temple had not been in existence when Kīrtivarma I and Mangaleśa planned the foundation of the 'Mahā Viṣṇu gṛha' Cave temple why did they not prefer to have the temple in the place of the Śaiva cave which provides readily a spectacular view of the grand temple even from the ground level too? Was there already the Śaiva temple? Obviously, the inevitable conclusion is that there was already the temple. An on-looker can have only a bird's eye view from the distant i.e. northern edge of the lake, of the front view of the cave temple III at a much higher level than the Śaiva cave temple, therefore suitable to have a spectacular view of the temple.

There is an open ground in front of the cave temple III. Also, there is an east-west oriented parapet raised along the northern edge of the ground. Similarly, on the eastern side of the ground was a structural wall up abutting the steep side of the hill closing the access to go eastwards further up to the Jaina cave IV, if it was already in existence. Why was the wall for if the Jaina temple was not there? People at large would not prefer to come from the eastern end and to climb the hill to reach the cave temple III. It

appears therefore that there was already the Jaina cave temple visited by the devout people. Since these temples III and IV were visited then for worship almost exclusively by the members of the Royalty and high dignitary to the former, to avoid possible disturbance from the eastern side the wall was raised to close the access from either side. It is only in the early last century a part of the wall abutting the hill was removed to provide access to the Jaina cave temple IV from the cave temple III. In those days and later devotees used to go the Jaina temple not from the ground level climbing by the flight of steps via the Śiva and the two Vaishnava cave temples as is done in the present, but by the natural hill track from the Eastern- Southern border path of the Agastya tīrtha. This is generally the traditional practice. Even today some Jaina devotees climb the hill by the track

Now, these factors appear to be useful in examining the probable chronological range of the Jaina cave temple. It may relevantly be recalled here that in general as noted already some additions and alterations subsequently are made to some of the existing temples. The Jaina cave is one such temple. As already mentioned earlier it is a modest temple with narrow mukha maṇḍapa, oblong hall as narrow as the mukha maṇḍapa but not as long and a garbha gṛha with a colossal image of Tīrthaṃkara (Vardhamāna Mahavira?) seated in siddhāsana on a siṃha pīṭha with royal chaurī-bearers on the sides carved on the back wall. On the side walls of the front mandapa are by in-cut technique unlike the cut-out sculptures like the Mahānaṭa, Hari-Hara, Vīṇādhara Śiva of the Śaiva cave temple, are carved sculptures of Pārśvanātha with Dharanēndra Yakṣa holding an umbrella over the tīrthaṃkara's head and Padmāvati yakṣi on the sides and Bāhubali (unusually with hairs as if combed backwards unlike the ringlets of the Bāhubali of the Jaina cave temple in Aihole)) with his sisters, Brahmi and Sundarī on the sides. These were added slightly later but during the Cālukya period. In the 11th-12th century, were added on the left front wall a small image of seated Tīrthaṃkara with triple umbrella over the head with the image of a well-known devotee seated with folded hands, Jakkiyabbe on the left known from a Kannaḍa inscription close by, small images of a Tīrthaṃkara surrounded by the other Tīrthaṃkara-s on the pillars of the façade of the oblong hall, big sculptures of Parsvanatha with Dharanēndra Yakṣa and Padmāvati Yakṣi with her vāhana kukkuṭasarpa on the walls of the oblong hall that in all probability was then enlarged for the purpose. This would undoubtedly imply that the temple was actively in worship up to 14th cent.

The cave temple was originally quite simple and plain probably of the reign period of the first two kings of the dynasty: Jayasimha and Raṇarāga who were feudatories to the early Kadambas of Banavasi. In this context, it is pertinent to note that the Kadaṃba kings, the orthodox Brahmanas well-versed in the Vedic traditions and practices from the beginning almost to the end liberally patronized with dignity and reverence Jainism as pointed out above. This religious atmosphere might have influenced the Cālukya feudatories as well to support the foundation of the Jaina cave. But after the consecration of the cave temple III at the instance of Mangalēśa, people, mainly Jaina devotees after their worship in the Jaina temple would curiously come down to see the other cave temples and there might be problems between the people and the members of the royal family and of the dignitaries. If this cave temple was got done sometime after the end of the Cālukya rule the ground plan of the temple, pillar and sculptures would have been different in preference and style. And there would not have been a north-south oriented structural wall up to the hillside. All these factors would indicate the Jaina cave to be the earliest.

The Śaiva cave appears to have been the next in the series under the patronage of probably Raṇarāga who is said to be the worshipper of the 'Hara caraṇa' of the god Śiva. The Śaiva cave in Aihole more or less of the same period with some slightly later additions. The Vaishnava cave II in view of the sculptural style particularly the dvārapāla-s in comparison with those of the cave temples I and III, is the third in the series probably of the period of Pulakēśi I. And the splendid monument of the Cave temple III is the brilliant and the most spectacular stage of the cave temple tradition. After critically analysing the data the cave temples may be chronologically arranged as follows:

1. The Jaina cave temple (originally) IV in Badami: early sixth century
2. The Śaiva cave temple I in Badami: early sixth century
3. The Śaiva cave temple (originally) in Aihole: mid six century
4. The Vaishnava cave temple II of probably the period of Pulakēśi I

5. The Vaishnava cave temple IV of 578 CE by Kīrtivarma I and Mangalēśa in Badami.
6. The Jaina cave temple of early 7th cent, in Aihole

Thus, the rock-cut cave temples of the Badami Cālukya in the lower Deccan are probably chronologically in the range of early sixth—mid-seventh century.

The cave temple architecture and sculptural disposition: their regional distinctiveness

When the Cālukya were carrying out their military exploits in the upper Deccan up to the Narmada and conquered the entire region ruled by the Kalacūris then, in Ellora in particular cave temple architectural enterprises were vigorously progressive from about 6th century and onwards up to the end of the seventh century. Such activities seem to have provided the necessary boost for similar cultural activities in the capital of the Cālukya. But the impact of the Ellora tradition on the latter seems to be not of considerable significance. In Ellora some types of the ground plans and pillar forms were intimately similar in the contemporaneous monuments of both the Buddhist and Hind, for instance a large oblong hall with mukha maṇḍapa, central hall and side aisles and a garbha gṛha at the back detached from the side walls providing a pradakṣiṇāpatha as e.g. Cave temple no. 14. But in Badami and Aihole, the ground plan of the cave temples is strikingly different. It is of one type: a plan comprising narrow oblong mukha maṇḍapa wide open in the front with pillared façade, spacious pillared sabhā maṇḍapa trapezium in plan and a square garbha gṛha not independent of the side and back walls providing pradakṣiṇāpatha. The pillars are not as voluminous. The other type is a variant of the first with or without mukha maṇḍapa and with aisles on the sides of the sabhā maṇḍapa. The Cālukya especially Kīrtivarma I and Mangalēśa who were 'parama bhāgavata' preferred Bhū-Varāha and Trivikrama since in the pursuit of certain ideals, i.e. protectors of the kingdom like Varāha, etc.

In the Domain of Sculptural Art, a concomitant part of the cave architecture regional preferences is pretty obvious. In Ellora, the Hindu cave temples are generally adorned with the most popular Puranic themes such as Śiva playing chess with Pārvatī, Rāvaṇa bearing Kailāśa on his shoulders, Andhakāsurāri, Kalyāṇasundaramūrti (the marriage of Śiva with Pārvatī), Durgā, Lakṣmī, Bhū-Varāha, and some others. On the other hand, in Badami Cālukya region it is the Śiva Tāṇḍava nṛtya such as

Vasanta Tāṇḍava, Ānanda Tāṇḍava, Umā Tāṇḍava and others; Para Vaṣṇudēva, Lajjā Gauri of the popular cult, apart from Bhū-Varāha, Trivikrama, Vīṇādhara Śiva, etc. In this context, it is appropriate to note that the Cālukya patronized the performance art of Bharatanāṭyam. Acalan, the son of Dēvayyā, known by his title Naṭasēvya, a very eminent expert in Bharatanāṭya śāstra was probably in the court of Vikramāditya II. This explains for the repeated occurrence of the sculptures of Śiva Tāṇḍava nṛtya. Similarly, the Lajjā Gauri cult was considerably popular in the Krishna Valley region from about the beginning of the Common Era. Thus, regional cultural ethos had their own say in the preferences of themes for sculptural art.

References

Ananda Coomaraswamy; 1927. History *of Indian and Indonesian Art*. Boston: Museum of Fine Arts.

Brown, Percy; 1965 (5th ed). *Indian Architecture (Hindu and Buddhist), Part 1*. Mumbai: D. B. Taraporewala Sons &Co Pvt. Ltd.

Burgess, James; 1874.*Antiquities of Belgaum and Kaladgi*. Varanasi: Indological Book House.

Cousens, Henry; 1926.*The Cālukya architecture*. Delhi: Archaeological Survey of India.

Fergusson, James; 1899. *History of Indian and Eastern Architecture*. New York: Dodd, Mead, and Co.

Michell, George and Surendra Kumar; 2014.*Temple Architecture and Art of the Early Cālukya: Badami, Mahakuta, Aihole and Pattadakal*. New Delhi: Niyogi Books.

Harle, J. C.;1994 (2nd ed). *The Art and Architecture of Indian Sub-Continent*. Yale University, U.S.A: Pelican History of Art.

Meadows Taylor; 1941(Reprint of his three papers published during 1851-59). *Megalithic Tombs and Other Ancient Remains in the Deccan*. Hyderabad: Directorate of Archaeology and Museums.

Padigar, S. V.;2010. *Inscriptions of Early Cālukya*. New Delhi: ICHR.

Soundara Rajan, K. V.; 1981. *Cave Temples of the Deccan*. New Delhi: Archaeological Survey of India.

Sundara, A.; 2000.*The Early Kadambas and Jainism in Karnataka*. Arhat Vacana, Vol.12, No. 3. Indore: Kundakunda Jñānapīṭha.

Chronology of the Brāhmaṇical Caves at Shiur, District Nanded, Maharashtra: A Reappraisal

Vaishali M. Welankar

Abstract

Brāhmaṇical caves at Elephanta, Mandapeshvar, Jogeshvari and Ellora from western Maharashtra have been well researched and analysed from the perspectives of chronology and religious significance. Similar is the case with some eastern Maharashtra or Vidarbha examples like caves at Gaurala. First detailed reporting of these caves by J. Burgess (1882) and J. Fergusson (1880), Beglar (1874-75) stand valuable in this regard and many scholars like K. V. Soundara Rajan (1981), A. P. Jamkhedkar (1987), Walter Spink (1967), George Mitchell and Carmel Berkson (1983), Prabhakar Deo (1972) etc. have largely contributed for the further understanding of some of these caves. (Fig. 1&2)

In the absence of inscriptional evidences except for a few of these Brāhmaṇical caves, it is difficult to secure a definite chronological framework. A relative chronology therefore has been attempted based on stylistic considerations in all the aforementioned analytical and descriptive works. The Brāhmaṇical caves in western India especially in Konkan have been attributed to the Kalacūri era c. 6th c. CE while majority of the caves at Ellora are attributed to the Cālukya-Rāṣṭrakūṭa period 7th – 8th c. CE. The caves at Pataleshvar, Mahur, Takli Dhokeshvar and Kharosa show stylistic affinities and architectural similarities to those from Ellora and Konkan hence fall in the same time bracket i.e. c. 6th -8th c. CE. Architecturally and iconographically, the Brāhmaṇical caves from Vidarbha are more akin to the central Indian caves from places like Udayagiri in Madhya Pradesh and are considered contemporaneous to the latter i.e. c. 5th c. CE.

The present attempt is to analyse the architectural features and iconographic depictions in the three Brāhmaṇical rock cut caves at Shiur, district Nanded (Maharashtra). The caves were first reported by Shelke and Deo (1972: 64-72). A detailed description of these caves and a tentative date based on style of the images carved therein was provided by the authors. The caves were mentioned as belonging to Rāṣṭrakūṭa period c. 8th c. CE. Geographical proximity to the sites like Kandhar that is attributed to the Rāṣṭrakūṭa era, these rudimentary caves seemingly fitted in the chronological framework. However, while taking a review of the Brāhmaṇical caves from Vidarbha, Dr. Jamkhedkar (2009) offers a different chronology. On the basis of the rudimentary architectural features he assigns a period between Vakataka and Cālukya rule i.e. c. 5th to 7th c. CE.

The present paper is an attempt to reassess these relative chronologies for Shiur caves, again on the basis of architectural features and the iconographic scheme which is quite unique as compared to the Brāhmaṇical caves from Vidarbha as well as Western Maharashtra.

The caves at Shiur (Fig.3)

Shiur is a small village situated on the right bank of river Penganga in Hadgaon Taluka of Nanded district, Maharashtra. There are three small excavations in the eastern face of a low rock formation located on the southwest of the modern village of Shiur.

Architectural features

On plan, the excavations are simple rectangular pillared halls. Two of these caves exhibit attempts of carving out a shrine in the rear wall, one with a rudimentary circumambulatory passage. The caves are 20 x 13 ft, 45 x 20 ft, and 42 x 28 ft in size. Compared to the highly developed architectural plans and massive scale of the Brāhmaṇical and Buddhist caves from western India, the caves at Shiur reveal a small, simple and humble nature of the excavation (Fig.4). The simplicity of the cave plans at Shiur is similar those found from Vidarbha specifically from the caves at Bhatala, Gaurala and Salbardi.

However, unlike the small boulder shrines from Bhatala (Fig. 5), and slightly bigger caves from Gaurala (Fig.6) and Salbardi that exhibit a developed nature of excavation with architectural features such as the typical 'T' shaped doorway, that

Figure 20:

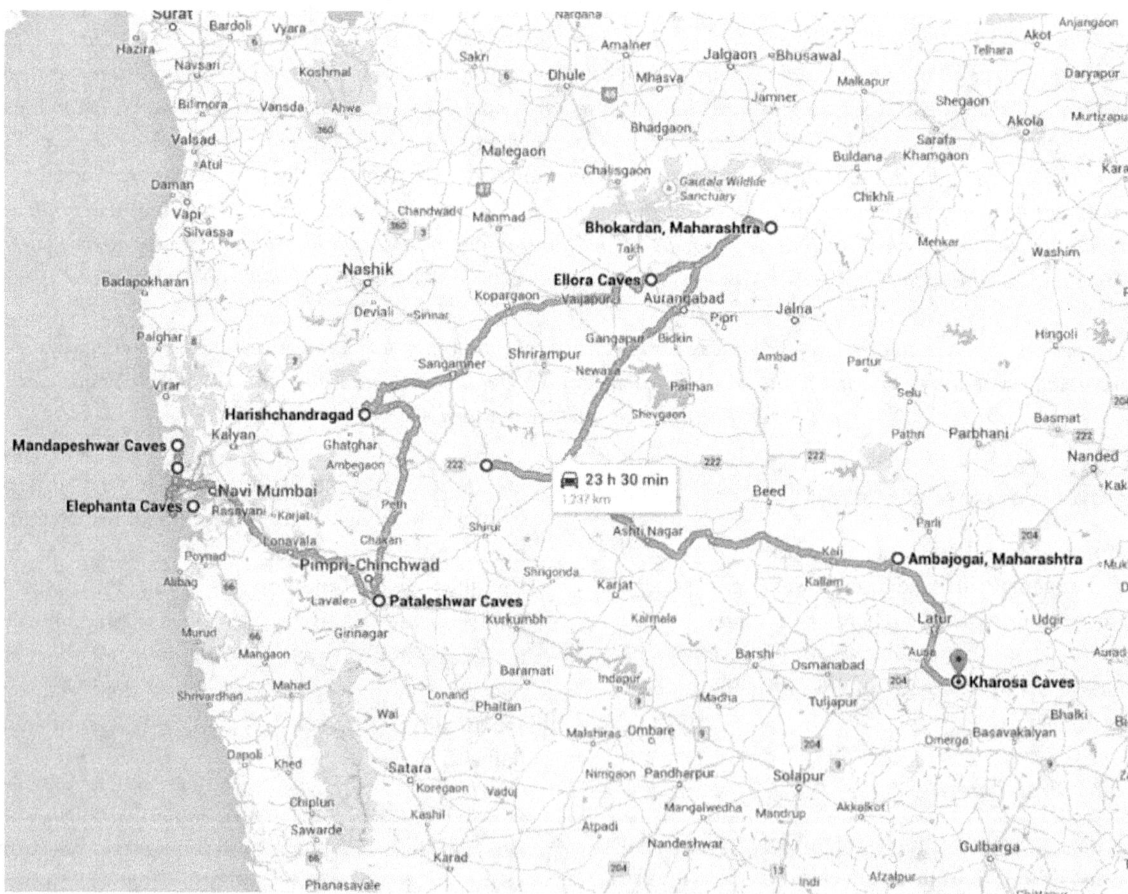

Figure 21:

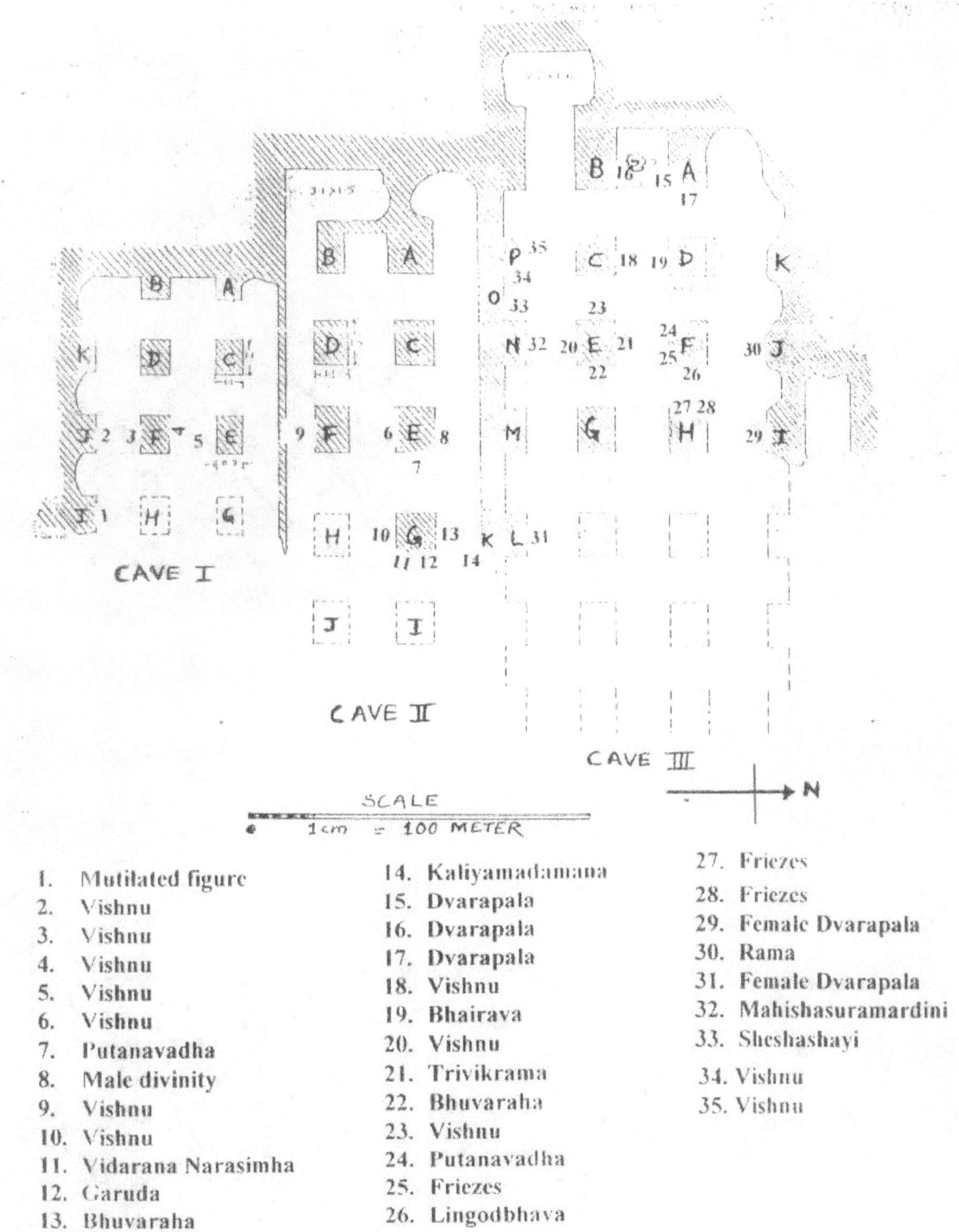

1. Mutilated figure
2. Vishnu
3. Vishnu
4. Vishnu
5. Vishnu
6. Vishnu
7. Putanavadha
8. Male divinity
9. Vishnu
10. Vishnu
11. Vidarana Narasimha
12. Garuda
13. Bhuvaraha
14. Kaliyamadamana
15. Dvarapala
16. Dvarapala
17. Dvarapala
18. Vishnu
19. Bhairava
20. Vishnu
21. Trivikrama
22. Bhuvaraha
23. Vishnu
24. Putanavadha
25. Friezes
26. Lingodbhava
27. Friezes
28. Friezes
29. Female Dvarapala
30. Rama
31. Female Dvarapala
32. Mahishasuramardini
33. Sheshashayi
34. Vishnu
35. Vishnu

Figure 22: The caves at Shiur. The alphabets in inverted comas show the pillars.

was in practice during 4th -5th c. CE, the caves at Shiur are devoid of any neatly carved entrances or façade and doorways.

The interior of each of the cave at Shiur is simple and plain, except for the images on the pillars. There are no well-cut ceilings and architraves above the crude and massive square pillars. The walls between these three adjoining caves are dilapidated at some places; however enough remains to show the crude nature of the excavation. The Brāhmaṇical caves from western India on the other hand, show a highly developed form of architectural components such as

Figure 23:

Figure 24:

Figure 25:

beautifully and precisely carved entrances, ceilings, decorative pillars in the interior with architraves and brackets etc. The caves at Shiur are thus devoid of any precision in architectural design and finesse, which is a major hindrance for securing even a relative chronology. The iconographic scheme and style of the images carved on the pillar, therefore, is the only clue.

Iconographic scheme

The Brāhmaṇical caves from western Maharashtra and those from Vidarbha are similar when it comes to the placement of the images in the interior. The images in these caves are mostly carved on the maṇḍapa and mukhmaṇḍapa walls. However, the images from the interior of all the three caves at Shiur are carved on the faces of the massive cubical and crude pillars. This could be the result of smaller scale of the excavation coupled with the selection of a low hillock for the excavations.

The style and type of images show a significant difference from those found in the other Brāhmaṇical caves of India. The images in all these three caves are mostly pertaining to Vaishnavism i.e. Viṣṇu and his various forms, and the scenes from Harivaṃśa such as putanāvadha, kāliyāmardana etc. The only śaiva images found are a highly mutilated image of Bhairava and a śivaliṅga flanked by Viṣṇu

seated and touching the liṅga with his upper left hand on the right side and four-armed Brahma seated with hands in namaskāramudrā showing the reverence to the liṅga on the left.

Majority of the Brāhmaṇical caves from Konkan and Ellora belong to shaivism, some of them specifically show the evidence for Pāśupata cult. Similar is the case with the caves from Vidarbha where majority of the caves are dedicated to Shiva worship. The caves belonging to the Vaiṣṇava sect from Western India on the basis of iconography are the cave at Bhokardan and cave no. 27 at Ellora. The Vaiṣṇava caves from Vidarbha are two boulder shrines from Bhatala dedicated to Kevala Narasiṃha, an avatāra of Viṣṇu and the big fowl cave at Gaurala showing the Vaiṣṇava images on the interior walls. However, the original dedications of the caves at Gaurala and cave no. 27 at Ellora have been questioned by various scholars.

The images on the interior wall of the Big Fowl cave at Gaurala, Dist. Chandrapur in Vidarbha region of Maharashtra though thought to be intrusive indicate the existence of Vaiṣṇava worship. And based on the stylistic analysis of the images can be traced back to late 5th c. CE. The images carved therein include Viṣṇu as eight armed Trivikrama, Bhū-Varāha, Śeṣaśāyī, Nārāyaṇa, and Kevala Narasiṃha and an image of Mahiṣāsuramardinī. At least two of the many boulder caves from Bhatala, Dist. Chandrapur, Maharashtra, exhibit the existence of worship of Kevala Narasiṃha form of Viṣṇu. The existence of Vaiṣṇava sanctuary at Ramtek, Dist. Nagpur with structural temples dated to 5th c. CE dedicated to the worship of Kevala Narasiṃha, Varāha, and eight armed Trivikrama and a double-shrined temple probably dedicated to the worship of Vriṣṇi viras i.e. Vāsudēva and Balarāma supports the popularity of Vaishnvaism in the region. The existence of Sātvata cult during the Vakataka realm is further supported by Mandhal copper plates of Vakataka King Rudrasena II and the images of Śeṣaśāyī, eight armed Trivikrama, thematic sculptures from Harivaṃśa and Ramayana from Paunar. It can be thus deduced that during the 5th century CE, eastern Maharashtra witnessed the sanctuaries dedicated for the worship of Satvata cult with the worship of Trivikrama, Varāha and Narasimha Avataras of Viṣṇu along with the worship of Vasudēva and Balarama.

While the Satvata cult was prevalent in the Vidarbha, the Vaiṣṇava caves from Bhokardan and Ellora indicate the evidence of Pancharatras. The architectural features of the cave at Bhokardan resembles the cave plan of the 5th-6th century cave temples from Mamandur in Tamil Nadu excavated during the Pallava regime (Fig.7). The imagery on the interior walls of Bhokardan cave shows the images of Śeṣaśāyī Viṣṇu, Balarāma and Revati, and the three Vaiṣṇava gods probably Aniruddha, Pradyumna and Sāmba. The images of Surya and Mahiṣāsuramardinī carved on the façade walls of this cave also fit in the iconographic scheme of Vaiṣṇava shrines from Southern India. The existence of Śeṣaśāyī image and the Vaiṣṇava vyuhas indicate the leaning towards the 'Pāñcharātra Sect' of Vaishnavism. On the basis of architectural and iconographic features the cave has been attributed by the scholars as belonging to 7th-8th c. CE.

The images in cave no. 27 at Ellora again pertain to Pancharatra sect as the iconographic panels on the walls of the verandah depict Bhū-Varāha, Brahmā-Viṣṇu-Maheśa, Vāsudēva-Ekānaṃśa-Balarāma, Śeṣaśāyī and Mahiṣāsuramardinī. The evidence of Śeṣaśāyī and two of the five vriṣṇī vira-s indicate the existence of Pāñcharātra sect of Vaishnavism. Although, the cave except for these panels on the walls of the verandah remains an unfinished one, on stylistic grounds the images can be dated to c. 7th c. CE.

Iconography at Shiur caves

Cave I: The first cave of the group on the eastern end is cave I. This cave consists of a rectangular hall, divided into the central nave and aisles by the two rows of six extremely plain, square and crude pillars. The front two pillars, one of each row is totally broken. Apart from the four pillars there are three pilasters in the eastern wall of the cave and two pilasters in the rear or southern wall of the cave. The inner faces of some of these pilasters and some of the faces of each of the square pillars bear Vaiṣṇava images.

1. Mutilated figure: The inner face of the first eastern pilaster, 'K' of the façade is a mutilated male figure. Nothing more about this image has survived through the ravages of time.

2. Viṣṇu (148 x 72 cm): The inner face of (second eastern) pilaster 'J', of the cave bears an image of four-armed Viṣṇu. He is shown here as standing in alidha pose. His lower right hand is on his right thigh. The upper right hand holds a discus. The attribute in the raised upper left hand is beyond identification due to the mutilated state of the image. The image is shown as wearing a kiriṭamukuṭa, earrings, a sacred thread, and a lower garment.

3. Viṣṇu (140 x 76 cm): On the inner face of the first extant eastern pillar 'F', of the façade is carved an image of Viṣṇu. Here Viṣṇu is carved as standing erect. He is four armed. In the lower right hand, he holds a mace with its butt downwards. In the raised upper right hand, he holds a discus. Both his left hands along with the attributes held in them are mutilated. The image is shown as wearing earrings, necklace made of coins and a lower garment. The crown and the face of this image are broken.

4. Viṣṇu (144 x 69 cm): The western face of the same pillar 'F', of the cave is carved an image of Viṣṇu. Here Viṣṇu is shown as standing erect. The image is partially mutilated. The image is four armed. The upper two hands are broken. The lower right hand holds mace with its butt downwards and the lower left hand of the image is akimbo. The image is shown as wearing a necklace, a sacred thread, and a lower garment. The remaining ornaments are not discernible.

5. Viṣṇu (139 x 63 cm): On the eastern face of the pillar 'E' of this cave, depicts an image of Viṣṇu as standing erect. He is four armed. In the lower right

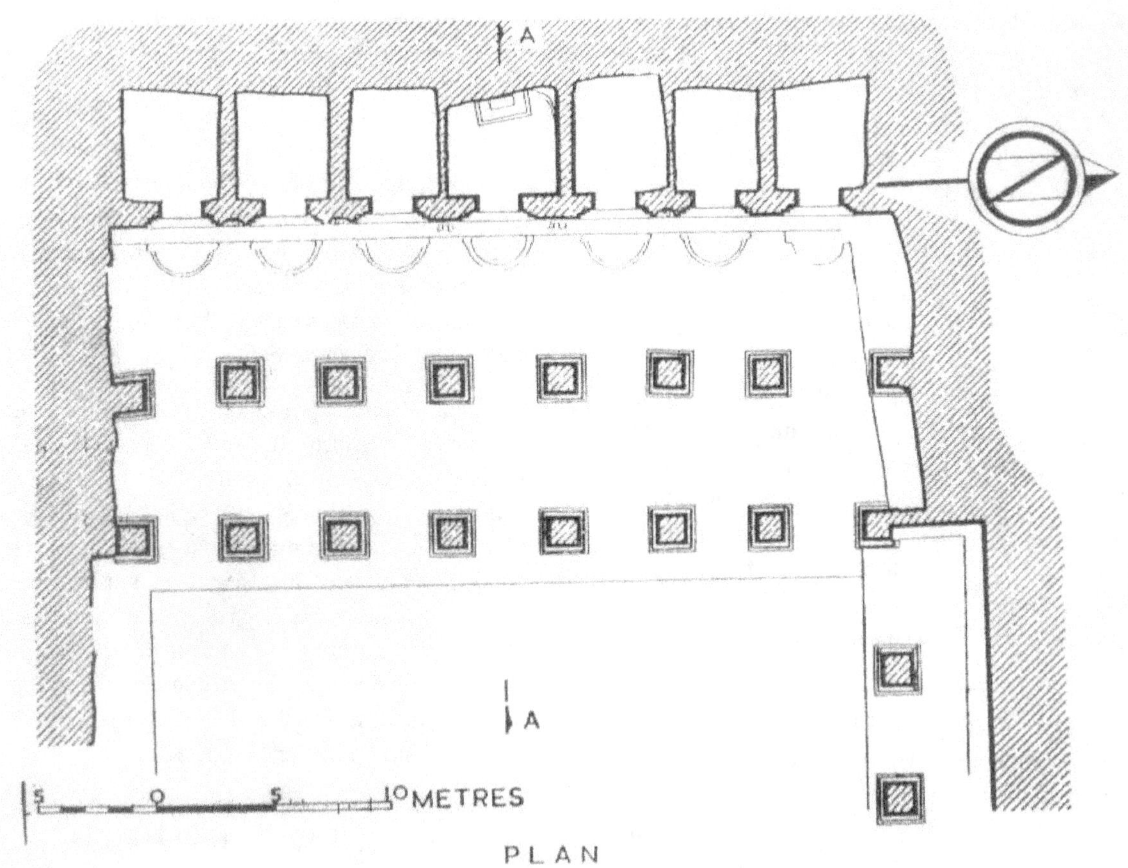

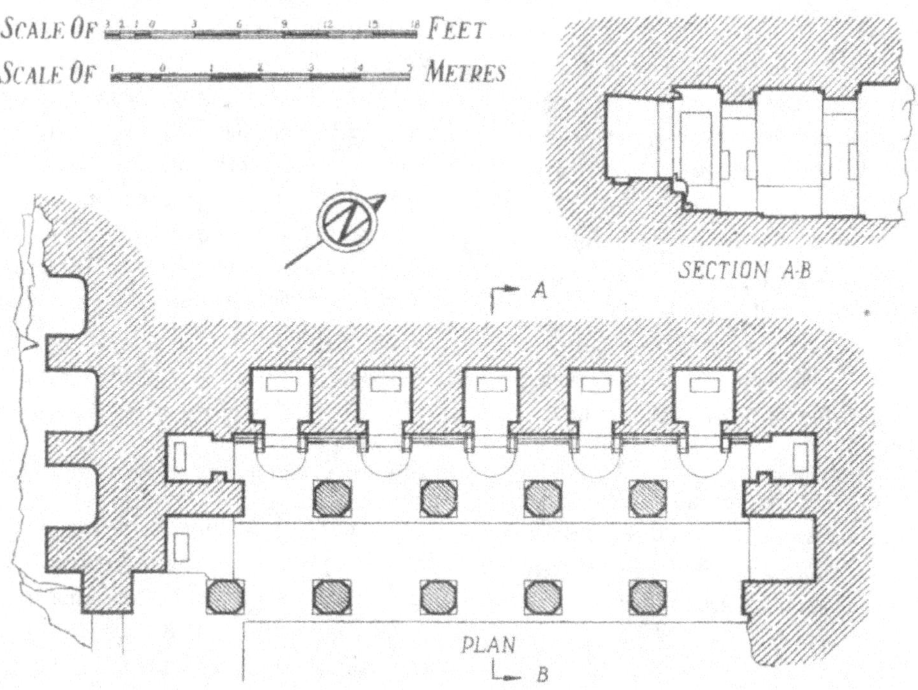

Figure 26: (A, above) Bhokardan and (B, below) Mamandur

hand, he holds a mace. The upper right hand along with the attribute is broken. It is the case with the upper left hand. His lower left hand is akimbo and devoid of any attribute. His image is shown as wearing a kiritamukuta, earrings, a sacred thread, and a lower garment.

Cave II: The middle cave in the group of three caves at Shiur is Cave II. This cave is also rectangular in plan and is divided into the central nave and aisle with two rows of pillars. An attempt of carving out a square shrine in the centre of the rear wall of this rectangular hall is clearly visible with the unfinished remnant portions at the rear. The pillar type shows a stylistic affinity to the ones from cave I at the site. These pillars are square and crude devoid of any base or capital. Some of these pillars in cave II bear Vaiṣṇava images on some of their faces. Following are the images found on the pillar faces.

1. Viṣṇu (151 x 75 cm) (Viṣṇu / Pradyumna): On the eastern face of the pillar E, is carved an image of Viṣṇu, standing erect. He is carved here as a four-armed divinity. In his lower right hand, he holds a mace with its butt downwards and the attribute in the upper right hand is broken. In his upper left hand, he holds a conch and his lower left hand is akimbo and without any attribute in it. The image is shown as wearing a kiritamukuta, earrings, armlets, wristlets and a lower garment. The face is highly eroded but he has obliquely set eyes. The central portion of mace bears a decorative band.

2. Putanāvadha (99 x 76 cm): The northern face of the same pillar 'E' is carved an image depicting Putanāvadha. Here Putanā is shown as seated with her right leg folded and the left knee raised. She is two armed. Both her hands are raised above her head, leaving her breasts bear. Child Kṛṣṇa is depicted as suckling the right breast of Putanā. He is shown as squeezing her breast to death with his two hands. The image of Putanā is shown as wearing a plain kiritamukuta, earrings, and a thick necklace. The image of Kṛṣṇa is shown as wearing armlets, and a lower garment.

3. Male divinity: The western face of the same pillar 'E' of this cave is a highly eroded standing image of a male divinity. The features including the attributed held in the four hands are not discernible due to the mutilated state of the image.

4. Viṣṇu (150 x 76 cm): The eastern face of the eastern pillar 'F' is carved an image of Viṣṇu standing erect. The upper portion of the body is highly mutilated including the face of the image. Here Viṣṇu is carved as a four-armed divinity. In his lower right hand, he holds a mace. The upper portion of the upper right hand and the attribute held in it are mutilated. Same is the case with upper left hand of this image. The lower left hand of this image is akimbo and without any attribute held in it. The ornamentation of the image is not clear due to the mutilated and eroded state of the image except a few traces of the lower garment.

5. Viṣṇu (Hriśikeṣa) (143 x 54 cm): On the eastern face of the western pillar of the façade i.e. 'G', is carved an image of Viṣṇu in erect posture. He is a four-armed deity. In his lower right hand, he holds a mace with its butt downwards. In his upper right hand, he holds a plain discus. The attribute in the upper left hand is mutilated. His lower left hand is akimbo and he holds a conch in it. His image is shown as wearing a plain kiritamukuta, earrings, a sacred thread, armlets, and a lower garment. The face is highly broken and eroded.

6. Vidaraṇa Narasiṃha: The northern face of the same pillar 'G', in the cave bears two figures in the upper and lower registers. The upper register (a) bears a mutilated portion of Viṣṇu carved as Vidaraṇa Narasiṃha. The upper portion of the image is totally mutilated. It is on the basis of the remnant portion, which is akin to the other Vidaraṇa Narasiṃha images from Maharashtra and elsewhere too, that this image can be identified as that of Vidaraṇa Narasiṃha. Here the image of Narasiṃha is shown as standing in alidha posture, forming a lap, on which lies the demon Hiranyakaśipu. The remnant portion of the image of Narasiṃha indicates the traces of lower garment. The image of Hiranyakaśipu is comparatively intact. It shows the demon lying on the lap of Narasiṃha, with his head hanging off the left thigh of the god. The demon is two armed. In the right hand he holds a sword and in the left he holds a shield. The image is highly eroded. The lower two hands of Narasiṃha with long nails are extant and are shown as tearing the belly of the demon.

7. Garuda (63 x 54 cm): On the lower register (b) of the same pillar is carved an image of Garuda. The image of Garuda is shown here in a flying posture, turned to his left. He is two armed. Both his hands are raised above the shoulders and there is a serpent held in each of them. The image of Garuda is shown

as wearing a high kiritamukuta, earrings, a sacred thread, armlets, and a lower garment.

8. Bhū-Varāha (126 x 72 cm): On the western face of the same pillar 'G' is carved an image of Viṣṇu as Bhū-Varāha. Here Bhū-Varāha is shown as standing in alidha, facing to his left, with the right leg firmly placed and the left one lifted and probably kept on the nāga hood, which is not discernible now. The image of Varāha is carved as a four-armed divinity. His lower right hand is akimbo. The attribute in the raised upper right hand is mutilated. The upper left hand and the attribute held in it are mutilated. The lower left hand of Varāha is raised and bent at the elbow on which is carved a seated image of Bhūdēvī. In the same hand he holds a mace. The image of Bhūdēvī is carved as seated on the elbow of Varāha, facing front. She is two armed. Her right hand is on the snout of Varāha and the left hand is on her left thigh. The image of Varāha is shown as wearing two thick and plain necklaces, a rope like sacred thread, armlets, wristlets, and a lower garment with the central loop falling in front.

9. Kaliyāmardana (144 x 86 cm): On the eastern face of the westernmost pilaster i.e. 'K' of the cave bears an image of Kṛṣṇa killing the demon Kāliya. Here Viṣṇu as Kṛṣṇa is shown as standing in alidha with his right leg on the ground and the left leg that is lifted and kept on the body of the zoomorphic serpent Kāliya. The image of Kṛṣṇa is four armed. His lower right hand is akimbo. In the raised upper right hand, he holds a discus. The attribute in the raised upper left hand is broken. And with his lower left hand, which is seen near his chest, he is controlling Kāliya probably by stretching his tongue or by stretching the string he had tucked in the nostrils of the serpent. This act is called 'Natthiya'. The zoomorphic Kaliya has a serpentine body and his hood is erect. The image of Kṛṣṇa is shown as wearing a kiritamukuta, earrings, a sacred thread, armlets, wristlets, and a lower garment.

Cave III: This cave closely resembles the other two caves from the site, in regards to the plan. It is rectangular and the central nave and aisles are separated by the two rows of crude, square pillars; but it is bigger in dimension than the other two caves and there is a crude but approximately finished square shrine in the rear wall of this cave. The shrine is devoid of any proper doorway and the circumambulatory passage is unfinished. Inside this shrine is a Śivaliṅga on the floor, which seems to be

a later addition, so also the monolithic Nandi kept in front of the shrine in the central nave of the cave. On faces of the pillars and pilasters of this cave are carved various Vaiṣṇava images.

1. Dvārapāla: On the eastern face of the western pilaster 'A' of the shrine is carved an image of Dvārapāla. He is standing erect and is two armed. His right hand is akimbo and the left hand is broken. His head is also broken. The image shows the traces of a necklace, a sacred thread, and a lower garment.

2. Dvārapāla: On the western face of the eastern pilaster 'B' of the shrine is depicted another Dvārapāla. Standing in tribhaṅga, he is two armed. In his right hand he holds a mace and his left hand is akimbo. The face of this image is highly eroded. The image is shown as wearing a crown. The remaining ornaments are not discernible due to the eroded state of the image.

3. Dvārapāla: On the northern face of the pilaster 'A' is carved another Dvārapāla. Nothing much can be described about the image due to the eroded state of the image.

4. Viṣṇu (Keśava) (156 x 85 cm): On the western face of the pillar 'C', is carved an image of Viṣṇu. He is depicted here as standing in erect posture. He is four armed. His lower right hand is akimbo. In the upper right hand, he holds a conch. In the upper left hand, he holds a discus and the lower left-hand rests on the mace near the waist. The image is shown as wearing a crown, earrings, beaded sacred thread, waistband, and a lower garment. He has obliquely set eyes and curved eyebrows.

5. Bhairava: On the eastern face of the pillar 'D', is a mutilated image. The lower portion of the image is totally broken. The right hand and the face and the crown are also partially broken. But the remaining left hand, which holds a human head, makes the identification of this image clear, as that of Bhairava. And if this identification is correct, this is one of the only two Śaiva imageries found at the site, the other being the Liṅgodbhava panel.

6. Viṣṇu (149 x 69): On the eastern face of the pillar 'E' of the cave is carved an image of Viṣṇu. Here the deity is carved as standing in tribhanga. He is four armed. In the lower right hand, he holds a mace. The attribute in the raised upper right hand is not clear. The attribute in the raised left hand is broken. The lower left hand is akimbo. The image is shown as

wearing a crown, earrings, a sacred thread, armlets, necklace made up of coins and a lower garment.

7. Trivikrama (156 x 95 cm): On the western face of the same pillar 'E' is carved an image of Viṣṇu as Trivikrama. Here the deity is depicted as standing with right leg firmly planted on the ground and the left one is lifted up to the shoulder level. He is carved as a four-armed divinity. His lower right hand is on his right thigh. In the raised upper right hand, he holds a discus. His upper left hand is in sucimudra and his lower left hand, which is kept on the left thigh, holds a conch. The image is shown as wearing a crown, earrings, beaded sacred thread, chest-band, waistband, beaded armlets, and wristlets. A Gandharva flanks his head on the left side.

8. Bhū-Varāha (130 x 56 cm): On the northern face of the same pillar 'E' is carved an image of Viṣṇu as Bhū-Varāha. He is depicted as standing in alidha posture with his right leg firmly placed on the ground and the left one is lifted and kept probably on the nāga hood. He is carved as a four-armed deity. His lower right hand is akimbo. Both the upper hands and the attributes held in them are mutilated. The lower left hand is folded at the elbow probably supported the anthropomorphic image of Bhūdēvī. The image of Bhūdēvī is mutilated except the right hand that is visible on the snout of the Varāha. The image of Varāha is shown as wearing a crown, a sacred thread, armlets, and a lower garment.

9. Viṣṇu (Janārdana) (156 x 85 cm): On the southern face of the same pillar 'E' is carved an image of Viṣṇu. Here the deity is shown as standing in erect posture. He is four armed. His lower right hand is akimbo. In the upper right hand, he holds a discus. In the upper left hand, he holds a conch, and the lower left hand is kept on the head of gadādevi who is shown as standing erect. The image of Viṣṇu is shown as wearing a crown, a necklace, a sacred thread, armlets, beaded wristlets, and a lower garment.

10. Putanāvadha: On the upper register of the eastern face of the pillar 'F' in the cave is a panel depicting Putanāvadha (88 x 67 cm). Here Putanā is depicted as seated with her left leg folded and right one hanging. She is two armed. Both her hands are raised high to bear open the breasts. Child Kṛṣṇa is carved as suckling her right breast, squeezing it to death. The image of Putanā is shown as wearing a low crown, earrings, necklace, a band on the stomach, waistband, and a lower garment. The image of Kṛṣṇa is shown as wearing a lower garment.

11. Friezes of divinities: On the lower register of the eastern face of the same pillar 'F', below the image of Putanā, are two friezes of divinities carved in a standing posture. The identification is difficult due to the small size of each figure and the attributes held in their hands are even smaller and eroded.

12. Liṅgodbhava panel: The northern face of the same pillar 'F' in this cave bears two depictions, one each in upper and lower register. The upper register depicts the Liṅgodbhava myth. Here the images of Brahma and Viṣṇu are shown as seated, flanking the Śivaliṅga, to the left and right respectively. The image of Brahma is carved as having three faces. His image is shown as wearing a jaṭāmukuṭa, a single beaded necklace, armlets, waistband, a sacred thread, and a lower garment. Brahma is carved as holding his two hands in namaskāramudrā near his chest. His image is turned slightly towards śivaliṅga. The image of Viṣṇu on the right side of the śivaliṅga is shown as seated in sukhāsana. He is four armed. His lower right hand is in varadamudrā and in the raised upper right hand he holds a discus. His upper left hand is touching the liṅga, and his lower left hand is kept on his left thigh. The image of Viṣṇu is shown as wearing a kiriṭamukuṭa, earrings, a sacred thread, waistband, armlets, wristlets, and a lower garment. Though the panel appears to be Śaiva, the marked difference in its representation than is usually found in Maharashtra and elsewhere, doubts the Śaiva leanings. Usually, in the Liṅgodbhava panel, the failure of both Brahma and Viṣṇu in swan and boar incarnations respectively, to find the upper and lower end of the śivaliṅga is depicted as the core of the myth. Here, in this panel the images of swan and Varāha are missing. It is also important to note that the image of Brahma is two armed and holds his hands in namaskāramudrā slightly facing to the śivaliṅga, while the image of Viṣṇu is four armed, and none of his gestures and attributes indicate his submission to the Śivaliṅga. Instead, the upper left hand of Viṣṇu that touches the upper part of the Śivaliṅga probably depicts the success of finding the upper end of Śivaliṅga. This very feature along with the gesture of his lower right hand i.e. Varadamudrā indicates that this seemingly Śaiva panel is depicted here with Vaiṣṇava leanings. And this along with the remaining Vaiṣṇava images found in all the caves and the absence of Śaiva and Śākta images except

the image of Bhairava indicate the original Vaiṣṇava dedication of the caves.

13. Friezes of divinities: The lower register of the northern face of the same pillar 'F', and below the Liṅgodbhava panel; are carved small figures of standing divinities in two rows.

14. Friezes of divinities: On the southern face of the pillar 'H' in this cave also bears the similar friezes like that on the northern face of the pillar 'F', in this cave.

15. Female Dvārapāla/ Lakṣmī (127 x 62): On the eastern face of the first western pilaster 'I' of the cave bears an image of a female Dvārapāla. The image is depicted as standing in tribhaṅga. The image is two armed. In the right hand she holds a full-blown lotus while the attribute in her left hand is mutilated. Near her left leg is a small attendant figure holding an umbrella above her head, which is seen above the head of the main figure. Her image is shown as wearing a plain crown, earrings, and a lower garment.

16. Rama (150 x 64 cm): On the eastern face of the second pilaster 'J', on the west of this cave is carved an image of Viṣṇu as Rama. This probably is the earliest independent depiction of Rama as an avatāra of Viṣṇu. Here the divinity is carved as standing erect. He is two armed. His right hand is akimbo and in the raised left hand he holds a bow. A quiver can be seen tied behind the right shoulder of Rama. He wears a jatāmukuṭa, earrings, a single beaded necklace, a sacred thread, beaded armlets, waistband, and a lower garment. The nose of this image is partially broken and he has obliquely set eyes and curved eyebrows.

17. Female Dvārapāla: On the western face of the eastern pilaster 'L' of the cave also depicts a Dvārapāla. The image is highly eroded to discern any other features except revealing that this also was a female Dvārapāla.

18. Mahiṣāsuramardinī (152 x 85 cm): On the western face of the first eastern pilaster 'N' of the cave is carved an image of Mahiṣāsuramardinī. She is carved as facing the front. She is four armed. In her lower right hand, she holds a sword. In the upper right hand, she holds a trident, the lower end of which is kept on the back of the Mahiṣa demon. In her upper left hand, she holds a goad and with the lower left hand she pushes down the hind portion of the zoomorphic Mahiṣa demon. The force in the panel is depicted through the posture of the demon who is depicted in a zoomorphic form as being killed by the Dēvī and the figure of the Dēvī herself who is shown as standing with her left leg firmly placed and with the right one she tramples down the head of Mahiṣa demon, and with her lower left hand presses down the hind portion of the demon. She is shown as wearing a jaṭāmukuṭa, earrings, a thick necklace, armlets, wristlets, waistband, and a lower garment.

19. Śeṣaśāyī (130 x 40 cm): The first panel 'O', on the eastern wall of the cave, facing the west is carved an image of Śeṣaśāyī. The image is carved in an extremely shallow relief and therefore most of the features are not clear. The image shows Viṣṇu as lying supine on a serpent bed. The outline of the coils of Śēṣa is seen under the body of the god. The image of Śeṣaśāyī is four armed. His lower right hand is seen as stretched out on the serpent bed. Both the right and left upper hands of the image are raised but the attributes are not clearly seen. The lower left hand of the image is also stretched out and kept on the left thigh. On the same wall and on the southern face of the pilaster 'N' are carved nearly four to five images, above the image of Śeṣaśāyī, facing the latter, and holding their hands in namaskāramudrā.

20. Viṣṇu (Acyuta) (146 x 85 cm): On the northern face of the second pilaster 'P', of the eastern side of this cave, is carved an image of Viṣṇu. He is carved as standing erect and has four hands. In the lower right hand, he holds a mace with its butt downwards. His upper right hand is raised, but the attribute in it is broken. He holds a discus in the upper left hand. His lower left hand is akimbo and he holds a conch in it. His image is shown as wearing a high kiritamukuta, earrings, necklace, a sacred thread, armlets, wristlets, and a lower garment.

21. Viṣṇu (Trivikrama/ Govinda) (148 x 82 cm): On the western face of the same pilaster 'P', is carved an image of Viṣṇu. Here Viṣṇu is shown as standing erect. He is four armed. His lower right hand is in varadamudrā. In the raised upper right hand, he holds a mace with its butt downwards. The attribute in the raised upper left hand is mutilated. His lower left hand is akimbo and holds a conch in it. His image is shown as wearing an elaborate kiritamukuta, earrings, a thick necklace, a sacred thread, waistband, and a lower garment. The image has a roundish face and obliquely set eyes with curved eyebrows.

Figure 27:

Figure 29:

Figure 28:

Figure 30:

From the above description and possible identification from the remnants of the images, it is certain Shiur caves present an iconographic scheme that is different from the other Vaiṣṇava cave temples from western Maharashtra, Vidarbha and central and south India dated between 5th to 8th c.

CE. The iconographic scheme at Bhatala, Gaurala, and Bhokardan and cave no. 27 at Ellora indicates that the dedication and worship pertained to the Satvata-Pāncarātra sect of Vaishnavism with Śeṣaśāyī, eight armed Trivikrama, vyuhas, Vaiṣṇava Triads and Avatāras like Narasimha and Varāha and also the imagery from the Harivamśa and Rāmāyaṇa. The Vaiṣṇava images from the Śaiva caves at Ellora also indicate this nature of Vaiṣṇava religion popular in the region.

However, the caves at Shiur differ in the sectarian leanings. Significant changes in iconography can be seen at Shiur. The image of Trivikrama at Shiur (Fig. 8) is four armed as compared to the eight-armed images from Ramtek, Gaurala, Pauar, Bhokardan and Ellora. The smaller size and not-so-specific placement of the image of Trivikrama in the iconographic scheme here suggests a deviation from the sātvata leanings as seen during the Vakataka rule of the region. Instead of Rāmāyaṇa panels one can witness for the first time, an image of Rama (Fig.9) as one of his avatāras like the Bhū-Varāha, and Trivikrama. The image of Śeṣaśāyī Viṣṇu, though carved crudely, is the only image in Shiur caves that is carved on the interior wall between the pillars.

A major sectarian difference is the introduction of vyuhantaras or twelve of the twenty-four forms of Viṣṇu. The images of Vāsudēva or Balarāma or Pradyumna or Aniruddha as four main vyuhas or their depiction as a triad is no more a part of the iconographic scheme here. They are replaced four armed Viṣṇu figures, identical, except for the permutation of attributes in their hands. The caves at Shiur thus provides the evidence for Viṣṇu as Keśava, Acyuta, Janārdana, Hriśikeṣa, Viṣṇu/ Pradyumna, Trivikrama/ Govinda (Fig. 10 & 11) and six similar forms (unidentifiable due to the mutilated attributes). The two small friezes with a row of twelve such small identical four-armed figures of Viṣṇu also indicate the importance of vyuhāntaras in the overall iconographic scheme.

The doctrine of Shrivaishnavism is closely connected with the Pāncarātra doctrines. Both these sects believe that Viṣṇu manifests himself in five ways. For Pāncarātrins they are Para (the ultimate source), vyuha (the four principles deified as Vāsudēva, Samkarṣaṇa, Pradyumna and Aniruddha), Vibhāva (the incarnations), Antaryamin (the one that resides within) and Archa (the image). The Shrivaiṣṇavas call it Sarvavyāpin, Puruṣa (conciousness), Satya (matter/ Universe), Acyuta (time-invariant) and Aniruddha (ultimate atomic particle of all existence). The concept of vyuha of the Pāncarātrins can be seen proliferated in Shrivaishnavism, with vyuhāntaras or various forms emanating from the four principles Vāsudēva, Samkarṣana, Pradyumna and Aniruddha. These total vyuhāntaras were considered to be twenty-four. With the growth of Shrivaishnavism during 10th century by Rāmānujāchārya, Andhra Pradesh became the centre of this sect. However, the emergence and popularity of the sect in Andhra Pradesh is dated as early as 7th -8th cycle.

It is important to note here, that the region where the Shiur caves are located was for a short period under the rule of the Viṣṇukundins, a dynasty from Andhra Pradesh, during the 6th c. CE. The cave temples at Undavalli in Andhra Pradesh are attributed to the period of Viṣṇukundin rule c. 6th c. CE. Although the original dedication of the two storyed Brāhmaṇical cave at Undavalli is doubtful, a huge image of Śeṣaśāyī and the other Vaiṣṇava images like Bhū-Varāha carved on the pillars of the maṇḍapa indicate its Vaiṣṇava leanings. The caves at Undavalli and Shiur differ in many respects like the scale, plan and finesse, however, like the caves at Shiur, Undavalli cave also shows some of the main images of Viṣṇu and his forms carved on the pillars and not on the walls of the maṇḍapa and façade. Therefore, although the caves at Shiur follow the models of the small, crude boulder caves from Vidarbha, the iconographic scheme and placement of images is more akin to some of the caves in Tamil Nadu and Andhra Pradesh under the rule of Pallavas and Viṣṇukundins.

The caves at Shiur therefore can be safely attributed as the effort during the post Vakataka period under the rule of Viṣṇukundin kings in the region.

References:

Beglar, J.D.M 1873-74. Archaeological Survey of India Report Vol. III; Calcutta: Office of Superintendent of Government Printing

Burgess, James 1882. Report on the Elura Cave Temples and the Brāhmaṇical and Jaina caves in Western India, Vol. V of Archaeological Survey of Western India; (Reprint 1971), Varanasi: Indological Book House.

Fergusson, James and J. Burgess 1880. The Cave Temples of India, London: W.H. Allen & Co.

Jamkhedkar, A.P 1987. 'Vaishnavism in Vakataka Times', Parimoo R. (Ed) Vaishnavism in Indian Arts and Culture, New Delhi: Books & Books; pp. 335-342.

O'flaherty, Wendy, George Michell and Carmel Berkson 1983. Elephanta: The Cave of Shiva; New Jersey: Princeton University Press.

Shelke, G.C. and P.R. Deo 1972. 'Brāhmaṇical Caves of Shiur'; Marathwada University Journal vol. XI. Aurangabad. pp.64-72.

Spink, Walter M. 1967. Ajanta to Ellora, Bombay: Marg Publications.

Soundara, Rajan, S.V. 1981. Cave Temples of India, New Delhi: Archaeological Survey of India.

The Hiatus in Buddhist Cave Architecture in Maharashtra: Contesting Claims

Yashadatta Alone, Jawaharlal Nehru University, New Delhi

Abstract

The very idea of hiatus emerged in the historiography of the western Deccan is deeply rooted in the readings into the political events. Political narratives have been responsible for making 'hiatus' as a historical event not only in the case of early Thēravādin caves but also in the case of later Mahayanist caves. It has become a narrative of the present discourses on the caves. How art historical studies have grown under the shadow of the polemics of political history is worth noting and needs to be contested. Contestation has to be based on the acceptable propositions that would create a very different understanding as well as provide impetus to the new issues and problematize the cave monuments in its historical context. In case of early caves, the Sātavāhana chronology has become the issue of contestation and in order to place the Puranic genealogy in a unilinear fashion, historians have read event of a conflict between the Sātavāhanas and the Kṣatrapas as a mark of hiatus in the process of cave excavation. Such generalization, time and again has emerged out of belief in the textual tradition that the Sātavāhana genealogy in the Puranas has to have greater authenticity. Therefore, one has to contest the idea based on the very reading of inscriptions, for example, if one of the Sātavāhana kings is mentioned to have ruled for 52 years, then why there is no visible evidence to corroborate his rule or is it because of the fictitious nature of the evidence, our understanding gets controlled by such evidence? Similarly, the Mahāyāna phase in the western Deccan has always been dated as the development of the fifth century AD as if the western Deccan was immune to the Mahāyāna Buddhism, consequently, was averse to the Buddha image representation, and therefore, the Hinayāna/Thēravada caves went on getting excavated till about fifth century AD, thus it is concluded that the Mahāyāna caves began only in the fifth century AD. Moreover, when it comes to the Vakatakas, the hiatus at Ajanta, as has been highlighted by Prof. Walter Spink needs to be contested in the light of the dated Vada inscription of the Konkan Mauryas, and the image tradition that gets developed at Kanheri itself. One pertinent example would be that of cave complex at Ajanta patronized by the local king Upēndragupta. The lower portion of the attendant figures in the shrine of cave 20 of Ajanta is incomplete and the inscription of the Upēndragupta in Ajanta cave 17 claims that he had defeated the Aśmakas. If the war between the two local kings was that paramount then why the artisan left unfinished the lower portion of the attendant images in cave 17 at Ajanta? No doubt that the Ajanta cave 20 was also patronized by the Upēndragupta and he might have initiated its excavation only after the war. Besides, how do we understand the imagery at Ajanta itself in the light of the observation that only the later caves of Ajanta have marked the influence of the eastern Vidarbha sculptural tradition whereas the early phase is devoid of such influences? Can we show any connection between the coastal tradition and Ajanta when it comes to the Mahāyāna caves sculpture? Why the pictorial conventions of shrine Buddha images at Ajanta cave 11, 15, lower 6 and 7 do not fall under the conventions of the late fifth century AD developments of sculpture at Ajanta itself? Can there be a better reading of the development of conventions in the light of the Vada inscription of the Konkan Mauryas and its palaeographical implications? The paper attempts to seek answers to the questions raised above with appropriate examples.

Introduction

Historical reconstruction of the past is always dependent on the nature of the evidence available, but at the same time, the framework of understandings will always become a guiding tool to decode the available evidence. Decoding though is an exercise involving nature of objectives, also at times, becomes relative in presenting a picture of remote past as a mere romantic admiration and glorification. Nature of glorification as a part of political thinking, maintaining dominance of thought process are some of the important embedded categories that enter in the realm of thought process, and perhaps may not empower to make a viable meaningful understanding of the monuments of the past. Meaning as read and understood through the expressible signifiers are located in the historical contexts and its subjective positions. Numerous ideas have emerged through the historical reconstruction of the past, and hiatus is one such idea that is in circulation ever since disciplines of history, archaeology, art history and cultural studies have emerged during colonial times in India. Disruptions are always conceived as hiatus in the process of historical continuities, how does one attempt to understand certain traits of historical continuity in the reading of art historical monuments, depends on the very basis of objective formulations that go in the historical reconstructions and imaginations.

The very idea of hiatus emerged in the historiography of the western Deccan cave is deeply rooted in the readings into the political events. Narratives on political histories have been responsible for making 'hiatus' as a historical event not only in the case of early Thēravādin caves but also in the case of later Mahāyānist caves. Broadly, historical reconstructions have produced 'three hiatuses' in studying the Buddhist cave tradition of western Deccan- 1. Sātavāhana-Kṣatrapa conflict, 2. Hiatus between the Thēravādin caves and the Mahāyāna caves that consequently produced extended chronological framework in the dating of the late Thēravādin caves, 3. 'Hiatus' in cave excavation activity in Ajanta's Mahāyāna caves as has been proposed by Prof. Walter M. Spink (1966, 1967, 1972, 1974, 1975, 1981, 1981A, 1985, 1989, 1991, 1992, 1992A, 1992B. 1993, 1994, 2005). All three have become narrative of the present discourses on the caves. How art historical studies have grown under the shadow of the polemics of political history is worth noting, and needs to be contested. Contestation has to be based on the acceptable propositions that would create a very viable understanding as well as provide impetus to the new issues, and problematize the cave monuments in its historical context. In case of early caves, the Sātavāhana chronology has become the issue of contestation, and in order to place the Purāṇic genealogy in a unilinear fashion, historians have read event of a conflict between the Sātavāhanas and the Kṣatrapas as a mark of hiatus in the process of cave excavation (Dehejia, 1972). Such generalization, time and again, has emerged out of belief in the textual tradition that the Sātavāhana genealogy in the Purāṇas has to have greater authenticity. Therefore, one has to contest the idea based on the very reading of inscriptional evidence, for example, in the Purāṇas one of the Sātavāhana king is mentioned to have ruled for 52 years, then why there is no visible evidence to corroborate his rule, or is it because of the fictitious nature of the evidence that made us to read the account in the texts as a historical reality, and our reading of the text depends on the idea that text being sacred, therefore, it has to be read without questioning the text itself? It appears that the reading of the text is often considered to be a screed process, and words are used as evidence itself, consequently, the process of reading the religious texts have controlled understandings unquestioned.

Let us examine the cases of the hiatus i.e. the conflict between the Sātavāhanas and the Kṣatrapas producing disruption of rock-cut cave excavation activity. It was Vidya Dehejia (Ibid) who attempted to read the conflict between the two political dynasties as a reason for hiatus. All the historians have read the Purāṇic account as an authentic source of information and have not questioned its veracity. One of the Sātavāhana king Sātakarṇi is mentioned to have ten sons but their names are not mentioned in the Purāṇic list (Pargiter 1962). Their names are obtained through inscriptions and coins. Joe Cribb (1998) has assigned the conflict between the Sātavāhana and Kṣatrapa to have happened in 60-70 AD/CE, but certainly, no specific dates can be assigned and therefore, consequently, it is difficult to imagine hiatus as for the fact that cave excavation process continued even after the Kṣatrapas take over. It would be worth to see the political manifestation of patronage. Nasik and Karle are the sites to have records of such incidents. Nasik being important cave site, the Sātavāhanas issued orders to its administration to take care of the fraternity of the monks (Senart, 1905; Luder, 1912) despite the fact that they were followers of the Brāhmaṇical religion. The local rulers mainly the Mahārathīs had active participation in the excavation of the Buddhist cave at Nasik, mainly the chaitya cave (LL 1141; Senart No. 18). When Nahapāna ruled western Deccan, the son-in-law of the Nahapāna patronized the excavation of cave 10 at Nasik as well as made land donations at Karla (Senart, 1905: 59-96; LL 1131, 1132, 1133; Senart, 1902-3: 47-74; LL 1099). After regaining of the territory by the Sātavāhanas under the rule of Gautamiputra Sātakarṇi, the Sātavāhanas patronised the excavation of cave 3 at Nasik and continued the land grant revenue that was offered by the earlier political rulers (LL 1126; Senart, 1905, no. 5; LL 1100; Senart, 1905, no. 14). It is also interesting to observe that while acknowledging the glory of the Gautamiputra Sātakarṇi, the inscriptional record at Nasik mentions that Gautamiputra Sātakarṇi stopped the intermixing of the varṇas (LL 1125, 1126; Senart 1905, no. 4 and 5). It shows how the Brāhmaṇical code of social functioning was getting imposed by the Sātavāhanas. Perhaps, because of such political move, Nagarjuna wrote letters to Gautamiputra Sātakarṇi mentioning the ethical moral principles of behavior1. The cave excavation activity seems to have been a continuous process. A margin of one or two years, or even ten years or so is difficult to make out in the absence of dated inscriptional evidence. There are numerous cave sites in the southwestern Deccan that have been excavated and only formalistically its date brackets are determined, and accordingly, they are assigned to the first and second century AD/CE.

The next idea of hiatus has been located between the Thēravādin and the Mahāyāna cave excavation. While the earlier scholarship regarded that the Hīnayāna/Thēravādin cave excavation went on till about second-third century AD/CE and the Mahāyāna cave excavations are assigned from fifth century AD/CE onward, and more specifically after late fifth century AD/CE, therefore, there is a hiatus between the Thēravādin and the Mahāyāna cave excavations. It may be observed that later it was observed that the Hīnayāna/Thēravādin cave excavation process continued for a very long time, and accordingly, few caves are assigned to even fourth century AD/CE in order to show continuity of cave excavation process in the western Deccan (Dhavalikar, 1984). Thus, either hiatus is accepted as a possible reason for the resumption of cave excavation activity.

It may also be observed that the nature of readings in the political events has also produced the ideas of hiatus in the dating of the Mahāyāna caves. The Mahāyāna phase in the western Deccan has always been dated as of the development of the late fifth century AD/CE as if the western Deccan was immune to the Mahāyāna Buddhism, consequently, was averse to the Buddha image representation. Therefore, the Hīnayāna/Thēravāda caves went on getting excavated till about fifth century AD/CE. It is further concluded that the Mahāyāna caves began only in the fifth century AD2. The other reason for this dating is cited as the political chronology in the region and the ways in which certain inscriptional evidence has been dated so far. There are two sets of inscriptional evidence, one comes from Ajanta and the other comes from Kanheri. Ajanta cave 16 inscriptions mention the Vākāṭakas whereas the

Kanheri copperplate inscription mentions the Traikūṭakas. Besides, there is also inscriptional evidence of the Konkan Mauryas that mentions the date Śaka 322 (Ramesh, EI, vol.40,1973-75: 575). It needs to be considered in order to reconstruct the political history of the region afresh.

Kanheri copper plate inscription of the Traikūṭakas mentions the date of 245 without specifying to which era it belonged. V. V. Mirashi has assigned Kanheri copper plate inscription to the Cedi-Kalacūri era, and accordingly, the date arrived at is 495 AD/CE (Mirashi, CII, vol. V). The inscription has also been used as a marker for the dating of the Mahāyāna cave excavations at Kanheri. Nevertheless, Vada inscription of the Koṇkaṇa Maurya is the only dated inscription. Koṇkaṇa Mauryas in western Deccan rued after the Traikūṭakas. Thus, reading of inscription becomes extremely problematic and has thrown two separate dates. As there is a specific date mentioned in the Vada inscription of the Koṇkaṇa Mauryas, it should be taken as a yardstick. It is also evident that the Traikūṭakas will have to be dated earlier than the Koṇkaṇa Mauryas. The date of Vada inscription of the Konkan Maurya is Śaka 322 i.e. 322+78= 400 AD/CE. It may be observed that Joe Cribb, while proposing the chronology of the early Kuṣāṇas, questions the very viability of the Śaka era and more specifically the year 78 as marker for the Śaka era (Sims-Williams, Nicholas and Cribb, Joe 1996: 75–142), however, such a proposition becomes false as for the fact that the calculation of the Śaka era is based on the inscriptional evidence of Badami (Kielhorn F., EI, 54-57). Therefore, year 78 cannot be disputed for the calculation of the Śaka era. Rabatak inscription as described by Joe Cribb throws light on the early Kuṣāṇas and their possible chronology but the year 78 remains a perfect number for the calculation of the Śaka era.

As mentioned above, the Traikūṭakas will have to be dated earlier than the Koṇkaṇa Mauryas, and then the question arises, what is the possible date of the Traikūṭaka copper plate inscription in Kanheri? If the era considered is that of Śaka era then the date we arrive at is 245+78= 323 AD/CE. The proposed date of early fourth century AD/CE then goes well with the Koṇkaṇa Maurya's inscription's date of 400 AD/CE. If one really sees the palaeography of the inscription and applies to the inscriptions of the Kanheri caves, then the imagery that gets developed at Kanheri needs a total rethink. Ajanta by that time was not a significant site all. Kanheri remains a nodal site.

The proposed dates show early decades of fourth century AD, which is earlier than 400 AD date of the Koṅkaṇa Maurya inscription. Thus, the pertinent question would be how do we understand the proliferation of the Buddha images in Kanheri? Kanheri cave 2c and Kanheri cave 3 are full of Buddha images with inscriptions. Shobhana Gokhale (1991) observes the similarity in their palaeography with that of the Traikūṭaka inscription. One such inscription is also observed under the seated Buddha carved on the façade of cave 3 (Fig. 3). The image is seated shown in pralambhapadāsana and the inscription mentions the gift of Shakya monk Dharmagupta. (Gokhale, 1991, Ibid, Inscription no. 8) Therefore, their pictorial conventions need total reconsideration. It also predates to the Buddha images carved at Ajanta. It may be observed that the Buddha images carved on the courtyard pillar at Kanheri cave 3 (Fig. 1 and 2) are of both varieties-1. Plain transparent drapery, and 2. The non-transparent variety. So, such conventions cannot be attributed to the Gangetic valley alone. The region of western Deccan also could develop such qualities, perhaps much before the Gangetic valley. Importance of these images has considerable bearings on the later Buddha images that are developed at Kanheri itself. At the same time, one will have to segregate images sculpted in early fourth century AD/CE, and later times such as late fourth century AD/CE and the fifth century AD/CE. Based on this logic, then a distinct phase of loose Buddha images in the cave shrines at Kanheri as observed by Marylin Edward Leese (1983) and at Kondivaṭē and Ajanta cave 8, will have to be dated in the mid-third century AD. In this context, the development at Kondivaṭē becomes important in terms of the doorframe decoration as well architectural plan.

Moreover, when it comes to the Vākāṭakas, the hiatus at Ajanta, as has been highlighted by Prof. Walter Spink (Walter Spink, op cit.) needs to be contested in the light of the dated Vada inscription of the Koṅkaṇa Mauryas, and the image tradition that gets developed at Kanheri itself. Terminating era of the Vākāṭaka rule is based on the dating of the Kanheri copper plate inscription as Cedi-Kalacūri era. It cannot be a case anymore considering the date mentioned in the Vada inscription of the Koṅkaṇa Mauryas.

Fig. 1 & 2. Buddha images on the courtyard pillar in Kanheri cave 3.

Fig. 3. Buddha image on façade of Kanheri cave 3, having an inscription of monk Dharmagupta.

Now let's turn to Ajanta, caves nos. 11, 15, 6, and 7 are important excavations. What is important to note here is the pictorial convention of the shrine Buddha images. Except cave 6 Upper main shrines and the shrines at the right left of the back wall, all others have different pictorial conventions, when they are compared with each other and the shrine images in other caves at Ajanta mainly the cave nos. 16, 17, 19, 20, 26, 1, 2, and 4. In the case of shrine images in caves 11, 15, 6, and 7, there are two distinct body types followed and they have their genesis in Kanheri. It may also be observed that the pictorial conventions of the Vidarbha sculptures are observed in sculptures of Ajanta caves 16, 17, 19, 20, 26, 1, 2, 4 and including painting.

Fig. 4. Buddha image in the shrine of Ajanta cave 11.

All agree that Ajanta cave 11 is the early Mahāyāna cave in the cave complex. Its façade design is very different from the later caves at Ajanta itself. Ajanta cave 11 façade is adopted from Panhāḷēkājī cave 6, which is dated to fourth century AD by M. N. Deshpande (1986: 30). On the other hand, the interior pillars in the hall have its antecedent at Kondivaṭē cave 13. As far shrine image is concerned (Fig. 4), it is huge and neatly carved out. Head of the image has considerable projection against its throne plane with a round face and well-proportioned torso. Shoulders are broad and proportionately carved. The contours of muscular curves make the torso slender but the spread of the thighs balances the weight of the image. The plain drapery in this sculpture is noteworthy. The overall outline of the figure is sharply delineated. The kneeling devotee is slender, its folded legs are noteworthy for its muscular bulge. The image follows conventions that are considerably different from the later caves at Ajanta itself. Thus,

the shrine Buddha image can be assigned to the second half of the fourth century AD.

Fig. 5. Buddha image in the shrine of Ajanta cave 15.

Another Buddha image at Ajanta that needs attention is the shrine image in cave 15 (Fig.5). There is a shrine antechamber and there are also intrusive images carved in it. The shrine Buddha image is seated in the padmāsana with the dhammacakramudrā like Ajanta cave 11 shrine image. The head of the image is big. The area of Uṣaniṣaha's dense hair-knot and is considerably bigger in proportion to the face. The face is round. Eyebrows and eyes are not elongated. The nose is straight and the nostrils are not wide. Protrusion of the lips is not wide. The neck is slightly more elongated than that of the Buddha image in cave 11. The torso is slender and stands straight. Shoulders are not heavy and broad. Muscles are tightened. Drapery is transparent and covers both the shoulders. Contours are diffused, giving the effect of sweeping line. Besides, the image sticks to the wall plane. The halo behind the head is large. Two Gandharva figures are carved at the top level of the hallow. Transparent drapery covering both the shoulders of the Buddha image is often attributed to the northern tradition, especially of Mathura and Sarnath. However, western Deccan had already developed these conventions at Kanheri (cave no. 3) dated to the late second century AD (Fig. 1 &2), i.e.

much earlier than fifth century AD when such conventions were developed in Sarnath. Sarnath Buddha images are dated to late fourth century AD/CE onward and there is inscriptional evidence to date those images[3].

Thus, at Ajanta, two distinct body types emerged one like cave 11 and another like cave 15. Both get followed at a certain point of time especially at Ajanta cave 6, and 7. Both the types get followed further and different conventions get developed in the shrine images of later Ajanta caves. Therefore, it becomes pertinent to separate sculptural conventions at Ajanta itself. Spink would like to locate reasons for incomplete nature of the shrine chamber as well as carving of images to the conflict between the two feudal kings (Spink, 1975: 155-168). Incomplete nature of cave shrine at the back in cave 11 is often cited as evidence. There is a big room carved on the right shrine chamber wall without any access to it. A square hole is the only access to this chamber. It indicates that the room was carved from a large square hole and rock was removed gradually. The entire room was carved but no proper access in the form of a door was ever carved. The backside of the floor remained unfinished but the cave was painted and must have been used. Either it was thought that the pradakṣiṇāpatha was not that important or there was no sufficient patronage to complete the excavation of the cave. Painted inscription in this cave needs to be compared paleographically with the inscription of the Vada inscription of the Koṅkaṇa Maurya[4]. As has been mentioned earlier, the shrine Buddha image will have to be dated in the late fourth century AD/CE and accordingly, development at Ajanta will have to be mapped.

Ajanta cave 6 upper level has numerous Buddha images and also its interior show different stages of excavations. While there is a difference in the delineation of the outer wall sculptures and the interior sculptures, their differences indeed show different chronological positions as well, for example, the outer shrinelet Buddha images and the shrine Buddha image in the front interior aisle of the cave. The front aisle shrine-images on the left of the cave have different conventions and are no match with the later shrine Buddha images as well as the one that is carved within cave 6 itself. The lower cave 6 of Ajanta, has the shrine Buddha image that is followed from the cave 11, on the other hand, main shrine Buddha of cave 6 upper level has different

Buddha image and show affinity with the later shrine Buddha images that are carved in late fifth century AD/CE. Therefore, the logic of hiatus needs to be rethought and cannot be attributed to the one sole reason of the conflict between the two feudatory kings. It is equally difficult to trace out exact nature of reasons as to why excavation in the cave shows such remarkable differences in the execution of the cave. Only formalistic analysis offers to mark out the different stages of cave excavation along with the carving of the pillars and their bases and capital portion. The nature of reason remains a conjecture, however, patronage must have played an important role in the process.

Another pertinent example would be that of cave complex at Ajanta patronized by the local king Upēndragupta. Upēndragupta, a feudatory king of the Vakatakas, patronized Ajanta caves 17-20.5 In the courtyard of chaitya cave 19 shows marked similarity in space division on the façade as well as in the courtyard chambers. Walter Spink observes several intrusive images in the courtyard; however, there is considerable stylistic similarity among such images. Ajanta cave 20 is an interesting cave. The lower portion of the attendant figures in the shrine of cave 20 of Ajanta is incomplete and the inscription of the Upēndragupta in Ajanta cave 17 claims that he had defeated the Aśmakas. If the war between the two local kings was that paramount then why the artisan left unfinished the lower portion of the attendant images in cave 20 at Ajanta? There is every possibility that the artisans used short–cut methods towards carving. Instead of sculpting the entire lower portion from the waist, it is likely that artisans used clay and made lower portion accordingly as artisans were aware that the entire surface would be painted (Fig. 5).

Undoubtedly Upēndragupta patronized Ajanta cave 20, and he might have initiated its excavation only after the war. Besides, how do we understand the imagery at Ajanta itself in the light of the observation that only the later caves of Ajanta have marked the influence of the eastern Vidarbha sculptural tradition whereas the early phase is devoid of such influences?

Thus, it may also be observed that unfinished nature/rough carving at the back of the wall/shrine wall perhaps becomes a part of methods employed by artisans and may not be always an indicator of disruptions. In this context, an earlier example of the Karle chaitya cave may be a case to such pointers.

The back wall of the great Chaitya cave at Karla remained roughly carved as artisans were aware the utility of such spaces at the back wall. It does not mean that the great hall at Karla witnessed phases of excavation and there was a disruption of carving activity. It was part of the process rather than disruption. Hence, hiatus as a concept, at times, becomes indecisive and needs further interrogation. It perhaps remains applicable only in certain cases and cannot be considered as generic, applicable to the entire site. At the same time, conventions do not change overnight. There are equally trivial issues of unfinished nature of caves such as Ajanta cave 5, 23, 24, etc. Many intrusive images are observed in cave 6, 9 and around cave 10 and 26. Ajanta cave 9 and 10 are part of the early complex whereas cave 6 becomes one of the early Mahāyāna cave. Complexity in its placement of images needs to be understood from the politics and importance of the site. Thus, one has to be very cautious while adopting a deterministic framework in the case of the western Deccan caves and more specifically site such as Ajanta.

Notes and references:

Cribb Joe, 'Western Satraps and Sātavāhanas: Old and New Ideas of Chronology', in Ex Moneta Vol-I, (Eds.) A. K. Jha and Sanjay Garg, Harman Publishing House, New Delhi 1998.

Dehejia Vidya, 1972, Early Buddhist Rock Temples A Chronological Study, London.

Deshpande M. N., 1986, The Caves of Panhāḷēkājī, p-30, Archaeological Survey of India, New Delhi.

Dhavalikar M K, 1984, Late Hinayāna Caves of Western India, Deccan College Post Graduate Research Institute, Pune.

Gokhale, Shobhana, 1991, Kanheri Inscriptions, Deccan College Post Graduate Research Institute, Pune.

Kielhorn F., 'Aihole Inscription of Pulakesin-II Śaka 556', in Epigraphia Indica (EI) vol. VI, pp54-57.

Leese, Marylin Edward, 1983, The Traikuta Dynasty and Kanheri's Second Phase Buddhist Cave Excavation, unpublished Ph D. thesis, University of Michigan U.S.A.

Luder H, Appendix to Epigraphia Indica (EI), Vol. X.

Mirashi V. V., Corpus Inscriptionum Indicarum (CII), vol. V.

Pargiter F. E. 1962 (first published 1913), The Purana Text of the Dynasties of the Kali Age, reprint, Delhi.

Ramesh K.V., 'Vada Inscription of Suketuverman, saka 322', in Epigraphia Indica (EI), vol.40,1973-75.

Senart E. 1902-3 'The inscriptions in the caves of Karle' in Epigraphia Indica, Vol. VII

Senart E. 1905, 'The inscriptions in the Caves at Nasik in Epigraphia Indica VIII pp. 59-96,

Sims-Williams, Nicholas and Cribb, Joe 1996, "A New Bactrian Inscription of Kanishka the Great", Silk Road Art and Archaeology, volume 4, 1995-6, Kamakura, pp. 75–142.

Spink Walter-1966, 'Ajanta and Ghatotkacha: Preliminary Analysis', Ars Orientalis, pp 135-156.

-1967, Ajanta to Ellora, in Marg XX, 1967.

-1972, 'Ajanta- A Brief History', in Pal P. P. (Ed.) Aspects of Indian Art, Leiden.

-1974, 'The Splendours of Indra's Crown: A Study of Mahāyāna Development at Ajanta', in Journal of the Royal Society of Arts.

-1975, 'Ajanta's Chronology: The Problem of Cave Eleven', in Ars Orientalis vol. VII, pp. 155-168.

-1981, 'Ajanta's Chronology: Politics and Patronage', in William Joanna (Ed.) Kaladarshan, pp. 104-126, New Delhi.

-1981, 'Ajanta's Chronology: Politics and Patronage', in Chhavi, Bharat Kala Bhavan, Benaras.

-1985, 'Cave 7's Twice Born Buddha Images', in Studies in Buddhist Art of South Asia, (Ed.) A. K. Narain, pp 103-116, Kanak Publication, New Delhi.

-1989, 'A Recently Discovered Buddha Image at Aurangabad', in Ratna-Chandrika Panorama of Oriental Studies (Eds.) Devendra Handa & Ashvini Agraval, Harman Publishing House, New Delhi 1969, pp 189-198.

-1991, 'Vakatakas: Flowering and Fall', in ParimooRatan& Others (Eds.), Art of Ajanta: New Perspective, pp71-99, Books and Books, New Delhi.

-1992, 'Before the Fall: Pride and Piety at Ajanta,' in Miller Barbara Stoller& Blitzer C. (Eds.), Powers of Art, Patronage in Indian Culture, pp 64-77, Oxford University Press, Delhi.

-1992, 'The Archaeology of Ajanta', in Ars Orientalis vol. XXI pp 67-94.

1992, Pathik vol. 13, no.4, July, pp16-25, Maharashtra Tourist Development Corporation, Mumbai.

1993, 'The End of Imagery at Ajanta', in (Eds.) Nayak B.V. &Ghosh N. C., New Trends in Indian Art and Archaeology, pp. 337-348, Aditya Prakashan, New Delhi.

-1994, Ajanta: A Brief History and Guide, Asian Art Achieves of the University of Michigan, 1994.

2005, Ajanta History and Development, Brill Indological series.

1. Considering the nature of content in the inscription, it appears that as Sātavāhanas enforced Brāhmaṇical code of conduct, it is likely that it compelled Nagarjuna to write letters to Gautamīputra Sātakarṇi where ethical, moral values are described in order to achieve Nibbāna by gaining Buddhahood. For a detailed description of the letters, see Nagarjuna's Letter to King Gautamiputra, translated by Venerable Lozang Jamaspal, Venerable Ngawang Samten Chophel, and Peter Della Santina, Motilal Banarsidass Delhi, 1978, 1983 (reprint).

2. Burgess and all others assigned the Mahāyāna excavations at Ajanta to fifth century AD/CE, see Burgess Jas., 1880, Cave Temples of India, London, however M N Deshpande observed that Ajanta cave 15 is likely to be earlier in date as the plan of the cave is almost like the early Hinayāna caves, he further observed that the cave was likely to be altered from the Hīnayāna to Mahāyāna. See Deshpande M. N. in Ghosh A (Ed.), 1961, Ajanta Murals, pp 14-21.

3. For a detailed discussion on Sarnath and Mathura images of fifth century AD, see William Joanna, Art of Gupta: Empire and Province, 1986.

4. Painted inscriptions in the cave 11 was observed by M. K. Dhavalikar, and he considers them palaeographical to fifth century AD/CE, thus, Walter Spink uses this evidence to strengthen his argument that the cave 11 began getting excavated in 462 AD/CE i.e. after few years of 458 AD/CE which is based on Hisseborala inscription. See Dhavalikar M. K. 1968, 'New Inscriptions from Ajanta', Ars Orientalis, VII, pp. 147-53.

5. For the inscriptions of cave 17 and 20, see Mirashi V. V. Corpus Inscriptionum Indicarum, Vol. IV, Inscriptions of the Vakatakas, and also Gupta Chandrashekhar, 1991, 'Authorship of Ajanta Cave 17 to 20', in Art of Ajanta: New Perspectives, pp 100-104, Books and Books, New Delhi.

Newly Discovered Buddhist Rock-cut Caves of Maharashtra: An Appraisal

Shrikant Ganvir, Deccan College Post-Graduate and Research Institute, Pune

Abstract

The present paper aims to examine the significance of the newly discovered caves in Maharashtra after the post-independence period. An attempt will be made to discuss how newly discovered caves have facilitated our knowledge of different aspects of the rock-cut architecture of the region. The role of these caves to comprehend the religio-cultural setting of Maharashtra will also be examined in the present paper. The architectural, sculptural and iconographic features of these caves will also be taken into consideration in this paper.

Introduction

An extensive documentation of Buddhist caves of Maharashtra was carried out in the nineteenth century and the first half of the twentieth century and subsequently published in the articles and monographs (Abbot 1891, Bradley 1853, Cousens 1891, Dikshit 1941, Frere 1850, Johns 1976, West 1861, West and West 1862, Westergaard 1844, Wilson 1850; 1853). The first comprehensive account of the rock-cut caves of India was published in The Cave Temples of India (1880) by Fergusson and Burgess. Burgess (1883) later on published a

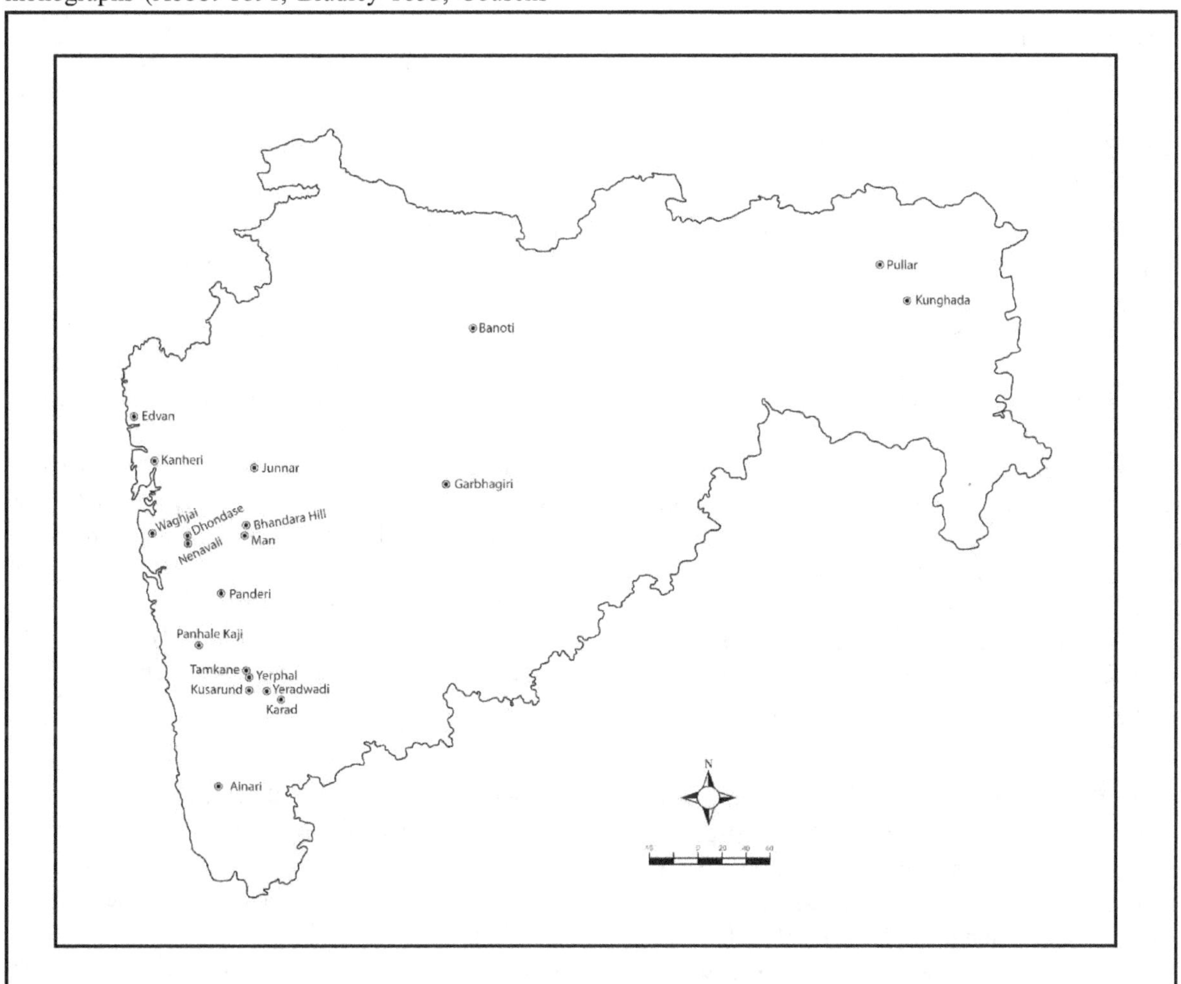

Figure 31: Map showing locations of newly discovered Buddhist caves (Prepared by Hemant Dalvi)

brief account of some of the Buddhist caves of western India in 'Report on the Buddhist Cave Temples and Their Inscriptions'. Cousens (1897) published an inventory of the archaeological sites in the 'Revised Lists of Antiquarian Remains in the Bombay Presidency', which includes some of the unknown or less-known Buddhist caves.

The present paper deals with newly discovered Buddhist caves in Maharashtra in the Post-independence period. An attempt has also been made to comprehend their architectural significance and also to analyse some important features such as their location, sectarian affiliation, functional aspect, etc. The newly discovered Buddhist caves have been classified into four groups based on their location and size. The caves have been dealt here in chronological order, i.e. in order of their discovery. These caves were reported either through systematic exploration or by accidental discovery. Locations of most of these caves are shown in the map of Maharashtra (Fig.1).

The first group includes the newly discovered caves from the known Buddhist rock-cut groups. In this group newly discovered caves at Bhaja, Ajanta, Nenavali, Junnar, Jivdane, Kanheri and Tamkane have been included.

Two more caves, one a vihāra cave and the other, a caitya cave were discovered by M. N. Deshpande during 1955-56 (IAR 1955-56:71-72). These two caves have been studied in detail by Nagaraju (1981: 126-127, fig.25). The vihāra, cave 25 and caitya, cave 26 seem to be the earlier caves in the Bhaja group, based on their architectural features. The unfinished vihāra cave has a large rectangular hall with three cells in the left wall, two cells in the right and a cell in the back. The caitya cave is circular on the plan with a flat roof (Fig.2). There is a stupa in the centre, which is simple in execution with a cylindrical mēdhī and a hemispherical aṇḍa. The presence of a circular socket on the top of the aṇḍa is indicative of an arrangement to fix a loose harmika.

During the clearance of debris of a retaining wall which had collapsed in a landslip, a new vihāra cave was discovered at Ajanta by Abdul Waheed Khan in 1956 (IAR 1955-56:72). The vihāra cave has a hall and three cells within the right, left and back walls. This cave, now numbered as '15-a' belongs to the early phase of the rock-cut excavation of the Ajanta caves. The cells have two benches and their door

frames of the cells are canopied by caitya arches, which are interconnected by railing pattern (Nagaraju 1981: 103, fig.19).

Figure 32: Cave 26, Bhaja (Photograph courtesy: Dr. Abhijit Dandekar)

A group of Buddhist caves at Nenavali was discovered by Rev. Abbott (1891:121-123). The caves are not mentioned in 'The Cave Temples of India', as the caves were discovered after its publication. A brief account of these caves was later published by Cousens (1891). M. N. Deshpande, who had carried out an extensive study of the Nenavali Buddhist caves in 1981-82, noticed a group of five vihāra caves, locally called Camār lēṇa, a quarter kilometre from the main group on the southern side (IAR 1981-82:96-98). These caves are in a bad state of preservation and the front portion of these caves have been collapsed (Fig.3). These caves consist of a hall, mostly provided with cells.

A brief account of the Buddhist caves of Junnar was first published by James Burgess (1877). A comprehensive study of these caves was further carried out by Dr. Suresh Jadhav (1980). A group of 5 caves was reported at Dudharya, 5 kilometres south-east of Junnar. All caves are simple without any decoration. Most of the caves are single cell type excavations. The absence of inscription and water cistern in this small monastic site is striking. In the absence of either epigraphic record or any notable

Figure 33: Exterior view, Nenavali Caves (Photograph: Dr. Shrikant Ganvir)

architectural feature, it seems difficult to date this group of caves (Nakatani et. al. 2010: 225-232). Three more caves were reported at Jivdane by Dr. S. Nagaraju (IAR 1978-79: 99). These are plain vihāra caves. Two more plain caves were reported by Pravin Patil at Tamkane (Tal. Patan, Dist. Satara). Both caves have a veranda and an inner cell (Patil 2012:143-144).

A group of seven caves at Kanheri was reported by Dr. Suraj Pandit. These caves are located on the eastern hill (Pandit 2012:51-60). Natural caverns were modified into these Buddhist caves. Cave 1 is a simple cell with veranda. Cave 2 has two seats and a bench. Cave 3 has a bench in recess, whereas cave 4 consists of a small bench and a water cistern. Cave 5 is the most significant in this group. This cave has along bench along the back wall and consists of two stupas carved on the back wall. The stupas are carved in deep relief and exhibit all the architectural members such as mēdhī, aṇḍa, harmika, yaṣṭi and chatrāvali. These stupas can be dated to the first century CE on the basis of stylistic features. Such relief stupas are also noticed in Kōṇḍaṇē cave 2 and Mahad cave 27 (Nagaraju 1981). Cave 6 is simple

hall type cave, consisting of 'L' shaped bench in a recess along the back and right walls. Cave 7 is also hall type cave, showing the remains of benches on the sidewalls of the veranda followed by a simple hall (Pandit 2012:51-60). Dr. Suraj Pandit has recently discovered another group of seven vihāra caves at Kanheri, which can be considered earlier in the Kanheri caves. One of them is showing the remains of harmika. The architectural features of the caves suggest that these caves were functioning as temporary shelter for monks in the rainy season (Times of India, Pune Edition, Date:17 January 2016).

The second group includes the newly discovered major group of rock-cut caves. This group includes a group of 29 caves at Panhāḷēkājī. The Department of Archives and Archaeology, Maharashtra State undertook exploration in 1970, which resulted into a significant discovery of a group of 29 Buddhist and Hindu rock-cut caves at Panhāḷēkājī (Tal. Dapoli, Dist. Ratnagiri) on the Konkan coast (IAR 1970-71:67). The State Department of Archives and Archaeology, Maharashtra (IAR 1972-73:95, IAR 1973-74:22) and the South-Western Circle of the

Figure 34: Façade of caves 4 and 5, Panhāḷēkājī (Photograph: Dr. Shrikant Ganvir)

Figure 35: View of cave 12, Panhāḷēkājī (Photograph: Dr. Shrikant Ganvir)

Archaeological Survey of India (IAR 1977-78:41) carried out scientific clearance of the debris, which brought about the architectural, sculptural and archaeological remains. This is the most significant discovery of rock-cut caves in the western Deccan. These caves are associated with Hinayāna and Vajrayana sects of Buddhism as well as Nātha and Gāṇapatya sects of Hinduism. Cave 1 to cave 15, cave 18, cave 21 and cave 27 are associated with Hinayāna and Tantric Vajrayana phase of Buddhist architecture (Figs. 4 and 5). The entire Buddhist activities at the site can be dated from the third century CE to the tenth century CE. These caves show advanced architectural features. The Buddhist caves at Panhāḷekājī are of special significance as they provide pivotal evidence regarding Vajrayana Buddhism in the coastal Maharashtra (Deshpande 1986).

The third group includes the newly discovered minor groups of rock-cut caves. It includes caves at Induri, Kunghada, Pullar, Yerphal, Yeradvadi, Digevadi, Dhondase, Kharbala, Bahirampada, Panderi, Garbhagiri and Edvan.

A group of four caves was reported by R. L. Bhide in the Bhandara hill, near Induri (Tal. Maval, Dist. Pune). The group consists of a caitya and three vihāra caves (IAR 1957-58:66, Bhide 1964:148-149). The caitya is rectangular on plan and is open to the sky. The sockets on the top of the walls of this caitya suggest that there was a provision to fix a ceiling on its top. These caves can be dated to the second-third century CE on the basis of the architectural features. A group of five caves at Kunghada (Tal. Nagbhir, Dist. Chandrapur) was discovered by L. K. Srinivasan of the Archaeological Survey of India (IAR 1962-63:15). The caves are plain and three of them have façade. Remains of the caves were reported from Pullar (IAR 1970-71:49). Two Brahmi inscriptions were also reported from the site.

A group of two caves at Yerphal (Tal. Patan, Dist. Satara) located on the Karad-Patan road was discovered by Prof. M. K. Dhavalikar and Dr. Suresh Jadhav in December 1979. The caitya cave is apsidal on plan and consists of an astylar hall with a stupa in the apse. The vaulted roof of the caitya cave does not show any evidence of the arrangement of wooden ribs and rafters on it. The stupa has high mēdhī and a hemispherical aṇḍa with a squarish socket on its top, which is meant for fixing harmika. The traces of a caitya arch were reported by Dhavalikar and

Jadhav. The vihāra consists of two cells, one of them has a bench. The caitya cave can be tentatively dated to the first half of second century CE on the basis of its stylistic affinity with caitya cave 6 at Karad and the isolated caitya at Junnar (Dhavalikar 1984:33).

A group of four rock-cut excavations was discovered at Yeradvadi (Tal. Patan, Dist. Satara), twenty-five kilometres northwest of Karad and two kilometres west of Malhar Peth by Dr. David Efurd (2006: 11-14). This group consists of a caitya, a vihāra and rest are the unfinished excavations. The caitya is under worship as a Śaiva shrine, locally called 'Rudrēśvara'. The caitya is apsidal on plan and has twenty-one pillars, out of which nineteen pillars are octagonal, where the front pillar on either side is squarish (Figs. 6 and 7). The cave has a vaulted ceiling with grooves, which meant for wooden ribs and rafters. Interestingly, the principal object of veneration, i.e. the stupa is absent in the cave. The façade has a caitya arch, which shows a strong influence of blind caitya arch. The caitya can be considered as one of the earliest caityas of the western Deccan. The caitya cave has been dated to the second century CE by Efurd. A group of three caves was discovered at Digevadi (Tal. Patan, Dist. Satara), near Yeradwadi on the Karad-Chiplun road by Dr. David Efurd (2006: 16). The group consists of a caitya, a vihāra and a cluster of cells. The caves are in a bad state of preservation. The caitya is apsidal on plan with an astylar hall. The ceiling is vaulted and a stupa is absent, similar to Yeradvadi caitya.

A group of nine caves at three sites was reported by the present author in 2009 in the vicinity of the Buddhist caves at Thānāḷē and Nenavali Buddhist caves, while carrying out an extensive study of the Thānāḷē and Nenavali caves as the Departmental Research Project of the Deccan College Post-Graduate and Research Institute, Pune. A group of two caves is located near Dhondase (Tal. Pali, Dist. Raigad) about 13 kilometres east of Pali, the Taluka headquarter in Raigad district and 5 kilometres northeast of the village Dhondase. The group consists of cave 1, a vihāra and cave 2, an unfinished caitya cave (Ganvir 2014:55-59). The vihāra consists of a veranda, hall and three cells (Fig. 8). The hall had originally a running bench on both sides and at the back. When the cave was extended two more cells were added in the back wall through cutting the bench in the back wall. An attempt was also made to excavate a cell on the right side. Both

Figure 36: Façade, Yeradvadi Caitya (Photograph: Dr. Shrikant Ganvir)

Figure 37: Interior view, Yeradvadi Caitya (Photograph: Dr. Shrikant Ganvir)

the cells of the back wall have benches. The cells on the northern and southern sides in the back wall are completed whereas the cell on the right side is left unfinished. Cave 2, an unfinished caitya cave, consists of a veranda and a roughly squarish hall with an unfinished stupa (Fig.9). The cave is entered through a flight of steps which is now much damaged. The astylar hall is roughly square and flat-roofed. The hall has a squarish shaped mass of rock in the rear end, which was evidently intended for a stupa and it remains unfinished because of seepage of water in the back side of the hall.

Figure 38: Cave 1, Dhondase (Photograph: Dr. Shrikant Ganvir)

Figure 39: Cave 2, Dhondase (Photograph: Dr. Shrikant Ganvir)

Another group of two caves was reported at Kharbala, near Dhondase caves in the forest area near Sudhagad. The caves are remained unfinished probably because of the unsuitability of the rock for further excavations. The caves have a squarish or rectangular hall, without any traces of bench (Fig.10). It was also intended to provide the doorway to one of the caves; the remains of such arrangement are still visible (Ganvir 2014:55-59).

Figure 40: Exterior view, Kharabala Caves (Photograph: Dr. Shrikant Ganvir)

Another group of five caves was reported by the present author at Bahiramapada (Tal. Pali, Dist. Raigad) about 11 kilometres east of Pali, the Taluka headquarter in Raigad district and 3 kilometres northeast of the village Dhondase (Ganvir 2014:55-59). The group consists of two vihāra caves and three unfinished caves. Caves 1, 4 and 5 are unfinished caves, whereas caves 2 and 3 are vihāra caves and are identical on the plan. Both the caves consist of a bench in the back wall. The caves are simple and do not show any embellishment (Fig.11). On stylistic grounds, the Dhondase caves can be dated to the middle of the second century as these caves show many similarities with the Junnar caves. The Dhondase caitya is a quadrangular, astylar and flat-roofed caitya. According to Dhavalikar (1984:27), the quadrangular, astylar and flat-roofed caitya emerged in western India in the middle of second century CE. The Bahirampada caves seem to be earlier than the Dhondase caves on the basis of their architectural features and can be dated to the middle of first century CE.

Figure 41: Exterior view, Bahirampada Caves (Photograph: Dr. Shrikant Ganvir)

A group of three caves was discovered by Anjay Dhanavade and his team in 2009 at Panderi (Tal. Mandangad, Dist. Ratnagiri), located 15 kilometres away from Mhapral, a small riverine port on River Savitri (Dhanavade et. al. 2011-12:179-184). The three caves are mostly identical in plan and consist of a mandapa and shrine (Fig.12). Cave 1 faces east while caves 2 and 3 face north. Cave 1 has an outer mandapa and an inner cell. The outer hall has two benches carved on the northern and southern walls. Cave 2 is more elaborate than the remaining two caves. This cave has a pillared hall with two long benches excavated on the eastern and western walls, and a shrine in the back wall. The shrine of the cave has an ornate door with two dvāraśākhās and a lalāṭabimba. Cave 3 is smaller in dimensions, compared to the remaining two caves. This cave consists of an outer hall and an inner cell and the door of the cave is unadorned. As rightly mentioned in the scholars in the article (Dhanavade et. al. 2011-12:179-184), it is difficult to assign religious affiliation of the caves in absence of any contextual evidence, but on the basis of their striking similarity to the caves at Panhāḷēkājī, the possibility of their association with Tantric Buddhism cannot be ruled out.

*Figure 42:*General view, Panderi caves (Photograph courtesy: Dr. P. P. Joglekar)

A group of three caves at Edvan (Tal. and Dist.: Palghar) was discovered by Dr. Suraj Pandit and Siddharth Kale (2013:250-252). Edvan is located on the northern bank of Vaitarana creek and south of Palghar, the District headquarter. The caves have been altered and have been used for the worship of a goddess. These caves exhibit striking similarities with the Buddhist caves at Jivdane. Although it is difficult to ascertain religious affiliation of the caves, a tentative possibility of its association with Buddhist monks cannot be ruled out due to its proximity to Sopara.

A group of two caves, at Garbhagiri hill (Tal. Pathardi, Dist. Ahmednagar), 6 kilometres from Shirapur village and 25 kilometres from Pathardi was discovered by Dr. Shreekant Jadhav. The group consists of a caitya and a vihāra (Jadhav 2015:424-434). The caitya is apsidal on plan and has an unfinished stupa in the apse of the cave (Fig.13). The excavation of the pillars stopped as the remains of three pillars on the right side of the cave can be seen. The ceiling of the caitya is vaulted. The façade of the cave displays the remains of a caitya arch with stone ribs. The vihāra cave consists of a rectangular hall with cells on three sides of the cave. The vihāra has eight cells without benches, three each on the right and left sides and two in the back wall.

*Figure 43:*Interior view, Garbagier Caitya (Photograph courtesy: Dr. Shreekant Jadhav)

The fourth group includes newly discovered single or solitary cave in Maharashtra. Solitary Buddhist caves were reported from Man, Dhangwhan, Banoti, Gothe, Pomgaon, Waghjai, Kusarund, Dhareshvar and Ainari.

A solitary cave at Man (Tal. Haveli, Dist. Pune), 19 kilometres west of Pune was reported by R. L. Bhide (1964:148). The cave is located in a hill known as madhicā dōmgar, west of the village. The coins of the Western Kshatrapas were reported from the vicinity of the cave. It seems that this cave was functioning as a temporary shelter either for Buddhist monks or traders. A caitya cave was reported by the Department of Archaeology, Government of Maharashtra at Dhangawhan, near Kamshet (Tal. Maval, Dist. Pune). The cave is apsidal on plan and the stupa is in ruinous condition (IAR 1965-66:28).

T. M. Kesava of the Archaeological Survey of India noticed an unfinished rock-cut cave of the

Vākāṭakaperiod at Banoti (IAR 1982-83:136-137). The Banoti cave (Tal. Soygaon, Dist. Aurangabad) is only fifteen kilometres from Ajanta as the crow flies and seventy kilometres away from the road. The debris clearance was carried out by the Archaeological Survey of India to comprehend its architectural features (IAR 1989-90:55-56). The cave bears unique architectural features (Figs. 14 and 15).

Figure 44:Interior view, Banoti cave (Photograph: Dr. Shrikant Ganvir)

Figure 45:Doorframe of the shrine, Banoti cave (Photograph: Dr. Shrikant Ganvir)

The cave consists of a simple porch fronted by four pillars, a pillared shrine antechamber with shrine behind with unfinished ambulatory (pradakṣiṇāpatha). The plain hall of the cave has pillar-fronted extensions on either side with two cells at the right and a cell at the left. According to Spink (2005: 337), the cave is of particular interest because it has two distinct phases, in fact, it is the only Vākāṭaka cave in Maharashtra which was expanded a century or so later. The shrine doorway has a distinct stupa in its central motif, which confirms its Buddhist affiliation in the first phase of the excavation. This first phase must have started in the last half of the fifth century CE. The second phase of excavation, which can be dated to the last half of the sixth century CE which can be evident from the transformation of one of the two unfinished shrine antechamber pillars (Spink 2005:336-343).

Two caves were reported by Vikram Marathe, one each at Gothe (Tal. Mulshi, Dist. Pune), behind the hills of Deshmukhvadi and Pomgaon (Tal. Mulshi, Dist. Pune). The cave at Gothe, 3 kilometres from Paratevadi, is a vihāra, which has seven cells in the back wall (Marathe 1999-2000:161-162). Some of the cells have preserved the remains of benches. Remains of a water cistern were also reported at the site. Another cave at Pomgaon is located near Gothe village. It is a single cell without any bench. The strategic location of these two solitary caves on the ancient trade route going from Chaul to Junnar is of an immense significance. A detailed analytical study of the interrelation of Buddhist caves, ancient trade routes and ancient sites has been published in the article on the ancient port at Chaul (Gogte et. al. 2006:76-77).

A cave was reported in Waghjai hill in Agarav region (Tal. Alibag, Dist. Raigad) near Chaul in 2004 by Prof. V. D. Gogte and his team (Gogte et al. 2006: 76). The cave seems to be of caitya-cum-vihāra type of the late Hinayāna phase of the Buddhist rock-cut architecture in the western Deccan. The cave has a hall and inner central chamber enshrining a stupa (Fig.16). The cave is in a dilapidated state. The hall is squarish whereas the inner chamber is rectangular. The stupa is in a bad state of preservation, showing the remains of stepped inverted pyramidal capital. The cave can be approximately dated between the late second century CE to the early third century CE. It shows striking similarities with the caitya caves of Mahad and Kuḍā (Dhavalikar 1984:38-47).

Figure 46: Interior view, Waghjai Cave (Photograph courtesy: Dr. Abhijit Dandekar and Dr. Sachin Joshi)

A vihāra cave was reported at Kusarund (Tal. Patan, Dist. Satara) by Pravin Patil. The cave consists of a hall and ten cells with benches (Patil 2012:241). A circular impression of rock in the centre of the hall strongly confirms the possibility of a rock-cut or structural stupa. Another cave at Dhareshvar (Tal. Patan, Dist. Satara) reported by the same researcher seems to be affiliated to Buddhism as the cave has been undergone recent renovation and is under worship as Śaiva shrine (Patil 2014:242). The vaulted roof and the nature of the façade propose its association with Buddhist rock-cut architecture.

A cave was reported by Anjay Dhanavade at Ainari (Tal. Vaibhavwadi, Dist. Sindhudurg) on the Konkan coast (Dhanavade 2014:187-190). The cave is located 5 kilometres away from Ainari. There are three rock-cut excavations including a cave and two water cisterns. The cave is of caitya-cum-vihāra type, belonging to the late Hinayāna phase. It consists of a veranda supported by two octagonal pillars, a pillared hall and an apsidal room/hall with the provision of excavating a stupa. A big rock is seen standing in corner of the apsidal cell with the definite intention of carving a stupa. The cave has altogether four cells with stone benches, one cell on the left side and the remaining three cells are in the back wall. The stylistic affinity of this cave at Ainari to Pohale caitya, Karad cave 7, Kuḍā cave 7, Shelarwadi cave 7, Khed caitya and Wai caitya (Dhavalikar 1984:29-50).

Concluding remarks

Most of the caves seem to be located on the ancient trade routes or near the routes. Most of the newly discovered Buddhist caves to the late Hinayāna phase of rock-cut Buddhist architecture. The newly discovered caityas mostly follow the architectural traits of the late Hinayāna phase. The Banoti cave is a solitary example of the Mahāyāna phase of the Buddhist rock-cut architecture, whereas the Buddhist caves at Panhāḷēkājī mostly represent the Vajrayana phase of the Buddhist rock-cut architecture. Epigraphic records are almost absent in newly discovered caves. Discovery of minor Buddhist monastic complexes is more fascinating. These caves need further investigation to understand their functional aspect. Although many more Buddhist cave sites were reported either in Pre-independence period or Post-independence period, looking into the nature of geographic setting and landscape of the state, it seems that there could be still some more unknown Buddhist caves in the mountainous region which could not be visited due to their uttermost location, so it is essential to carry out more systematic and extensive exploration of the region for further investigations.

Acknowledgements

This is a revised version of my paper presented in the International Conference on the Rock-cut Caves of Maharashtra, organized by the Centre for Archaeology and the Centre for Extra-Mural Studies of the University of Mumbai. I am thankful to Prof A. P. Jamkhedkar, Dr. Mugdha Karnik, Dr. Suraj Pandit and Dr. Kurush Dalal for inviting me to present the paper in the International Conference. I express my sincere gratitude to the authorities of the Deccan College (Deemed University) for their constant academic support. I am grateful to Prof. Y. S. Alone for his valuable comments.

I am also thankful to Prof P. P. Joglekar, Dr. Shreekant Jadhav, Dr. Abhijit Dandekar, Dr. Sachin Joshi and Vikram Marathe for providing photographs of the newly discovered caves. I thank Hemant Dalvi for preparing the location map of the caves.

Bibliography

Abbott, J.E. 1891. "Recently discovered Buddhist Caves at Nadsur and Nenavali in the Bhor State, Bombay Presidency." Indian Antiquary 20: 121-123.

Bhide, Ramchandra. 1964. "Mahārashtrātīl Ajñāt Lēṇyāṃca Śōdh." Journal of the University of Poona 19:145-150 (in Marathi).

Bradley, W.H. 1853. "Buddhist Cave Temples in the circas of Buitalbari and Dowlatabad in the H.H. the Nizam's Dominions." Journal of the Bombay

Branch of Royal Asiatic Society 5: 117-24.

Burgess, James. 1877. Memorandum on the Buddhist Caves at Junnar. Bombay: Government Central Press.

Burgess, James. 1883. Report on the Buddhist Cave Temples and Their Inscriptions. London: Trübner &Co.

Cousens, H. 1891. An Account of the Caves at Nadsur and Karsambla. Bombay: Government Central Press.

Cousens, H. 1897. Revised Lists of Antiquarian Remains in the Bombay Presidency. Bombay: Government Central Press.

Deshpande, M. N. 1986. The Caves of Panhāḷēkājī (Ancient Pranalaka): An Art Historical Study of transition from Hinayāna, Tantric Vajrayana to Nātha Sampradaya. New Delhi: Archaeological Survey of India.

Dhanavade, Anjay, P. P. Joglekar and Abhay Kale. 2012. "Discovery of Rock-cut Caves at Panderi, District Ratnagiri, Maharashtra." Journal of Indian Ocean Archaeology 7-8: 179-184.

Dhanavade, Anjay. 2014. "Caves at Ainari." Journal of the Asiatic Society of Mumbai 86 (2012-13): 187-190.

Dhavalikar, M. K. 1984. Late Hinayāna Caves of Western India. Poona: Deccan College Post-Graduate and Research Institute.

Dikshit, M. G. 1941. "Fresh Light on Pitalkhora Caves." Journal of the Bombay Historical Society 6:112-21.

Efurd, David. 2006. "Caitya Halls: Evidence of a Rock-Cut Architectural Tradition in the Vicinity of Karād, Southern Mahārāṣtra." South Asian Studies 22:11-22.

Fergusson, James and James Burgess. 1880. The Cave Temples of India. London: W. H. Allen & Co.

Frere, H. B. E. 1850. "Memorandum on Some Buddhist Excavations Near Karad." Journal of the Bombay Branch of the Royal Asiatic Society 3:108-118.

Ganvir, Shrikant. 2014. "Recently Discovered Buddhist Caves in Konkan: Some Observations." In Bodhisiri: A Festschrift to A.V. Reddy, edited by P. Chenna Reddy and E. Śiva Nagi Reddy, 55-59. New Delhi: Research India Press.

Gogate, Vishwas, Shrikant Pradhan, Abhijit Dandekar, Sachin Joshi, Rukshana Nanji, Shivendra Kadgaonkar and Vikram Marathe. 2006. "The Ancient Port at Chaul." Journal of Indian Ocean Archaeology 3:62-79.

Indian Archaeology 1955-56 A Review. 1956. Edited by A. Ghosh. New Delhi: Archaeological Survey of India.

Indian Archaeology 1957-58 A Review. 1958. Edited by A. Ghosh. New Delhi: Archaeological Survey of India.

Indian Archaeology 1962-63 A Review. 1965. Edited by A. Ghosh. New Delhi: Archaeological Survey of India.

Indian Archaeology 1965-66 A Review. Edited by A. Ghosh. 1973. New Delhi: Archaeological Survey of India.

Indian Archaeology 1969-70 A Review. 1973. Edited by B. B. Lal. New Delhi: Archaeological Survey of India.

Indian Archaeology 1970-71 A Review. 1974. Edited by M. N. Deshpande. New Delhi: Archaeological Survey of India.

Indian Archaeology 1972-73 A Review. 1978. Edited by M. N. Deshpande. New Delhi: Archaeological Survey of India.

Indian Archaeology 1973-74 A Review. 1979. Edited by B. K. Thapar. New Delhi: Archaeological Survey of India.

Indian Archaeology 1977-78 A Review. 1980. Edited by B. K. Thapar. New Delhi: Archaeological Survey of India.

Indian Archaeology 1978-79 A Review. 1981. Edited by B. K. Thapar. New Delhi: Archaeological Survey of India.

Indian Archaeology 1981-82 A Review. 1984. Edited by B. K. Thapar. New Delhi: Archaeological Survey of India.

Indian Archaeology 1982-83 A Review. 1985. Edited by M. S. Nagaraja Rao. New Delhi: Archaeological Survey of India.

Indian Archaeology 1989-90 A Review. 1994. Edited by S. K. Mahapatra. New Delhi: Archaeological Survey of India.

Jadhav, S. 1980. Rock Cut Cave Temples at Junnar: An Integrated Study. Unpublished Ph.D. Thesis, University of Pune.

Jadhav, Shreekant S. 2015. "Relatively Unknown Buddhist Rock-cut Caves in Garbhgiri Hills (Dist. Ahmednagar)." Heritage: Journal of Multidisciplinary Studies in Archaeology 3:424-434.

Johns, G. H. 1876. "Notes on Some Little-Known Bauddha Excavations in the Poona Collectorate." Indian Antiquary 5: 252-253.

Marathe, Vikram. 2000. "Unveiling the Ancient Trade Route of Paratewadi." Puratattva 30: 161-163.

Nagaraju, S. 1981. Buddhist Architecture of Western India. Delhi: Agam Kala Prakashan.

Nakatani, N., F. Yoneda, A. Toyoyama and A. Uesugi. 2010. "Through Ports, Passes and Junctions: Reconsideration of the Excavational Patterns of Minor Buddhist caves in Western India with Special Reference to Junnar." In South Asian Archaeology 2007 Proceedings of the 19th Meeting of the European Association of the South Asian Archaeology in Ravenna, Italy July 2007, Vol. II, edited by P. Callieri and L. Colliva, 225-232. Oxford: Archaeopress.

Pandit, Suraj. 2012. "Few Lesser Known and Unknown Caves from Kanheri." Journal of the Asiatic Society of Mumbai 84 (2010-11): 51-60.

Pandit, Suraj, and Siddharth Kale. 2013. "Caves at Edvan." Journal of the Asiatic Society of Mumbai 85 (2011-12): 250-252.

Patil, Pravin. 2012. "Caves in the vicinity of Patan." Journal of the Asiatic Society of Mumbai 85 (2010-11): 140-144.

Spink, Walter M. 2005. Ajanta: History and Development. The End of the Golden Age, vol. 1. Leiden: Brill.

West, Edward W. 1861. "Copies of Inscriptions from the Buddhist Cave Temples of Kanheri and Caves in the island of Salsette, with a plan of the Kanheri Caves." Journal of the Bombay Branch of the Royal Asiatic Society 6: 1-14.

West, Edward W., and Arthur A. West. 1862. "Nasik Cave Inscriptions." Journal of the Bombay Branch of the Royal Asiatic Society 7: 37-52.

Westergaard, Niels, L. 1844. "A Brief Account of the Minor Buddha Caves of Beira and Bajah in the neighbourhood of Karli." Journal of the Bombay Branch of the Royal Asiatic Society 1: 438-43.

Wilson, J. 1850. "Memoir on the Cave-Temples and Monasteries and other Ancient Buddhist, Brāhmaṇical, and Jaina Remains of Western India." Journal of the Bombay Branch of the Royal Asiatic Society 3: 37-118.

——. 1853. "Second Memoir on the Cave Temples and Monasteries and Other Ancient Buddhist, Brāhmaṇical and Jaina Remains of Western India." Journal of the Bombay Branch of the Royal Asiatic Society 4: 341-375.

Origin and Development of Rock-cut Architecture of Vidarbha (Maharashtra)

Ganpatrao K. Mane, Amravati University, Amravati

Abstract

The Vidarbha region lies between 19°26'and 21°47' N and 75°56' and 79°23' E. It comprises eleven districts viz. Akola, Amravati, Buldhana, Washim, Yeotmal, Bhandara, Chandrapur, Gadchiroli, Gondia, Nagpur and Wardha. The Vidarbha region can be broadly divided into two zones, viz. Eastern Vidarbha and Western Vidarbha. The region between Ajanta and Gawilgarh hill ranges can be considered as the Western zone. The Eastern Vidarbha comprises a landscape of low elevation, irregular hills and slow-moving streams.

The early Iron Age sites of Vidarbha can be distinguished into three categories, namely, 1) burial, 2) habitation-cum-burial and 3) purely habitation sites. Our study is concentrated on megalithic dolmens which are reported from Pimpalgoan, Bhrami, Tiloti-khairi, Chamorshi and Hirapur. This type of megalithic burial is part of the early rock-cut architecture in Vidarbha. In Hirapur, megalithic burial 01 is a huge dolmen, which is made of laterite and sandstone. The dolmen is divided into two separate chambers each with a separate rectangular porthole. Besides this dolmen, two other dolmens have been found in dilapidated condition. After careful observation, Dolmen 01 was found to have two portholes which were intentionally prepared by the builder of the dolmen. The capstone of dolmen is huge and intact. This site was excavated by Deccan College. The depth of the dolmen is about 1.75 mother left chamber is just like a cave with a capstone. Similar types of caves are reported at Bhivkund and Satbhoki. The person who had excavated the cave might have known the dolmens of Hirapur, Pimpalgoan and Tiloti-khairi. They put a capstone in front of caves at Bhivkund and Satbhoki which are very similar to Pimpalgoan and Tiloti-khairi.

*Generally, it is accepted that the tradition of rock-cut architecture first got associated with the reformistic faiths like Ājīvikas and the Buddhists during the Mauryan period. During that period, itself, it got transplanted to Orissa and the Western Ghats where the earliest of the rock-cut caves are noticed. These are mainly associated with Buddhism. From here, it spread to different parts of India, especially to the south. **Eventually, the** tradition was taken over by the Śaiva Śāktas and Vaiṣṇavas and later from the 6th century onwards by the Jainas.*

In Vidarbha, another interesting document has been noted at Deotek, a small village not far away from Pauni Adam, Hirapur. There are two inscriptions on a large stone slab. Out of the two inscriptions, one dates back to the time of Ashoka and the other to that of the Vakatakas. The four-line inscription is issued by a Dharmamahāmātra in the 14th year after the coronation of Ashoka.

The excavations at Pauni and Bhon have yielded a large number of brick stupas. These pieces of evidence are helpful to know the religious activities of the Buddhist religion. Most of the earliest vihāras are concentrated near Pauni. It shows that the megalithic people might have merged into Mauryan society and the architectural activities may have transferred to Mauryan society. It indicates that the early rock-cut architecture was started separately during Mauryan Period. There is no influence of cave architecture of Lomas Rishi and Sudama caves of Bihar.

The megalithic people were the first community to learn about iron metallurgy. This technology helped to chisel the stone for building megalithic monuments i.e. dolmens, menhirs. This megalithic architectural construction was a milestone; for early Mauryan society of Vidarbha. They started small Vihāras which are very closely related to dolmens.

Introduction

The Vidarbha region lies in between Lat. 19°26' and 21°47' N and Long. 75°56' and 79°23' E. It comprises eleven districts i.e. Akola, Amravati, Bhandara, Buldhana, Chandrapur, Gadchiroli, Gondia, Wardha, Washim and Yeotmal, occupying an area of about 93654 Sq.km. The Vidarbha region can be broadly divided into two zones i.e. Eastern and Western Vidarbha. The region between Ajanta and Gawilgarh hill ranges can be considered as the Western zone. The Eastern Vidarbha comprises a landscape of low elevation, irregular hills and slow-moving streams.

Previous Work

A number of scholars have done intensive and exhaustive work in the field of western rock-cut architecture. Very few works have been done on Vidarbha rock-cut architecture by scholars like A. Cunningham, M.G. Dixit, S.B. Deo, A.P. Jamkhedkar, Pradeep Meshram, Shripad Chitale, and P.N. Phadake. It is, therefore, my endeavour to work on the origin and development of the caves in detail, taking into account every minor point which has not touched by earlier scholars.

A. Cunningham has written a report of a 'Tour in the Central Provinces in 1873-74 and 1874-75 which was published in 1879 and the reprint came in 2000. Dr. M.G. Dixit has prepared a list of caves in a book '*Madhya Pradēś kē Purātattva kī Rūparēkhā*' in 1954 when Vidarbha was under the Central Provinces and Berar. Dr. S.B. Deo published an article on "Joginkupi Cave Inscription at Pullar" but he untouched the architecture of the cave. Dr. A.P. Jamkhedkar works on Arts and Architecture of Maharashtra (Ancient Period). He discusses the plans of the caves and important features of Vidarbha caves.

Dr. P. S. Meshram published a book on '*Vidarbhātīl Buddha Dharmācā Itihāsa*' in 1993. His work on cave architecture is sketchy in nature. Dr. Shripad Chitale has written a small monograph on Vidarbha caves. He describes these caves from a popular and not from an archaeological point of view perspective. No one has touched the origin and development of caves and correlated to the cave architecture of western India.

The main purpose of my present study is to find out the origin and the development of caves as well as critical analysis of the rock-cut caves of Vidarbha.

Before going towards the origin of the caves, one knows about the urbanization process in Vidarbha.

In north India, the period around 7th-6th century B.C. was the time of emergence of new political entities and rise of cities, which are depicted in contemporary literature such as Aṣtadhyāyī and Buddhist literature. At the same time by 1000 BC Vidarbha witnessed a full-fledged Iron Age. Eastern part of Vidarbha was under the Aśmaka Janapada. The Early Iron Age megalithic culture succeeds the Chalcolithic culture of Vidarbha and the material remains of the former are known due to a sizeable number of excavated megalithic sites.

In Vidarbha region (Fig. 1) 125 megalithic sites are reported. Eight of them are habitational sites[16]. They are mostly noted in the hilly, barren, and forested wasteland region. However, only about 15% of these are excavated. The concentration of megalithic sites is in about 50 km radius of the city Nagpur. All these megaliths typologically belong to a single type i.e. pits bounded by a stone circle, except for a few dolmens and menhirs which have been noticed in Chandrapur and Bhandara districts.

The Early Iron Age sites of Vidarbha can be distinguished into three categories, i.e. (1) purely habitation sites (2) burial and (3) habitation-cum-burial sites. There are two trends of iron using people, one belongs to burial practices and the other related to non-burial practices. Junapani, Takalghat-Khapa, Mahurjhari, Bhagi Mohari, Dhamana Linga, Borgaon, Nagalwadi and Khairwada have given evidence of the use of iron and copper. The megalithic people used iron tools for hunting, agricultural and carpentry purposes. Apart from introducing iron technology in Vidarbha, the megalithic builders used copper. Primarily these objects are noted from some sites like Khapa, Gangapur, Takalghat, Mahurjhari, Raipur and Naikund. These mainly comprised of bells, bangles, dishes and bell-shaped objects. Copper bells with iron tongue are recovered from the sites of Junapani, Khapa, Mahurjhari, Naikund and Hingna. Dishes with lids, horse ornaments, gold and silver ornaments were also used by the megalithic people. As a result of this data available from excavated sites, it is realized that the megalithic people used the horse for riding purposes.

The introduction of the iron technology in the region

---

[16]Mane, G.K., 'Excavation at Nagalwadi - New light', Proceeding of the Indian History Congress, Delhi, 2007, p. 1001.

Figure 47: Vidarbha Region

as evident at Naikund in the form of iron smelting furnace has supported the above statement. The iron objects of Vidarbha are superior to those of south India. The iron objects found at Mahurjhari, Takalghat and Naikund are made of pure iron (99.1%, 99.6% and 82.2% iron and 1.8% - 0.4% carbon). This high content of iron in the tools suggests that the Vidarbha megalithic people knew the technology of iron smelting[17]. On the basis of C14 data, the megalithic culture of Vidarbha is dated to c. 700-500 B.C[18]. The dates for mid-level of megalithic habitations at Takalghat are 615 ± 100 B.C. and 465 ± 90 B.C[19]. The full-fledged use of iron goes back to 7th-8th century B.C.

Vidarbha people used iron for various activities. They started the chiselling of stones for preparing dolmens and Menhirs. The megalithic dolmens are reported from Pimpalgaon Brahmi, Tiloti-Khairi, Hirapur and Chamorshi. Menhirs are also recorded from Chandagarh, Nagbhir, Deulwada, Taibarva and

[17]Mane, G.K., 'Metal objects and Metallurgy of Megalithic Culture of Vidarbha, Proceeding of the Indian History Congress, Bhopal, 2001, p. 968.
[18]Deo, S.B. and Jamkhedkar, A.P., Naikund Excavations (1978-80), Bombay, 1982, pp. 7-8.
[19]Deo, S.B., 'Recent Researches on the Chalcolithic and Megalithic Cultures of the Deccan' (K.V. Raman, Ed.) Madras, Madras University Archaeological Series, 5, 1982, p. 37.

Yegaon Janva.

The dolmens of Vidarbha is a part and parcel of early rock-cut architecture of Vidarbha. Dolmen at Hirapur (Plate 1) is perhaps the biggest of the dolmens in Central India. In Hirapur[20], megalithic burial is a huge dolmen, which is made of laterite and sandstone. The dolmen is bifurcated into two separate chambers each with a separate rectangular porthole. The two small chambers, measure to the inside 5.8'x 8' and 5' x 8' respectively. Two portholes, were intentionally prepared by the builders of the dolmen (Plate 1). The cape stone of dolmen is huge and intact. A solid sandstone of 16' x 11.3' x 2.5' that might have been brought from Dongargaon hill, 3.5 kms away from the site, was laid upon three stone slabs. These orthostats are 6' above and 6' below the ground level.

Plate 1: Excavated Dolmen at Hirapur

Plate 2: Excavated Dolmen No. 3 - Capstone

Excavation of the Hirapur Dolmen were carried by the Deccan College during which copper coins, glass bangles, iron implements, stone polishers and seven

baked bricks were recovered[21].

Dolmen No. 2 was excavated and it was found that some capstone was used as a platform during the Sātavāhana period (Plate 2).

Dolmen at Pimpalgaon (Plate 3) has six pillars and the height of pillars is 1.20 m. The capstone is oval shaped (3.60 m long North-South, 3.70 m long East-West and 30 cm thick). There are 27 cup-marks on the capstone.

Plate 3: View of the Dolmen at Pimpalgaon

Dolmen of Tiloti-Khairi is somewhat similar to that of Pimpalgaon (Plate 4) in Bhandara district. The capstone rests on six pillars, is 4.30 m long, 3.40 m wide and 35 cm thick. The pillars are made of laterite stone. The height of the dolmen is 80 cm. Cup-marks are recorded on the capstone slab.

Plate 4: Front view of the Dolmen at Tiloti-Khari

In Vidarbha 132 caves have been reported by various scholars. The concentration of caves is in Nagpur and Chandrapur districts. The dolmens are erected in Bhandara and Chandrapur district which are near Bhivkund, Chandala, Jagankop, Kitali (Satbhoki), Pullar caves in Nagpur district and Bhatala,

---

[20]Mane, G.K., 'Hirapur Dolmen' Shodha Nibandha Sangraha, Yeotmal, 2000, pp. 25-26.
[21]Pawar, K.A., Archaeological Investigations at Parasgarh, Nagpur Hill in East Chimur Region of Chandrapur District of Maharashtra, Bulletin of the Deccan College, 70-71, 2010-11, p. 61.

Bhandak, Deulwada caves in Chandrapur district.

A detailed report on the important caves is given below.

Bhivkund

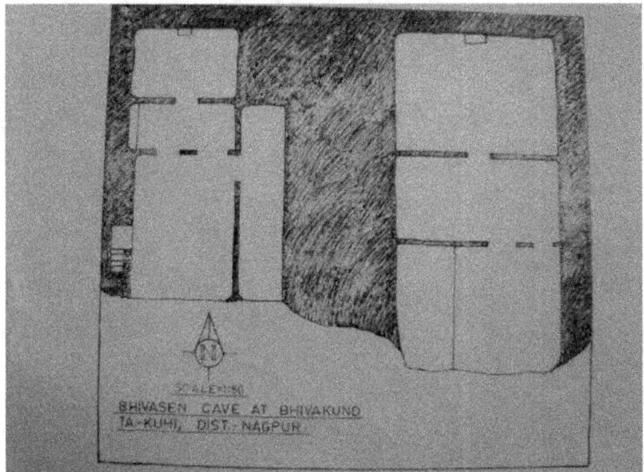

Figure 2: Bhivsena cave at Bhivkund

The site is situated on the high hill on Kuhi-Pachkhedi road. There are five caves. One is in dilapidated condition. Cave No. 1 faces south-west. The cave consists of two parts, a cell and veranda. This cave is excavated on a slope in the red sandstone hill. The cave is 5.5 m long, 2.55 m broad and 1.40 m high. The hill slopes gradually down to the west side.

In the front of the cell, a pillared veranda and the capstone rest on three pillars and the side wall. The capstone is 3.50 m long, 1.80 m broad and 0.30 m thick (Plate 5).

Plate 5: Front view of the Cave No. 1 - Bhivkund

Cave No. 2: This cave is in dilapidated condition. The capstone is lying on the high deposited material (Plate 6).

Plate 6: Cave No. 3 - Dolmen in dilapidated condition

Cave No. 3: This cave is known as Bhivsena Dev. Front of the cell is open veranda having capstone 3.60 m long, 1.00 m broad and 35 cm thick and 1.60 m height (Plate 7). There is an inscription which is incised on a stone portion of the upper wall of the cell. (Plate 8)

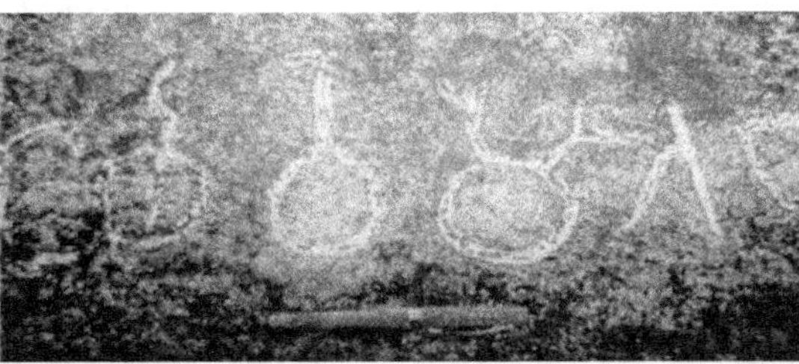

Plate 8: Inscription in Bhivsen Dev Cave at Bhivkund

Cave No. 5: Right side of the cave is having capstone measuring 2.60 m length, 2.30 m breadth and 1.40 m height.

Cave No. 4: The cave is known as Waghachi Dari (valley of the tigers). The cave is cuboid in form, with the following dimensions 4 m x 3.30 m x 1.40 m (Plate 9). Here also a capstone is used as a roof for the veranda.

Satbhoki

Plate 10: Front view of Cave Satbhoki

Plate 7: Bhivsen Dev Cave at Bhivkund

Plate 9: Cave No. 4 - Bhivkund

The sites of Adam, Mandal, Pauni, Pachkhedi (which have been excavated) are not far away from Satbhoki which is in Bhowari jungle (Plate 10). Pullar, Korambhi and Chandala caves are akin to this cave. Caves No. 2 and 3 have capstones. The measurements of the capstones are almost the same as of the Pimpalgaon and Tiloti-Khairi capstones.

Jagankopi cave at Pullar: The cave is divided into two parts: the cell and veranda which is open to the sky. The Jagankopi cave is cuboid in form, with dimension of 9'7" x 8'7" x 5'6". Below the right side of the door, there is a small water tank. There is an inscription on a stone partition slab set up above the water tank and at the right side of the entrance door to a cell of the cave. (Fig. 3)

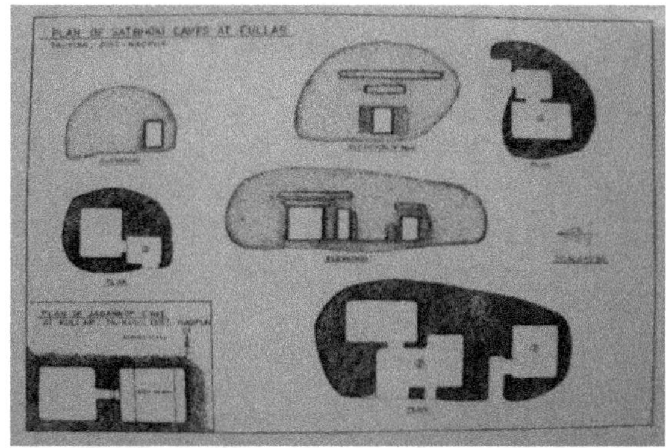

Figure 3: Plan and elevation of Jagankopi cave Satbhoki

Generally, it is accepted that the tradition of rock-cut architecture first got associated with the reformistic faiths like Ājīvikas and the Buddhist during the Mauryan period. During that period itself, it got transplanted to Orissa and the Western Ghats where the earliest of the then known rock-cut caves are noticed. These are mainly associated with Buddhism. From here, it spread to different parts of India, especially to the south. Eventually, the tradition was taken over by the Saiva Śāktas and Vaishnavas and later from the 6th century onwards by the Jainas.

In Vidarbha interesting document has been noted at Deotek, a small village not far away from Pauni, Adam, Hirapur. There are two inscriptions on a large stone slab. Out of the two inscriptions, one dates back to the time of Ashoka and the other to that of the Vakatakas. The four-line inscription is issued by a Dharmamahāmātra in the 14th year after the coronation of Ashoka.

The excavation at Pauni (Bhandara) and Bhon (Buldhana) have yielded a large number of brick stupas. These pieces of evidence help us to know about the religious activities of the Buddhists. The Hinayāna Buddhist establishment here goes back to the period of the NBP and subsequent times. The stupa was found to have been encased and enlarged in the initial centuries of the Christian era with the dome of the stupa built in boxes filled with rubble and brickbats. It has an elaborate lime concrete Pradakṣiṇāpatha, inner and outer railings with beautiful sculptures and majestic gateways recalling those at Sanchi. Since strategically located on the perennial river Wainganga, it has for the first time opened up the possibilities spread of Buddhism to the south through Vidarbha.

Most of the earliest Viharas are concentrated near Pauni. It shows that the megalithic people might have merged into Mauryan society and the autochthonous architectural activities may have been transferred to Mauryan society. This shows that the early rock-cut architecture was started separately during the Mauryan period. There is no influence on this cave architecture of the Lomas Rishi and Sudama caves of Bihar.

The megalithic people were the first community to learn about iron metallurgy. This technology helped them to chisel the stone for building megalithic monuments i.e. dolmens and menhirs. This megalithic architectural construction was a milestone, for the early Mauryan society of Vidarbha. They excavated small Viharas along with a capstone. During the first stage of excavation of Vihara, one can excavate veranda and cell; but in the earliest caves of Vidarbha, the veranda was excavated with a capstone. Capstone for veranda they used was similar to the capstone of the dolmens of Pimpalgaon and Tiloti-Khairi.

In the second stage, the capstone is not used on the top of the veranda. They excavated the whole veranda in a single stone and later on the development of cave architecture can be seen at Bhandak, Salbardi and Patur caves.

The development of caves can be understood on the basis of the Plan and Inscriptions, we can put these caves in chronological order as follows:

1] Some caves carry an Inscription in early Brahmi script i.e. Bhivkund, Pullar, Bhandak and use capstone for sheltering the veranda.
2] Small circular holes, about 3 feet in diameter, were made in the beginning in the hillside cliffs which could be closed with boulders. Following caves are noticed
   (1) Satbhoki
   (2) Bhivasena
   (3) Mansar
   (4) Kormbi
   (5) Deulwada
   (6) Ghugus.
3] The size of the cave has increased; façade with grooves for fitting the lintel and doors.
   (1) Bhivsena
   (2) Ramgad
   (3) Jagankopi.
4] The excavators of the caves were somewhat confident and the interior is neatly dressed creating a platform and a

pillar with a square room outside; sometimes with a small veranda.

    (1) Bhuyar
    (2) Muktagiri
    (3) Ramdigi
    (4) Deulwada
    (5) Kaladana.

5] Cutting a large size cave dug at foothills. Here the roof is domical, walls inclined and the span of the cave narrow. These types of are like a tunnel.

    (1) Ramgad and
    (2) Vipassana.

6] After gaining confidence and experience the artists created a cell with veranda.

    (1) Salbardi
    (2) Patur.

Caves Distribution and Developments

District	Sites	Caves	Inscriptions	District	Sites	Caves	Inscriptions
Nagpur	1. Bhimkund	05	01	Buldhana	1. Chandola	05	--
	2. Bhuyar	01	01		2. Motala	03	--
	3. Chandala	03	03	Chandrapur	1. Bhandak	07	03
	4. Gadpayali	04	--		2. Bhatala	22	--
	5. Gayadongari	02	--		3. Deulwada	06	01
	6. Jagankop	01	--		4. Gargamuni	01	--
	7. Kitali (Satbhoki)	07	--		5. Gavrala	01	--
	8. Pimpardol	05	--		6. Ghugus	03	--
	9. Pullar	03	03		7. Khadan Deulwada	01	--
	10. Ramgad	01	--		8. Kondeswar	01	--
	11. Ramtek	01	--		9. Mahali	05	--
Amravati	1. Devi lene	02	--		10. Mana	04	--
	2. Muktagiri	09	--		11. Nanak Pathar	02	--
	3. Nagziri	02	--		12. 12. Ramdigi	02	--
	4. Salbardi	09	--	Yeotmal	1. Kalamb	01	--
Akola	1. Patur	04	--		2. Nandi pera	03	--
Bhandara	2. Pauni	01	--		1. Shirpur Kavadasa	02	--
	3. Gaymukh - Bijli	02	--		2. Nimbadrhwa	02	--

P.N. Phadake has given some different chronological order of the caves[22].

The origin of the cave started during the Mauryan period and the development took place in the Sātavāhana period. The most perfection came during the period of Vakataka. The Salbardi caves can give as a clear example of the developed Vidarbha caves.

During the reign of the Vakatakas caves evolved into separate monuments and the earliest stone temples came into being. Such rock-cut caves are noticed at Salbardi. Certainly, this was not a sudden phenomenon. Its inspiration was perhaps to be seen in the caves at Ajanta. These caves, dated more or less securely because of the inscriptions of the Vakataka Kings.

We can see these caves into two complexes. Each complex consisting of two caves. Complex I is dedicated to Śaiva sect and II belongs to the Buddhist religion.

Complex II, Cave I (Lankeshwar Temple): This is the largest cave in all the caves and locally known as Lākhamahal of the Pāṇḍavas (Plate 11). It consists of a pillared veranda with cells on either side, an inner hall and cells on three sides. Here the cells are open. The cells of the inner hall are unfinished. In the inner hall, the platform is carved with four pillars. It is square on plan and measures 4.80 m (long) x and 3.90 m (wide). The inner square hall measures 7.75 m x 7.75 m. The beams are shown for the support of the platform of the ceiling. No doors are provided for the inner cells. Only three decorated doors are seen, two for the cells of the veranda and one for the entrance of the inner hall. The doors have grooves, cut all round their inner frames, probably to receive moveable wooden shutters.

Plate 11: Lankeshwar Cave at Salbardi

In the inner hall, as well as in cells neither an image is recorded nor any indication of an object which might represent a statue. The excavation of the cave is not complete.

Cave 2 (Pancāvatār Temple): The plan of Panchavatar temple is totally different from the Lankeshwar cave (Fig. 4). The cave consists of a front hall measuring 8.8 m (long), 2.58 m (wide) and 2.98 m (height). Viharas on eastern and western sides are measure 3.74 m (long), 3.64 m (wide) and 2.54 m (height) and 3.25 m (long), 3.25 m (wide) and 2.53 m (height), respectively. Both the viharas have the lintels over the doorways that face the west and east respectively; and the figure of a lion, couple, Gaṇēśa on either side and four figures in the centre of the lintel. The door frame has three śākhās. Behind the door jambs, sockets are provided i.e. 7.5 cm depth, with corresponding sockets on the ceiling for fixing the wooden door. There is an arrangement for closing the door and keeping it in position by means of a crossbar.

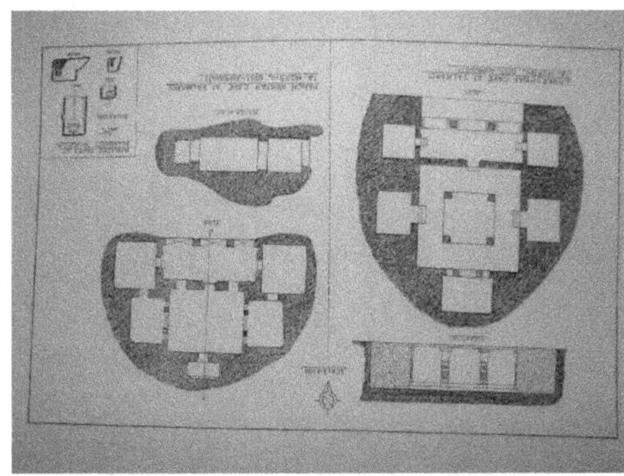

Figure 4: Plan - Caves at Salbardi

The inner mandapa is flanked by two cells. These cells are open and pillars are carved square. The upper part of the pillar is slightly smaller than the lower part. The ceiling of Mandapa is decorated with lotus medallions, one in the centre and four in each corner. The most noteworthy thing is that the cells are empty or without benches.

The small cell (2.38 m x 1.40 m x 1.94 m) excavation at the north end of the Mandapa contains a cell rectangular in form, provided with a Buddha (now headless) is flanked by Padmapāṇi and Vajrapāṇi. The figure of the Buddha is in Bhūmisparśamudrā. Below the Buddha figure are

---

[22]Phadake, P.N.;2001. 'Cave Architecture', *Shodha Nibandha Sangraha*, Ter. Pp. 63-64.

shown two human figures and in between the stem of a lotus. These figures are mutilated and beyond any identification. On the basis of figures and architecture, this cave can be dated to the Vakataka period. Originally the cave was curved during the Sātavāhana period and later on, it was occupied by the people of Vakataka period.

Discussion and Conclusion

The above discussion on the megalithic builder as a cave excavator shows that the megalithic people in Vidarbha region were in the know of the iron technology. They erected well-dressed dolmens, particularly Hirapur and the capstones of Pimpalgaon and Tiloti-Khairi are akin to the capstone of the Verandas of the caves. Whereas the caves that are provided capstone are earlier the ones without it are later. Later on, the cave excavators after developing ability and confidence do not use the capstone. This happened sometime during the Sātavāhana period. The development continues until the end of Vakataka dynasty.

Buddhist Rock-cut Caves: The Hinayāna—Mahāyāna Transition

Late M K Dhavalikar

Abstract

The large number of Buddhist rock-cut caves in Western India have been divided into two groups, labelled Hinayāna and Mahāyāna, on the basis of the absence or presence of the Buddha image in them and assigned to 200 BC-200 Ad and 6th cent. -8th cent. respectively with a hiatus of about four centuries in between. This gap has now been narrowed down because of Professor Walter Spink's dating the Ajanta Mahāyāna group to the latter half of the fifth century. However, it has been averred by Professor Schlingloff that the literary background of Ajanta paintings is Hinayāna, and therefore the latter group is Hinayāna.

The change in the layout of the caityagṛhas first occurs at Ajanta itself where Caitya 9 is quadrangular on plan which further develops into a quadrangular, flat-roofed and astylar caitya at Junnar in the first century. At Kanheri there is only one standard apsidal caitya (No. 3), whereas all others are small vihāras having a hall with benches and a meditation chambers and a veranda. They also probably served as shrines for loose images. Further evolution takes place at late Hinayāna sites such as Kuḍā, Mahad and Ajanta 8 which culminates in Ajanta 19 and 26.

So far as the problem of Hinayāna or Mahāyāna affiliation is concerned, it appears that Mahāyāna elements were already present in the third century at Kanheri such as Buddha images (Caitya 3) and meditations chambers, both contributions of the Mahayanists, as also the Mahāyāna formula of donative records at Junnar and Kanheri. There is evidence to show that monks of both the sects lived amicably in Western India and continued to do so at Ajanta as testified by Xuan Zang and I-Tsing.

Introduction

There are about 1200 rock-cut caves in India of which a thousand are in Maharashtra, and of these nearly two-thirds of it are Buddhist. They have been broadly classified by earlier scholars, particularly Fergusson and Burgess, under the rubric Hinayāna and Mahāyāna, on the basis of the absence or presence of the Buddha image, and dated them to about 200 BCE-200 CE and 500-1200 CE respectively, with a hiatus in between[23]. In many caves, Buddha images were added later in the 6th-7th century CE. However, a very pertinent question has been recently raised by Dieter Schlingloff, a renowned authority on Ajanta, in his recently published magnum opus in three massive tomes. Is there Mahāyāna at Ajanta? At the root of this query is Gregory Schoppen's article on Mahāyāna in the Encyclopaedia of Buddhism. He writes (2004: 492-93):[24]

'Textual sources placed the beginning of Mahāyāna in the second century CE with the first translation of Lōkakṣēma's Sukhāvatīvyūha-sūtra which is central to the Mahayanists. The evidence outside the textual corpus does not corroborate the conclusion that Mahāyāna started around the beginning of Common Era. The principal reason is the utter lack of inscriptional and archaeological

---

[23] James Fergusson and Jas. Burgess, Cave Temples of India, (London 1980).

The most exhaustive study of Ajanta and Western Indian cave temples is that by Professor Walter M. Spink. He has published several papers on Ajanta which have recently been published in six massive volumes. His first longish paper on Ajanta outlining his views in detail was presented at the XXXIV International Congress of Orientalists, Jan. 1964. See his "From History to Art History: Monuments of the Deccan," *Summaries of Papers*, pp. 242-43. For his later views, see his "Indra's Crown: A Study of Mahayana Developments at Ajanta", *JRSA*, Vol. CXXII, No. 5219, October, 1974), pp. 743-65. Professor Walter Spink's papers have been recently published in six volumes by E.J. Brill.

[24] Rajesh Singh, An Introduction to the Ajanta Caves, (Vadodara, 2012), pp. 34-35. See also David Schlingloff, Ajanta – Handbook of the Paintings, 3 vols., (New Delhi, Aryan Books International, 2014).

records in support of such a conclusion. There is just an isolated inscription and an image depicting Amitabha, the deity most central to Mahāyāna during the whole period of five centuries. The inscriptions refer to Hinayāna groups: the Sarvastivādins, Mahāsamghikas, Cētiyas, etc. Thus, it was not the period of Mahāyāna but of Hinayāna.'

Mahāyāna Buddhism

Broadly Buddhism is divided into three schools: Hinayāna, Mahāyāna, and Vajrayana or Tantric Buddhism. The beginning of Mahāyāna Buddhism goes back to the 2nd-1st century BCE and some would trace it to the 5th century BCE in the *Nikayas* in the first Buddhist Council which was organized at Rājagṛha (Rajgir in Bihar) to discuss Buddha's teachings which were till then not committed to writing. It is said that even Buddha is supposed to have had the philosophical leanings of Mahāyānism. The Second Council was held at Vaishali (Bihar) in 386 BCE where the differences between the *bhikkhus,* though minor, came in the open for the first time and the first schism occurred. One group was that of the traditionalists (*Sthaviravādins* or *Thēravādin*s), and the other of the *Mahāsamghikas,* who held opposite views The Thēravādins, therefore, excommunicated the *Mahāsamghikas*-s, so named because of they were powerful due to their majority; they branded the opponents as Hīnayānists (Lesser Vehicle). (Dutt, 1988: 79) The Mahāyāna school was firmly established when the Madhyamika school of *Nāgārjuna* and the *Yogacara* of *Maitrēyanāth, Asaṅga,* and *Vasubandhu* came into being.

The Hīnayānists believed in the chain of causation (*pratitya-samutpāda*), the eight-folded path (*Aṣṭāngika mārga*), and the four Aryan Truths (*catvāri ārya-satyāni*). In contrast, the sole objective of the Mahāyānists is *dharma-nairātmya* which may mean five elements *(Skanda-s)*. In Mahāyāna, *nirvāṇa* is individualistic; it is eternal state, powerful and happy, and is attained by eradication of impurities caused by ignorance. The great savant, A. K. Coomaraswamy (1956: 228-29) has cogently brought out the differences between the Hīnayānists and the Mahayanists.

The Mahāyāna or the Great Vehicle offers to all beings in all worlds salvation by faith and love as well as by knowledge, while the Hinayāna only avails to convey over the rough sea of becoming to the further ashore of *nibbāṇa* those few strong who require no external spiritual aid nor the consolidation of worship. The Hinayāna is exceedingly hard whereas the burden of Mahāyāna is light and does not require that man should immediately renounce the world and all the affections of humanity.

The adherents of the Mahāyāna sect are known as Bodhisattvas who are instructed to become Buddha ultimately. In other words, they reject the idea of *Arhat-hood* so dear to Hīnayānists but aim at Buddhahood through Bodhisattva state as it helps others to achieve salvation. Hence there are past and future Buddhas in Mahāyāna Buddhism. Finally, the most important difference is the image worship which is introduced with meditation as also elaborate rituals, formulae, charms and belief in heavens. But this ultimately led to its decline. It may be stated that the Mahāsamghikas found support in Maharashtra, (where Karla was their stronghold) and Andhra Pradesh. (Gokhale,1976:90)

The differences between the Hīnayānists and the Mahayanists were no doubt sharp but the issue is how they are reflected in art. There is no problem about the Hīnayānists as the absence of Buddha image, the symbolic worship and in their donative record, the words *dēya-dhamma* occurs. So far as the Mahayanists are concerned we can expect: (i) Images of Buddha and Bodhisattva whom they accorded a higher status than that to the Enlightened One; (ii)a room for mediation; (iii) Manuśi Buddhas; (iv) narratives according to the *Avadana* stories, and (v) the Mahāyāna formula of the donative record wishing happiness and well-being of all. It was probably due to Avalōkitēśvara's insistence that he would not accept salvation until all beings attain it.

The broad classification made by earlier scholars was simple and there was a hiatus of about four centuries in between the Hinayāna and the Mahāyāna rock-cut caves, but this gap is narrowed by the earlier chronology proposed by Spink who assigned the latter group of caves at Ajanta to about 460-480 AD (Gokhale,1976:90). It is averred that the Mahāyāna school was till then in the formative stage and therefore Schlingloff argues that there is no Mahāyāna at Ajanta (*Op.cit.*:75**).** This, however, is not tenable as it has been observed that the Mahāyāna elements were already present even in the second century. Buddha images were already present in the late second century at Amaravati, and in the early third century two Buddha images were carved—rather stealthily and not to be easily seen by the visitor - on the huge right pillar in the forecourt of Caitya cave 3 at Kanheri, the lower one standing and the upper one seated (Leese,1979: 83-93). Yet another, an unfinished one, is on a pillar of the apsidal caitya hall. Although Buddha image is not taken to be the monopoly of the Mahayanists, it is clear that it appears only with the rise of Mahāyāna. The earliest Buddha/Bodhisattva image carved in the second year of Kanishka's reign (79 CE) is in the Sarnath Museum. The Kanheri caitya is dated to the last quarter of the second century on the basis of an inscription in it which states that the donation was made in the sixteenth year of the reign of Yajñaśrī Sātakarṇi (170-99 AD). This epigraph also states that "the grant was given for the happiness and welfare of all" which is the Mahāyāna formula, and not *dēya-dhamma*, in the Hinayāna tradition (Gokhale, 1991, Inscription 5). There are a few earlier records at Junnar in which we come across the Mahāyāna formula. (Dhavalikar, 1982: 24, f.n.4). Meditation chambers first occur at Junnar and a little later at Kanheri.

Again, at Kanheri the domination of Mahāyāna is clear from Avalōkitēśvara images such as the eleven-headed, the litany of Bodhisattva (three panels), with Tārā and Bhṛkuṭi, and above all Akṣōbhya in Cave 56. At Ajanta too, there are Avalōkitēśvara images in painting and sculpture as well, his litany, and Manuśi Buddhas which all indicate the presence of Mahāyāna at Ajanta which Spink places in the fifth century. In this context I-Tsings's observation is significant. (Takakasu, 1896: 150-52)

"Priests and laymen in India make caityas or images with earth or impress the Buddha image on silk or paper, and worship it with offering wherever they go. Sometimes they build stupas of Buddha by making a pile and surrounding it with bricks. They put in the images or caitya of two kinds of *śarīras*: (1) Relics of the Great Teacher, (2) The *Gāthā* of the Chain of Causation."

It is likely that at Ajanta the Mahayanists may not have been dominant as at Kanheri and Ellora where even Vajrayana influence is discernible. The reason for this is that at most of the Buddhist cave monasteries in Maharashtra, both the Hīnayānists and Mahayanists were living amicably together as testified by I-Tsing. And this is probably the reason

why Schlingloff is not very emphatic in spite of the fact he has identified some of the narratives on the basis of *Avadana* stories which are Mahayanist. He states. (Schlingloff, *Op. cit.*: 75)

The majority of narrative paintings are based on the *Vinaya* of the Mūla-Sarvastivādins, and on the poems of *Aryaśura* and *Aśvaghōṣa* (*Saundarānanda*). All the works of literature connected with the paintings belong to the Hinayāna, and accordingly, themes that are particularly 'Mahayanistic' were not portrayed with the possible exception of the Avalōkitēśvara devotional pictures. The term Mahāyāna for the later caves, which originates from the time when the literary background of the paintings was still unknown, can therefore only be used as a label, it would be a mistake to form a conclusion about the ideology behind the paintings on the basis of this term.

Since the Mahāyāna affiliation of Ajanta is a crucial issue, it is better to analyse the textual evidence and collate it with that of art and architecture of the caves. The final products at Ajanta are the caityas 19 and 26 in which we find stupas with Buddha images carved on their front. This is a great leap from Hinayāna stupas and the problem, therefore, deserves to be examined threadbare. The early Hinayāna caitya is apsidal on plan which is divided into central nave and side aisles by plain octagonal pillars, with a rock-cut stupa in the apse; it has a huge arch on the façade. There is a major deviation in Ajanta caitya 9 which is quadrangular on plan but the pillars are disposed in an apsidal fashion. Interestingly, Aurangabad 4, a caitya, is also identical. Similarly, Kanheri cave 7 is quadrangular on plan but the post-holes in the hall are in the apsidal fashion. This is probably the earliest cave that was excavated at Kanheri and was in all likelihood meant for the residence of monks supervising the work; the apsidal portion was for their religious activities. These early examples indicate that the change in Ajanta 9 may not have been accidental but rather by design.

Junnar

Further development takes place at Junnar which, with 105 caves, is probably the largest Buddhist complex, next to Kanheri, but dispersed in different groups. Here Ganesh Leni 6 is a standard caitya conforming to the Hinayāna plan but the caitya arch is blind. This was not done deliberately but there was no alternative because of a loose stratum of rock. The same was the case with Amba-Ambika 26 of which the hall is not exactly apsidal but rather irregular. From this seems to have developed the quadrangular caityas at Junnar, as for instance, Bhimashankar 2, Ganesh Leni 14, Shivneri East 2 and so on. The apsidal and vaulted roofed caitya now becomes quadrangular, astylar and flat-roofed (Dhavalikar, 1984:12 ff).

This happened in the mid-second century when the Western Kshatrapas had pushed the Sātavāhanas into the southern Deccan and the rulers were not worried about changes in religious architecture which otherwise would have been blasphemous. The artists, therefore, had some freedom to experiment with their novel ideas. But in the latter half of the second century, the Sātavāhanas again assert their domination in Maharashtra under the leadership of Yajñaśrī Sātakarṇi (170-99) when the impressive Caitya 3 at Kanheri was excavated. It is the last standard Hinayāna caitya because the decline of the Sātavāhanas created political instability and economic degeneration resulting in a decrease in long-distance trade which affected the art activity. This is the most important reason for the hiatus between the Hinayāna and the Mahāyāna caves in Maharashtra when the art activity came to a grinding halt and picked up again only in the fifth century (Dhavalikar, 2002: 192 ff).

All these early caves are Hinayāna monuments but it seems that Mahāyāna elements were already being introduced. The donative inscription in Shivneri East 4, which is engraved on the right wall of its forecourt, mentions that it was donated by a merchant named *Vīrasēnaka* for *sava-loka-hita-sukhāya* which indicates Mahāyāna influence (*ASWI*, Junnar,No,4,p.93), and the same is the case with that in Kanheri caitya 3 which ends with *savvasa-cha-hita-sukhāya*. (Gokhale, *Op. cit.*: Inscription 53).

Kanheri

There are three early Buddha figures in the Kanheri caitya 3. Two of them are carved on the right (south) pillar in the forecourt and are taken to be the earliest anthropomorphic representations of the Enlightened One in Western India as they can be assigned to the early third century. The lower one is shown standing and the upper one is seen seated in meditation (*dhyānamudrā*); his right hand is in granting protection (*abhayamudrā*). The caitya 3 can be assigned to the end of the second century on the basis of an inscription in it., to the period of Yajñaśrī Sātakarṇi (170-99); the work on the forecourt and the pillars in it were probably carved a little later as its northern wall is not in alignment because of the adjoining memorial caitya4 which had to be excavated first even while the work on Caitya 3 was underway (Dhavalikar, in press).

There is yet one more Buddha figure on the base of the fifth pillar from the front on the left. It is unfinished and may have been intended to be Buddha. Besides this, one epigraph in this caitya recording the gift ends with *savvasa-hita-sukhāya* which is clearly the Mahāyāna formula. There is another example of this kind and there is therefore little doubt that Mahāyāna influence had started filtering into Maharashtra the mid-second century.

Equally important is the new vihāra at Kanheri which was probably the largest Buddhist establishment in Western India, with about 115 excavations. They can be divided into three different phases: I—Hinayāna (150-200 AD); II -Early Mahāyāna (200-350AD); III—450-700 AD). It is surprising that in such a vast complex there is only one caitya (3) and not a single *catuḥśālā* vihāra of the standard Hinayāna type. All the remaining vihāras are laid out according to the new plan which is not to be found at any other Buddhist site in Maharashtra. The Kanheri architects devised a new plan which basically consists of a squarish hall with a veranda at the front and a well-made forecourt. The hall has benches along its walls and small cells for worship and meditation. This simple plan resembling small bungalows at holiday resorts further develops in course of time with additions such as pillars in the veranda, recessed doorframes, stairs with moonstone (*candraśilā*), and above all sanctum in the rear wall. Almost every cave has a water cistern. The Buddha and Bodhisattva images were added later in the 5th -6th century AD.

The origins of this new vihāra plan can be traced at Junnar which is at a walkable distance from Kanheri through the Naneghat Pass. We have shown how the apsidal, vaulted roofed caitya evolves into quadrangular and flat-roofed one at Junnar, In the Tulja Leni group at Junnar Cave 13 is a roughly squarish hall with benches on three sides and a small cell in the left wall; its front, however, is completely ruined (Dhavalikar, *Op. cit.:12 ff*). The Shivneri East 25 is also a quadrangular hall with benches on all sides except at the front, and there is a projection in the middle of the backwall which may be for the chief monk or for placing the object of worship. But these are just halls (*maṇḍapas)* for congregations, and there are other examples such as Bhimashankar 2 and Amba-Ambika 27 and 28 which also are just squarish halls with verandas at the front (Jadhav: 1980). It may be noted that these are purely Hinayāna examples as is clear from the dedicatory formula of epigraphs in them. This plan appears to have been adopted at Kanheri with slight modifications. It is not unlikely that after the close of work at Junnar, the artisans came to Kanheri. Another important factor was such experiments in religious architecture could be carried out without much difficulty because of the rule of Western Kshatrapas who were of foreign origin.

In the II Group (200-350 AD) the first cave that was excavated according to the new plan is No. 21 at Kanheri which can be assigned to about 200 CE as it was excavated in the 16th regnal year of Yajñaśrī Sātakarṇi (170-99) and is thus contemporaneous with the Caitya 3. The cave 21 consists of a squarish hall (6m sq.) with a veranda and a well-made forecourt. The hall has benches in the rear and right walls and a small cell in the left-hand corner at the back with a bench. The veranda also has a bench in the left wall and the entrance to the hall is flanked by grated windows. There is a recessed cistern in the forecourt in the left wall above which is an inscription which the donation by Aparēṇu, a resident of Kalyan, with his relations, which was given on the fifth day of the Grīṣma season in the sixteenth year of the reign of Yajñaśrī Sātakarṇi, i.e. 186 AD. The donation was made to the *Sangha* of four quarters. (*ASWI, No. IV*, Junnar).

This record is of key importance in as much as it explicitly mentions *dēya dhammam*, the Hinayāna formula and also monks of the four quarters as also *sarvva-satvānām-hita-sukhāya,* which is the Mahāyāna formula. And above all, it can be firmly dated to 186 AD. The record is thus unique as it the first document indicating the advent of Mahāyānism in Western India. The Buddha images on the courtyard pillar are also assigned to the reign of Yajñaśrī. Much time, therefore, must not have elapsed between the caitya and the Buddha images in Cave 3.

Cave 22 is almost identical but has, in addition, a staircase and so is the case with No.26 the stair of which has a *candraśilā*. It also has a small niche in the back wall which, however, is a later addition as

it contains a Buddha image. The dedicatory epigraph displays developed forms of letters having ornamental flourishes suggesting a third-century date.

Caves 49-70 conform to the standard type evolved at Kanheri and belong to the first half of the third century. There are minor variations but for Buddha sculptures of the 5th-6th cent.

Cave 32 is a well-planned and meticulously excavated vihāra with a spacious forecourt having holes for wooden posts supporting a canopy that may have been erected on special occasions. The veranda has octagonal pillars with square bases and the pilasters have hour-glass decoration, as also benches which are adorned with vodka rail pattern on the back. The squarish hall (4 m sq.) has a bench in the rear wall and a cell with bench in the right wall. The discovery of a wooden image of Tara in this cave is its important feature for it shows that loose images were worshipped in the new vihāras. (Sankalia, 1986: 56-59)

Cave 50 marks further development as it has a niche in the rear wall surrounded by holes possibly for lamps or for some wooden attachment for the object of worship which obviously was portable. The cave has two cells in left walls and a running bench in the rear and right walls. Another noteworthy feature is the absence of pillars in the veranda but the pilasters bear the hour-glass decoration which later fully develops at Ajanta into medallions of great beauty. The cave can be dated to the late third or early fourth century on the basis of palaeography of the records which resembles the Kadaṃba or early Pallava inscriptions. It mentions the gift of a perpetual endowment of 1600 *kārṣāpaṇas* by stone masons of *Kallivana* (present Kalwan near Nasik). A wealthy trader, Sulabhati, among them, repaired the washed away road to the vihāra while his relations donated the benches for two monks who were living in it.

There appears to be a hiatus of about a century (350-450 AD) between the Early and Late Mahāyāna groups at Kanheri. Politically this period was marked by instability, and the economic activity was also on the decline as trade with Mediterranean countries was reduced to a dribble. The local chieftains like the Mahārathīs and Mahābhōjas do not mention their overlords, as for instance, Kuḍā inscriptions of the Mandava family. It was only from the mid-fifth century that the activity picks up again with the Vakatakas gaining supremacy. As a matter of fact, the post-Sātavāhana epoch is marked by degeneration in all fields of human life. At Kanheri the new standard plan continued with minor variations and at other places, small caves were excavated but many of them have remained unfinished possibly due to lack of patronage. The activity continued at Kanheri because of the ports of international trade such as Sopara, Chaul, Kalyan, etc in its vicinity. In such an unstable environment it is surprising that small bungalow like vihāras were created at Kanheri. They are all Mahayanist with images of Buddhas and Bodhisattvas, Avalōkitēśvara, with their litanies, Tara and Bhṛkuṭi, and above all, the *Dhyānī* Buddhas which herald the advent of the Vajrayana Buddhism. Kanheri perhaps is the only stronghold of Mahāyāna Buddhists in Western India save that at Ellora which again represents the Mahāyāna—Vajrayana transition.

The high-water mark of Mahāyānism at Kanheri is Cave 41. Located on the south side of the stream, it has a pillared veranda, but the hall has no benches but a cell in each of the side walls of which the central one is the shrine containing a seated Buddha in the teaching attitude (*vyākhyānamudrā*). The side walls of the hall are profusely decorated with sculptures, mostly showing Buddha seated, which probably is the delineation of the Miracle of Shravasti that he is supposed to have performed.

The cave follows the standard plan devised at Kanheri but is later (6th cent) with pillars having cushion capitals and squarish shafts in the lower part. The doorframe of the hall is recessed and is carved with the vase motif (*pūrṇa-ghaṭa*), the symbol of prosperity. The lintel is adorned with five arches. The shrine has Buddha in the *dharma-cakra-pravartana-mudrā*. He is flanked by attendants of whom that on the right is Avalōkitēśvara. In the right end of the veranda is Buddha in meditation with attendants. On the left is a unique representation of the eleven-headed Avalōkitēśvara which is the only of its kind in India. The image in the shrinelet in the forecourt is in all likelihood Amitabh in meditation. The earliest mention of Amitabh is to be found in the *Sukhāvatīvyūha-sūtra* and he is also known as Amitāyus. He is said to be residing in heaven where he is constantly in meditation. He is supposed to have brought forth Avalōkitēśvara.

Bodhisattva Avalōkitēśvara is the most exalted divinity of Mahāyāna Buddhism and occupies a higher position than that accorded to Buddha. He prominently figures in the *Saddharmapuṇḍarīka* and the *Sukhāvatīvyūha-sutra* which describe him as far superior to other Bodhisattvas; only Maṃjuśrī is his equal. The lotus and rosary are his attributes, making him comparable with Brahma and Vishnu. He is the only Bodhisattva who is shown with four arms (not even Buddha) which carry the attributes of Brahma viz. rosary, lotus, and *kuṇḍikā* (water vessel) and the fourth hand is in *varadamudrā*. The idea of Avalōkitēśvara goes back to the third century BC, during the time of Asoka. It was originated by the *Mahāsaṃghikas* in their *Mahāvastu Avadāna* whereas the images came to be made from the early first century AD.

It will thus be clear that the Mahāyāna phase in Western India starts from the last quarter of the second century when a new form of vihāra was introduced as is exemplified by Cave 21. Although it looks like a small compact residence, it could provide accommodation a number of occupants at a time because of the running benches on the side walls. Another advantage was that the benches and small cells in walls were more useful for keeping the object of worship, a stupa or an image like that of Tara which was found in Cave 32. The planning of the vihāras at Kanheri has elicited high praise from discerning critics.

More than any such monastic establishment in India, that at Kanheri displays order and refinement at a place for multiple residences. Each cell shows a natural but considered siting which produces a living environment (for monks in the monsoon) that could be well emulated by planners today. (Meister M,1981: p. 163)

The religion was undergoing a paradigm shift at the beginning of the Common Era with the rise of the Mahayanists, but although there was rivalry among them and the Hīnayānists, in Western India the adherents of both of them were living amicably.

Kuḍā

When the Mahayanist influence was being felt at Kanheri, changes were being introduced in the layout of the caityas at other centres, as for instance Jakhinwadi. These were small excavations as patronage had almost dried up for imposing caityas like that at Karla. A most noteworthy site of this change is Kuḍā (Dt. Raigad) on the western coast which has a complex of 28 caves datable to the third century on grounds of palaeography. Many of them were donated by a family of four brothers and their wives. They themselves were writers and the inscriptions engraved are probably the most beautiful records as they can be read like signboards.

Considerable development took place at Kuḍā. Caitya 9 is a quadrangular chamber with a stupa and having a veranda and a cell with a bench on the left. Cave 15 is identical and has a room each at either end of the veranda. Caitya 1 is like a temple with a veranda, a hall and a shrine joined to it by a vestibule (*antarāla*). The development is complete with Caitya 6 with the addition of benches on three sides of the hall. Cave 4 is similar but incomplete. The Kuḍā epigraphs end in *dēya-dhamma*, the Hinayāna formula.

Mahad

Small, modest caves combining caitya and vihāra were thus coming up in the interior of Maharashtra most of which have remained unfinished for want of adequate patronage. At Kanheri, however, the art activity continued possibly because of patronage available in the neighbouring commercial centres such as Sopara, Kalyan, and Chaul. Among the architectural experiments that were underway in the post-Sātavāhana era, the most remarkable is that at Mahad, an ancient trading centre on the Mumbai-Goa highway. In its group of 28 caves, Nos. 1 and 8, both caityas, are noteworthy. They can be said to be the link between the Hinayāna and the Mahāyāna caves at Ajanta as they bear a striking resemblance with Ajanta 8 and 11 respectively. Of the two, Mahad 8, which is well planned, consists of a squarish hall (4.50.m sq.) with benches on three sides and a shrine in the rear wall, flanked by a cell with bench. The veranda is ruined but its pillars have survived; they have squarish bases and are ornamented with lotus medallions. The bell capital has stepped abacus above like that at Kuḍā. The shrine once contained a rock-cut stupa as the circular mark on the floor and the *chatra* in the ceiling indicate but is completely destroyed.

An inscription on the back wall of the hall states that the *caityagṛha*, eight cells, and two cisterns are the gift of prince Kāṇabhōja Vēnupalita. The record conforms to the Hinayāna formula—*dēya-dhamma*. I would place it in the latter half of the third century although Nagaraju assigns it to 90 AD (Nagaraju: 1981) and Dehejia to 100AD. (Dehejia, 1972: 182-8).

Mahad caitya 1 is probably later than No,8 and is problematic. It consists of a quadrangular hall (17.54 x 10.52, 3.20 m height) with a pillared veranda and a squarish shrine in the back wall. The hall has four cells in the left wall and four more in the rear wall, all unfinished, besides two each flanking the shrine chamber. It also has a running bench on all four sides. The shrine chamber (6.10 x 5.19 m) has two pillars, one each on either side, and an entrance flanked by a large window as in Kuḍā caitya 6. Inside there is a squarish mass of rock from which an attempt seems to have been made to carve out a stupa, but what we see at the front is a Buddha image in the *pralambapādamudrā* as in Ajanta 19 and 26 and in Ellora 10. On the throne below is the *dharma-chakra* and deer, male attendants with fly whisk flank Buddha and *Vidyādharas* hovering above in the sky. At the top is a *Makara-tōraṇa* with flying figures holding a crown. Unfortunately, the face, the chest and the abdomen of Buddha have been scooped out.

On the back of the rock mass has been carved an outline of a seated Buddha and on the left face of the rock is Vajrapāṇi who has a stupa in his crown whereas on the right face is Padmapāṇi. All this imagery belongs to the 5th-6th cent. which is betoken of the domination of the Mahayanists.

The cave appears to be a late excavation of the late third or early fourth century, including the rock mass intended for a stupa and possibly the Buddha figure at the front; the other imagery is later. According to Vidya Dehejia and Nagaraju, it is a Mahāyāna caitya and hence they have not included it in their studies. Burgess also does not say anything about its religious affiliation obviously because of the images of Buddha and Bodhisattvas in the shrine.

Ajanta 8

This cave is absolutely unknown even to the scholarly world as it is completely in ruins and is used for housing generators supplying power to the site. According to Burgess, it was a Hinayāna excavation (James Fergusson and Jas. Burgess,1880: 289) but the late Dr. Suresh Vasant meticulously studied it and prepared its plan from whatever remains of it and assigned it to the Mahāyāna group at the site (Suresh Vasant, 1987: 249-53).The cave consists of a hall (7.60 m sq., 3.5 m hit) with three roughly squarish cells on the side walls and two each flanking the shrine which has a bench or a platform in the rear wall. There are some early features in the cave such as its plan which is identical with Mahad

8, and holes in the platform/bench in the shrine for fixing a loose image (of Buddha) which, as we have shown was already in vogue at Kanheri earlier. The veranda is totally ruined. The cave shares many features with Mahad, Kuḍā and Kanheri and may be assigned to the late third or early fourth century.

Ajanta 11

This cave is most crucial as it forms the link between the Hinayāna and the Mahāyāna groups. Even Walter Spink is of the opinion that it is the earliest in the latter group (Spink, 1968: 155-62). It has some early and some later features. It consists of a hall with veranda at the front and a shrine in the rear wall. The veranda pillars have square bases, but the shafts are octagonal with bracket capitals. At either end of the veranda is a cell each and its right wall is carved with three panels showing Buddha figures. The hall is supported by four pillars with moulded bases and octagonal shafts which are crowned by *ghaṭapallava* capitals. There are three cells each in the back and left walls and a bench along the right wall as at Junnar, Kanheri and other sites. The shrine contains a Buddha image in teaching attitude; it is carved against an unfinished stupa; the image is also unfinished and recalls that in Mahad 1 which further develops in caitya 19 and 26 at Ajanta.

There is a painted inscription in the cave which can be palaeographically assigned to the latter half of the fifth century. However, Spink has shown that there are two phases of painting in the cave and dates the cave to the mid-fifth century.

Conclusion

The foregoing analysis of evidence available at Junnar, Kanheri and some of the minor cave sites indicates the transition between the Hinayāna and the Mahāyāna caves during 200-450 AD. In fact, the beginning was made at Ajanta 9 where an apsidal caitya is found in a quadrangular hall, developing in course of time in Ajanta 19 and 26 which represent the culmination of the idea of having both the image and stupa together as at Nāgārjunakoṇḍa, where in some of the Ikṣvāku vihāras there are two shrines side by side, one for stupa and the other for the Buddha image (Sukumar Dutt, 1965: 191). They were separated obviously because they were worshipped by to two different sects viz. the Hinayāna and the Mahāyāna respectively. An attempt was made to combine them in Mahad 1 as also in Ajanta 11 and 1, and perfected in Ajanta 19

and 26 as also in Ellora 10. This clearly suggests that both the Hīnayānists and the Mahayanists were living together amicably in Maharashtra. When Yuan Chwang visited *Konkaṇapura*(Konkan, Western India), he found a hundred *saṃghārāmas* and about ten thousand *bhikkhus,* including Thēravādins and Mahayanists, living together, and later I-Tsing noted that the Mahayanists worshipped Bodhisattva and read *Mahāyāna sutras,* and those who do not read, are Hīnayānists (B G Gokhale, 1976: 98-99). This would suggest that the Hīnayānists may not have been worshipping the Buddha image in the initial stages and hence the two small Buddha images were carved in low relief on the massive pillar in the forecourt.

The image worship in Buddhism has rightly been credited to the Mahayanists as also that of Avalōkitēśvara, Manuśi Buddhas and Tara which are all present in the latter group at Ajanta, besides Avalōkitēśvara litany. Manuśi Buddhas are depicted in Caves 1, 2, 7, and 26 in stone and paint. It should be noted that the Mahāyāna donative formula of inscriptions, as for instance in Ajanta 26, which suggests the sharing of the merit achieved, certainly points to the presence of Mahayanists at Ajanta and shows that adherents of both the sects were living together. The only conclusion that we can draw is that neither of the sects was dominant at Ajanta which can be said to represent the overlapping phase between the Hinayāna and the Mahāyāna. The earliest influence of the Mahāyāna is discernible at Junnar and Kanheri in donative records, and the Buddha images in Kanheri caitya 3 which, however, appear to have been executed rather surreptitiously. The attempt to carve out the Buddha image in the shrine on the rock-cut stupa at Mahad is noteworthy. The Mahayanists appear to have succeeded in Mahad Cave 1 where there is a Buddha image in the shrine and on the back of the rock mass is an outline of a seated Buddha with Padmapāṇi on the right face and Vajrapāṇi on the left face. This belongs to the fifth century when the Mahayanists become dominant as is supported by the evidence from Ajanta, particularly Caves 19 and 26 where there are images of Buddha, Bodhisattva, Avalōkitēśvara, Tara and even Manuśi Buddhas which may have provided the inspiration for the donor of Mahad 1. Spink has assigned most of the important Mahāyāna caves at Ajanta to 460-480 AD and has classified them at Mahayanist.

References

ASWI, Junnar, No,4, p.93.

Coomaraswamy A.K, *Buddha and the Gospel of Buddhism,* (Bombay, 1956), pp. 228-29.

Dehejia Vidya, *Early Buddhist Rock Temples—A Chronological Study,* (London, 1972), pp. 182-8.

Dhavalikar M K, *Late Hinayāna Caves of Western India,* (Pune, 1982), p. 24, f.n.4

Dhavalikar, "Kanheri—A Re-discovery". (in press).

Dutt Nalinaksha, *Mahāyāna Buddhism,* (Delhi, 1988), p. 79.

Dutt Sukumar, *Buddhist Monks and Monasteries in India,* (Delhi, 1965), p.191.

Fergusson James and Jas. Burgess, *Cave Temples of India,* (London, 1880), p.289.

Gokhale B.G., *Buddhism in Maharashtra,* (Bombay, 1976), p.90.

Gokhale Shobhana, *Kanheri Inscriptions,* (Pune, 1991), Inscription 5.

Jadhav S.V., *Rock-cut Cave Temples at Junnar—An Integrated Study,* Ph.D. thesis, University of Poona, (1980).

Leese Marilyn, "Early Buddhist Icons in Kanheri Caves, *Artibus Asiae,* Vol. XLI (1979), pp. 83-93.

Meister Michel, "Suburban Planning and Rock-cut Architecture of India, "MADHU, Dr. M N Deshpande Felicitation Volume, (Delhi 1981), p. 163.

Nagaraju S., *Buddhist Architecture of Western India, (250 BC-300 AD),* (Delhi, 1981).

Sankalia H D, "A Unique Wooden Idol of Buddhist Goddess Tara from Kanheri Hills, *Jr. of Asiatic, Bombay, Dr. Bhagwanlal Indraji Felicitation Volume,* (1986), pp. 56-59.

Schlingloff David, Ajanta—Handbook of the Paintings, 3 vols., (New Delhi, Aryan Books International, 2014).

Sharma R S, *Urban Decay,* (New Delhi, 1987); see also Dhavalikar, *Environment and Culture—A Historical Perspective,* (Poona, 2002), pp.192 ff.

Shoppen Gregory, "Mahāyāna", Encyclopaedia of Buddhism, Vol.2 (2004), pp. 492-93, cited by Rajesh Singh, An Introduction to the Ajanta Caves, (Vadodara, 2012), pp. 34-35.]

Spink W., "Ajanta Chronology—The Problem of Cave 11", *Ars Orientalis,* Vol. VII (1968), pp. 155-62.

Suresh Vasant, "Ajanta Cave 8—A Study, in M S Nagaraja Rao (ed), *Kusumanjali—Dr C Sivaramamurthy Comm. Vol.,* (Delhi 1987), pp. 249-53.

Takakasu J., *A Record of the Buddhist Religion,* (Oxford, 1896), pp.150-52.

Buddhist caves at Nasik: An Analytical Study

Manjiri Bhalerao, Tilak Maharashtra Vidyapith, Pune

Abstract

The Buddhist caves at Nasik are one of the most important groups of monuments for the period c. 1st century B.C. to c. 6th century A.D. They also attest to the importance of Nasik from ancient times. Nasik (N. lat. 20o, E. long. 73o 51'), the headquarters of the district of the same name, is located on the banks of river Godavari.

The Pāṇḍavalēṇī, as these caves have been called for the last few centuries, is a group of twenty-four Buddhist caves preserving twenty-seven inscriptions. The caves were excavated from c 1st century B.C. till early 6th century A.D. Many caves enjoyed the royal patronage and some received donations from the rich lay devotees. The architecture, art, images and the epigraphical data at the site are the testimony of the changes that were taking place in the religious practices and philosophy of Buddhism. The recent changes in the chronology of the Sātavāhanas and Kshatrapas have repercussions not only on the chronology of the dynasties but also of the caves with dated inscriptions of these royal patrons. This, in turn, have some bearing on the chronology of the early Buddhist rock-cut caves. This review paper will address such issues related to this site.

Strategic Location

Nasik, in the district of the same name, is an ancient town, located on the banks of river Godavari. Being a famous pilgrim place for the Hindus, Jainas and Buddhists, this city is visited by the devotees throughout the year due to its proximity with the famous Trimbakeshwar, one of the twelve Jyotirlingas. The holy place of Trimbakeshwar is also famous for being the place of origin of the river Godavari.

The Buddhist caves at Nasik are one of the most important groups of monuments for the period c. 1st century B.C.E. to c. 6th century C.E. and attest to the importance of Nasik from ancient times. The location of the Buddhist caves in this region near the highway going to North India indicates the importance of the site chosen for the carving of the caves. These caves are locally known as the Pāṇḍavalēṇī. But the real name of the hill, in which they are carved, is Triraśmī, as can be seen through the inscriptions. The caves are located eight km to the west of the modern city of Nasik. Today the location of the caves has become very conspicuous as a memorial has been constructed in the memory of Late Dadasaheb Phalke and a modern stūpa has also been constructed nearby. It has become a very popular tourist place. However, the remains of the ancient rock-cut tanks can still be seen in the campus of a dargah near the base of the hill.

The Pāṇḍavalēṇī, as the caves have been called for the last few centuries, is a group of twenty-four Buddhist caves preserving twenty-seven inscriptions. The caves have been numbered by the Archaeological Survey of India from West to East. The caves were excavated from c. 1st century B.C.E.

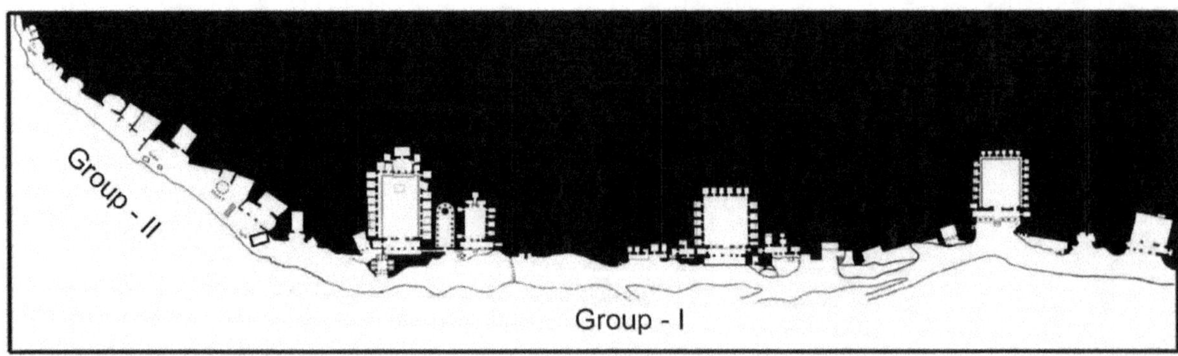

Figure 48: Plan of the cave site, Nasik

till early 6th century C.E. (Nagaraju 1981: 262 ff). The strategic location of this place can also be understood from the tussle between the Sātavāhana and the Western Kṣatrapa rulers over the acquisition of this area in the 1st century C.E. A detailed record of this tussle has been found in the form of inscriptions in these caves. These caves are also very important as they have received the royal patronage by the Sātavāhanas and the Western Kṣatrapas along with the rich Indian, Śaka and Yavana traders. The inscriptions in the caves have helped immensely to understand the contemporary political, religious conditions in ancient India.

Chronological development of the site

The beginning of the rock-cut activity was done with the excavation of the caityagṛha i.e. Cave no. 18 and the vihāra i.e. Cave no. 19. The earliest cave on this hill i.e. Cave no. 19 was excavated by the orders of the officer of the Śramaṇas from the court of the Sātavāhana ruler Kaṇha. This is a typical residential cave with six cells around a square hall fronted with a small veranda having a bench. The inscription is written on the sill of the grilled window in the veranda which opens into the interior hall. The rule of Kaṇha is ascribed to 30 to 12 B.C.E. Hence this cave is also dated approximately to this period. All the scholars who have worked on the caves at Nasik unanimously consider this cave as the earliest of the group.

The next cave at the site was the caityagṛha i.e. Cave no. 18 in the group. This is the only caityagṛha in this group. The donatory records and the present state of the cave suggest that there were various stages in the life of this cave. This cave has a stone facade. In the development of the rock-cut caves, this caityagṛha shows the second stage of development. The caitya gṛhas made prior to this one had wooden facades e.g. the caitya gṛhas at Bhaja, Pitalkhora, Ajanta 10, Kōṇḍaṇē, etc. But due to various reasons, most of them unknown to us, this caityagṛha at Nasik could not be completed. The interior and especially the pillars inside the caityagṛha show various stages in the excavation of this hall.

The interior of the hall shows a finished upper part of the hall and the lower part of the hall suggests some changes made in the original plan. The pillars at the back of the stūpa are plain octagonal and those in the front are plain octagonal with the pot base. The stūpa is also not finely finished till the base of it. It is smoothly chiselled only halfway and the lower

portion is rough, clearly indicating two different stages of excavation. This conjecture is supported by the inscriptional evidence also. There are three inscriptions in this cave, two on the facade and one inside the hall on the pillars. The inscription inside the hall is the dedicatory inscription mentioning the completion of the cave by one Bhaṭapālikā. The two inscriptions on the facade record the donation of a village by the people of Nasik and the donation of a railing and the figure of the yakṣa by one Nadasiri.

The decoration on the moulding of this cave is very peculiar, the first of its type in the entire western Indian caves. This decoration consists of the projecting beam ends carved in the fashion of dentils and the alternate dentils decorated with human, actually women's' faces. The depiction of the dentils, in case of all the earlier caves, was of rectangular projections, placed horizontally and the surfaces were devoid of any kind of decoration. But at Nasik, that too on the lower railing of the facade, the dentils are depicted placed vertically and their surfaces are decorated with human faces. (Bhalerao 2004:406). Hence this whole moulding, the arch, the inscription recording the donation and the figure of the yakṣa, the railing, the doorway and the decoration on the doorframe, all are considered to belong to a later phase. Similar decoration of the dentils is also found on the facade of the Cave nos. 17 and 4. Because of this particular feature, they are grouped close to each other in the chronological bracket.

It was probably before the completion or immediately after the completion of the caityagṛha that this whole region was taken over by Nahapāna, probably in the third decade of the first half of the 1st century CE. This rule of the Śaka Kṣatrapa probably accelerated the rock-cut activity at this site. The influx of the foreign merchants was probably promoted by the ruler and with this, the excavation of the caves donated by some foreigners started at Nasik, Karle, Junnar, etc.

At Nasik the creation of the Cave nos. 17, 4, 10 and 24 can be placed during this phase. This phase is the second phase of rock-cut activity at the site starting probably with the completion of the caityagṛha and ending with the defeat and death of Nahapāna at the hands of Gautamīputra Sātakarṇi in around 78 CE. Before the completion of the Cave no. 18, some excavation might have started to the eastern side of the group i.e. going towards Cave no. 24. It is quite probable that one or some of the small cells (which were broken later on and were converted into many shrines of the Mahāyāna phase) were created at this time. There is another possibility of the creation of the cemetery over there as per the convention of the contemporary period. One of the images of the Buddha was probably created by removing a rock cut stūpa, the remnants of which can still be seen along the wall. At many sites, stūpas were either carved in relief or round or constructed with brick and stone in the memory of the monks who probably died at that place. Cemeteries with multiple memorial stūpas have been noticed at Bhaja, Nadsur, Pitalkhora, Kanheri, etc.

The rock-cut activity at the site continued immediately to the west of Cave no. 18 after climbing a flight of steps. This is Cave no. 17, excavated by the donation of a Yavana merchant called as Indrāgnidatta, who had come from Dattāmitri, a place somewhere in North India. He had donated money for the creation of a cave which was a residential hall and inside which a caityagṛha was intended to be carved. He had also given a donation for the excavation of a cistern on behalf of his parents. The inscription recording this donation was carved in the veranda of this cave. The facade and the veranda of this cave are the two completely finished portions of the cave. The facade of the cave shows the typical rail decoration but the row of the dentils underneath the rail shows them placed vertically and alternately decorated by the human faces. The breadth of the veranda is lesser than that of the interior of the hall. It appears that the sacred location of being next to the caityagṛha was selected for this cave. But while starting the excavation it was probably not realized by the artisans that there was a very thin matrix of stone left between the caityagṛha and this cave. They might have started excavating the interior of the cave and this was probably realized. But by that time the veranda was completed and the interior was shifted towards the west and a separate entry was provided by extending the veranda in that direction. The wall between the caityagṛha and Cave no.17 was so thin that due to some attempt of work a small hole was made in the wall. Hence the work in the interior in the eastern wall was stopped and instead of carving cells a long niche was carved in the wall. Two cells were carved in the eastern wall and four cells were carved in the western wall. The extended portion of the veranda also has a cell in the western wall. The shrine at the back was started probably for the stūpa but was also left unfinished. Thus, a cave after a grand beginning

was unfortunately left unfinished.

It was immediately after this or contemporary to Cave no. 17 was the excavation of Cave no. 4. This cave is also an unfortunate excavation. The facades of Cave no. 17 and Cave no. 4 have many similarities between them. The railing pattern, the dentils with human faces, the pot base, inverted pot capital and animals with riders are some of the common features of these caves. In fact, the style of carving of these caves is also similar. Behind the pillars is a veranda. Inside the cave was carved a rectangular hall. In the wall between the veranda and the inner hall are carved two latticed windows. The rock of this cave is very bad and has many cracks in the ceilings and walls. Hence, one can imagine that there must have been a heavy leakage in the cave when it was initially excavated. This leakage must have troubled the excavators right from the beginning that is why no cells were carved inside. It was probably immediately after the completion of the facade that the decision of not making cells was taken and the floor of the cave was dug quite deep down. The whole interior was used to store water. On the basis of the similarity between Cave no. 17 and Cave no. 4 this cave is dated to the same period of Cave no. 17 i.e. 3rd or 4th decade of the 1st century CE.

Around the same time was excavated one of the most impressive caves on the hill i.e. Cave no. 10. This cave was the donation of Uṣavadāta, who was the son - in - law of the Western Kṣatrapa ruler Nahapāna. This is a finely finished excavation of one single scheme. This cave has a pillared veranda and a hall inside the cave surrounded by cells on all three sides. The relief stūpa at the centre of the back wall has been converted into an image of Kṣētrapāla Bhairava at a later date. There are remains of two cells in the courtyard also but they are in a very bad condition. The inscriptions in the veranda mention the donation of this cave to the monks of all quarters. The two cells in the veranda were donated by Dakṣamitrā, wife of Uṣavadāta and daughter of King Nahapāna. She had also donated two caves in the veranda.

Cave no. 24 was another cave which was the donation of a foreigner and was probably excavated during the rule of Nahapāna. This cave is in a dilapidated condition today. Only the finely carved entablature is extant and the walls of the cells are broken. There are two inscriptions in this cave, one

Figure 49: Cave No 10, Nasik

of them mentions the donation of the cave and two cisterns - one on the west side was by the donor and the other one was on behalf of his parents. The other inscription once again records the gift of one of the cisterns (Senart 1905 - 06:95).

One of the most controversial monuments in the entire range of the western Indian caves is the Cave no. 3 at Nasik. This cave is also known as the Dēvī Lēna or Gautamīputra's cave. This cave is very important for it contains four inscriptions. Two of them mention the donation of the cave. The first inscription dated in the 18th regnal year of Gautamiputra Sātakarṇi records the donation of land in the village Aparakakhadi, which was formerly enjoyed by Uṣavadāta, was donated to the monks of the Tekirasi hill. It also records that the donation was given by King Gautamiputra Sātakarṇi from the victorious war camp at Gōvardhana. The second inscription which mentions the 24th regnal year of this king states that the lands formerly granted in the village Kakhadi to the monks living in the cave which is our donation', having fallen fallow due to the desertion of that village, 100 nivartanas of land within the boundary of Gōvardhana was given

instead of the previous grant. The third record is the famous eulogy of Gautamiputra Sātakarṇi caused to be written by his mother Balaśrī and his son Vāsiṣṭhiputra Puḷumāvi in Puḷumāvi 19th regnal year. The fourth inscription written in continuation of the above is dated in the 22nd regnal year of Vāsiṣṭhiputra Puḷumāvi. It records that in lieu of the village Sudarśana granted earlier to the Bhadrāyaṇiya monks who had come from Dhanakata and residing in the 'Queen's cave', another village by name Sāmalipada was granted to them.

The inscriptions also record that this cave was especially dedicated to the monks of the Bhadrāyaṇiya sect. The architectural delineation of the cave indicates that there have been many stages in the excavation of this cave. The cave has a pillared veranda and an interior hall surrounded by cells. The most noteworthy feature of this cave is the presence of a relief stūpa on the back wall of this cave. Similarly, the decoration of the doorway like the Tōraṇas and the devotees holding lotus flowers are equally important. The backrests in the veranda, the beautifully decorated pillars and pilasters, the

Figure 50: Cave No 3, Nasik

Figure 51: Stupa in relief, Cave no. 3

ornamentation on the entablature and on the exterior

of the backrests, the huge beam ends being carried by the dwarves are also some of the noteworthy features of this cave.

The inscriptions in this cave are some of the most valuable documents of history recording the political achievements of the Sātavāhana family. Similarly, this is also the first inscriptional record of the presence of the Bhadrāyaniya sect in Maharashtra. All the other caves at Nasik were donated for the use of the monks of all quarters but only this cave was given exclusively for the use of the monks of the Bhadrāyaṇiya sect. This fact indicates the donor's special respect for this sect. Thus, the rock-cut activity for Cave no. 3 began at around 78 A.D. It probably halted after 84 A.D. and began and completed soon around 109 A.D.

Before the completion of Cave no. 3, two excavations had definitely started and one of them was completed. They are Cave no. 23 H and Cave no 2. The first cave i.e. Cave no. 23 H bears an inscription of the 2nd regnal year of Vāsiṣṭhiputra Puḷumāvi. Although the cave could not be completed the inscription was written down and is still in a very good condition. One does not know the exact reason for abandoning the cave but the poor quality of rock or the lack of resources could be imagined.

Cave no. 2 was excavated in the 6th regnal year of Vāsiṣṭhiputra Puḷumāvi. It was later on converted into a Mahāyāna shrine by breaking the partition wall between two cells. This seems to have been a two-celled cave with a veranda in the front. The wall of the veranda was also broken while converting this cave into a shrine but fortunately enough the first line of the inscription was not destroyed.

The excavation of Cave no. 1 started immediately after Cave no. 3 or could have been a simultaneous effort. This cave is also an unfortunate cave in this group. It began as a grand excavation following the footsteps of Cave no. 10 and 3. The entablature of this cave was almost finished on the lines of the same of Cave no. 3. The huge rock mass was chalked out for the pillars. The veranda was excavated and as the excavators proceeded towards the back of the hall a huge fissure in the rock gave in and the water started leaking in the hall. Many attempts were made to save this cave but the artists probably gave up and converted the whole cave into a tank for storing water. The floor was dug several feet deep and further work on this cave was abandoned.

The rock-cut excavation activity did not stop with these. Next to Cave no. 10, was started, the excavation for Cave no. 11. It was a donation of Rāmaṇaka, the son of Sivamita, a lēkhaka. This cave is located at a higher level and has to be climbed with a flight of rock-cut steps. The placement on a higher level of this cave is explained by the existence of Cave no. 10. So as not to break in Cave no. 10 such a location was chosen. The facade of the cave is almost exactly similar to that of Cave no. 10. But the interior of this cave is again a story of various alterations made in the original plan of the architect. Inside the hall, only one cell was carved in the left wall and in the back wall in the left corner a long bench of the shape of letter ` L' was carved. In the right side of the hall, cells were not carved as there was a danger of breaking into Cave no. 10, which actually took place and at one place in the right corner a hole can be seen in the wall. Hence the excavation was not carried out further. Later on, images of Jaina deities were carved on the back wall. Looking at the similarities in the facade decoration of this cave with that of Cave no. 10 and 2 it is quite possible that it was excavated sometime after 78 A.D. and somewhere near Cave no. 2.

Cave no. 12 was carved immediately next to Cave no. 11. This was actually an open hall without cells and without a veranda. There is an inscription on the front wall recording the donation given by one Rāmaṇaka son of Velidata. He records that the donation of one hundred kāhāpaṇas was given as perpetual endowment in the hands of the saṃgha, from which twelve kāhāpaṇas were to be given for clothes to the monk who keeps vassā in this cave. The approximate date of this cave could be c. 2nd century CE. It is difficult to date this cave exactly due to the lack of any sculptural decoration.

Around this time the only work that had started, was again in Cave no. 20. The inscription in this cave informs that it was initially donated by an ascetic Bopaki and was left unfinished for many years. Hence Vāsu the current donor wanted to complete it. But unfortunately, even she could not complete it and the cave was converted into a shrine with the image of the Buddha after the 6th century C.E.

Around the same time work seems to have started for the caves to the west of Cave no. 10. The caves numbered as 5, 6, 7, 8 and 9 were probably excavated around the same time. The Cave no. 5 is actually a completely broken excavation. There is no decoration on the facade of this cave. It originally had two cells but the walls are broken today. The floor of this cave was probably dug deep and it was converted into a tank.

Cave no. 6 is close to Cave no. 5 and was probably excavated immediately after the latter. It is in a broken condition today and the floor has been filled with concrete. The two octagonal pillars in the front are also the reconstructions made by the A.S.I. The inscription on the veranda wall informs us that this was a donation of a gahapati called Vīra. He had donated money for the excavation of this four-celled cave along with his wife and daughter. This cave can be dated to the later 2nd or the early 3rd century C.E.

The next cave in this row is Cave no. 7, a single-celled excavation donated by a nun, Tāpasini, a disciple of the ascetic Savvasa. Today it appears that the floor of this cave was dug deep as the cave looks placed at a very high level. On the basis of palaeography and the placement, this cave can also be dated to the late 2nd and early 3rd century C. E.

Cave no. 8 provides a very interesting record for the history of Buddhism. This cave was a donation of a

Figure 52: Caves No 17 to 20, Nasik

fisherman called Mugudāsa. He had donated money for the excavation of this cave along with his family. Another inscription in the same cave tells us that this donor was an upāsaka of the Caityaka sect and to his cave, another person called as Dhamanandin, had donated a field in Western Kaṇhahini for the expenditure of clothes for the monks living here. The entablature of this cave is also very interesting as it is a copy of the entablature of Cave no. 17 and 4. The only difference here is that all the dentils have been decorated with human faces on the contrary they are alternately decorated in the case of Cave no. 17 and 4. But the palaeography of the inscriptions and the hourglass motif on the pilaster of the cave help us in keeping it in the early 3rd century C.E.

Cave No. 9 shares its western wall with Cave no. 8. It has an altogether different facade in this group. The cave has a pillared veranda with two rooms at the back and one in the left end of the veranda. The room to the right of the two in the back wall is further excavated and another room was excavated inside it. The inverted pot capital and animals above them remind us of the animal abacus of the Caves numbered 3, 10, 17, etc. All these features make us

place this cave in the 3rd century C.E.

Approximately at this time caves were excavated beyond Cave no. 12. They are Cave nos. 13 and 14. Both of these caves were excavated simultaneously. Cave no. 13 has two rooms and a hall. Cave no. 14 has three cells. The ceiling of the hall is broken. The hourglass decoration suggests the dates of these caves as c. 3rd century C.E.

Sometime during this period, a cave was started just next to the Cave no. 18 i.e. the Caityagṛha. This was Cave no. 20. The inscription in the cave tells us that it was begun by an ascetic Bopaki. But it could not be completed. Hence a female devotee called as Vasu in the 7th regnal year of Yajñaśrī Sātakarṇi. However, after entering the cave, one comes across a renewed cave with a shrine containing a huge image of the Buddha flanked by the Bodhisattvas on both sides. It appears that probably in around 5th-6th century CE this cave was converted into a Mahāyāna shrine.

Sometime after this period Cave no. 21 and 22 were excavated. Cave no. 21 has two pillars in the front with square bases and octagonal shaft. Cave no. 22

is a very small and plain excavation. It can be put to somewhere around the end of the 1st century C.E. and the beginning of the 2nd century C.E.

Near the eastern end of the site what we have are many broken cells today converted into the shrines of the Mahāyāna phase. It appears that there were nearly five to six small caves or cells fronted by many tanks here. There is a possibility, that there were some memorial stūpas here, the remains of one can definitely be seen even today (one does not know whether it was for worship as a part of the monastic complex or carved in the memory of some monk). The excavation activity at the site had probably stopped after c. 3rd - 4th century C.E. We do not find any new cave coming up till around 6th century C.E.

Probably around the 6th century C.E. many small caves of the earlier period were converted into shrines with the images of the Buddha and Bodhisattva. This happened in the case of Cave nos. 2, 20 and many small caves in 23. Cave nos. 15 and 16 were also created at this time as shrines. But they seem to be fresh excavations and no remains of the early residential halls can be seen.

The earliest activity in this phase probably started in Cave no. 2. The veranda wall and the partition wall between the two cells at the back were broken down and images of Buddha and flanking Bodhisattvas were carved on the walls. The sculptures in the cave show typical Buddhist triads i.e. the image of the Buddha at the centre flanked by two Bodhisattvas.

The next excavation was probably carried out in Cave nos. 15 and 16. It appears that new shrines were excavated in this period as we do not find any marks in the walls or the ceilings indicating the existence of earlier cells. Both of these caves contain the images of the Buddha and Bodhisattvas carved in triads with combinations of the Padmapāṇi, Vajrapāṇi and Maitrēya.

The next activity at this site was carried out in the huge complex of Cave no. 23. Many cells and even a stūpa of the earlier period were broken and numerous images of the Buddha and some shrines containing the Buddha and Bodhisattva triads were carved. The front portion of the whole area of this cave is hollowed out by huge tanks. It was for this availability of water that so many cells earlier and so many shrines were excavated here.

The most impressive excavation of the Mahāyāna

phase can be seen in Cave no. 20. This cave has had three stages in its life. All of them are supported by inscriptional evidence. As mentioned earlier it was begun by an ascetic Bopaki and continued for a long time. It was during the 7th regnal year of Gautamīputra Yajñaśrī Sātakarṇi that one female devotee Vāsu took it as her responsibility to complete it. But it appears that even she could not complete it and whatever was the stage of the cave it was enlarged in the late 6th century C. E. and converted into a grand Mahāyāna shrine. There are distinct traces in the ceiling and the walls of the cave indicating the extension of the earlier cave. A sanctum with the image of the Buddha was created at the back of the cave. The shrine doorway was guarded by more than life-size images of Maitrēya and Padmapāṇi. Even these guardians have been provided with dwarf attendants. This is probably the last excavation or enlargement at the site.

Thus, the rock-cut activity at Nasik which started in c. 1st century B.C. came to a halt probably in c. 7th century C.E. In the case of many caves the patrons are known but in the case of many caves in the second phase, the patrons are not known at all. The religious inspirations of the donors can be understood but the origin of the artistic influences and conventions at this site are difficult to find out. The contemporary religious situation and the developments of various ideologies have been reflected to a certain extent in the form of sculptures at Nasik.

Inscriptions at Nasik

The inscriptions in the caves at Nasik have thrown light on various facets of ancient Indian culture. There are twenty-seven inscriptions inscribed in twenty-four caves at Nasik. They were written in the Prākṛt language using the Brāhmi script. These inscriptions have proved to be of immense importance for the reconstruction of the political as well as the cultural history of the region.

Inscriptions written in the caves with royal patronage have been studied by various scholars time and again. But those inscriptions which recorded the donation of ordinary people were not given due attention. Many such inscriptions reveal certain concepts which were hitherto unknown to us. The development taking place in various fields, at the abstract levels, was expressed through quite a few inscriptions.

The Buddhist caves at Nasik are noteworthy for the extensive historical data that is furnished through the inscriptions in the caves. Some of the most important inscriptions that have the bearing on the history of Maharashtra have been engraved in these caves. The earliest inscription recording name of the Sātavāhana dynasty is found in these caves. The other dynasties that find mention in the inscriptions are the Kṣatrapas and the Ābhiras. They are important mainly for the history and chronology of the Sātavāhanas and Kṣatrapas.

Inscriptions of the Śakas and Yavanas - Nasik, being located on the ancient trade route, was visited by many merchants. India had trading contact with the western world. Many foreigners came and settled down in India. Various new concepts and ideologies that were brought to this region by them. The inscription of a Yavana recording the donation of Cave no. 17 is very significant as it records the introduction of a new architectural design in Western India. This donation was given by Indrāgnidatta, a northerner who had come from a town called Dattāmitri (Senart 1905-06: 90). The inscription mentions his wish to create a combination of two different types of architecture i.e. caityagṛha and vihāra. (Senart 1905-06: 90). Unfortunately, this cave could not be completed but the wish expressed in the inscription was actually executed partially at Nasik itself and completely at other sites like Kuḍā, Mahad, etc.

Other inscriptions at the site are also significant as some of them record the donations by the Buddhist monks, nuns, women, traders, etc. Some important concepts in Buddhism are also expressed through these. One of them is the concept of Transfer of Merit. Inscriptions in the following caves - no. 17, 10, 24, 3, 23 and 8 express a concept called as "Transfer of Merit" i.e. sharing one's merit (puṇya) with another person. This has hinted upon the changing religio-philosophical scenario in this region i.e. the beginning of the Mahāyāna phase of Buddhism. Transferring or sharing of merit (Punya) with parents and the rest of the living beings for their spiritual welfare.

Unique motifs

Some caves at Nasik bear some interesting motifs e.g. – Caves no. 4, 8,17 and 18 Dentils (projected beam ends) with human faces. This is their earliest depiction in Indian caves. This concept has probably come from the European world. (Bhalerao 2003:

403-407). Triskelion is another motif. A symbol called the triskeles/triskelion occurs at only two places in the western Indian caves – Nasik and Junnar. But this is a common motif found on the coins in ancient India (Bhalerao 2005: 115-118). Similarly, some Greek mythological animals like Sphinx, Griffin etc. are also seen in these caves like in no. 17, 18etc.

Iconography

In the 5th -6th centuries A.D. many small viharas were broken and altered into shrines with images of the Buddha and his attendant Bodhisattvas, mostly Padmapāṇi and Vajrapāṇi. Sometimes Maitrēya is also carved. The Buddhist texts giving the details of the iconography of the Buddhist images were composed in the 12th century CE. The identification of the Bodhisattvas in the caves at Nasik has been a difficult task. One of the major problems for the identification of these is that there are no corresponding descriptions in the texts. It was so as this was a formative stage in Buddhist iconography. Especially in the case of Maitrēya the attribute water pot was changed to the branch of the nāgakesara flower (Kim 1997: 165). There is only one image of the goddess Tārā in the entire group of the caves and it appears that the rock-cut activity came to a halt until 12th century CE when the Jaina deities and Kṣētrapāla images were carved in Caves no. 10 and 11 (Thuse 2009: 177).

Thus, this group of 24 caves with 27 inscriptions, is a very significant group -

- To understand the internal chronology at the site.
- To see the place of Nasik in the development of the Buddhist rock-cut architecture at the pan Indian scale
- To determine the chronology of these caves in accordance to the recent researches in the political history of this region and the dates of various rulers
- To study the religio - philosophical developments that took place in Buddhism till the beginning of the Mahāyāna phase
- To study the reflections of these developments in inscriptions, architecture, sculpture.
- To understand the changes in iconography and religious practices through art and architectural evidence and try to search for probable reasons.

References

Bhalerao, Manjiri (2003) Dentils with human faces - A Unique motif at Nasik. In Sankarnarayan, K., R. Panth and I. Ogawa (eds.), Buddhism in Global Perspective. Mumbai: Somaiya Publications. Vol. 2, pp. 403 – 407

Bhalerao, Manjiri (2006) Triskelion on coins &monuments - An unsolved enigma, in Coinex 2006, International Society for the Collectors of Rare Items, Ahmadabad. pp 115-118

Kim, Inchang (1997) The future Buddha Maitrēya: An Iconological Study, New Delhi: D.K. Printworld (Pvt) Ltd.

Senart E (1905-06) Nasik Inscriptions Epigraphia Indica, VIII: 59 – 96

Thuse, Manjiri (2009) Buddhist Caves at Nasik – An Analytical Study, Unpublished Ph.D. Thesis, Deccan College PG & RI, Pune.

Patterns of Patronage in the Jaina Caves of Maharashtra

Viraj Shah, Foundation for Liberal And Management Education (FLAME), Pune

Abstract

The Jaina caves of Maharashtra are limited in number and simpler in design compared to the vast wealth of Buddhist and Brāhmaṇical caves of the region. These caves, scattered over nineteen sites, were excavated during 1st century BCE to 14th-15th century CE, most of which emerged during the 9th to 14th centuries. These caves, following the regional architectural trends, are mostly plain excavations; but depict a multitude of icons. In the absence of adequate epigraphic data, it has been very difficult to propose any conclusive accounts on the patronage of these caves.

The paper aims to explore the patterns of patronage to the Jaina caves of Maharashtra through a variety of sources such as epigraphs; architectural and iconographic trends; and donor sculptures. It probes into the issues of piety, pilgrimage and prominence of Jainism in medieval Maharashtra as reflected in the nature of these caves and the donative inscriptions; as well as other Jaina remains of the region.

Introduction

The Jaina caves of Maharashtra are limited in number and simpler in design compared to the vast wealth of Buddhist and Brāhmaṇical caves of the region. The Jaina caves, scattered over nineteen sites, were excavated during 1st century BCE to 14th-15th century CE (Shah 2008). These caves, following the regional architectural trends, are mostly plain excavations; but depict a multitude of icons. In the absence of adequate epigraphic data, it has been very difficult to propose any conclusive accounts on the patronage of these caves.

The paper aims to explore the patterns of patronage to the Jaina caves of Maharashtra through a variety of sources such as epigraphs; architectural and iconographic trends; and donor sculptures. It probes into the issues of piety and pilgrimage in medieval Maharashtra as reflected in the nature of these caves and the donative inscriptions.

Jaina caves in Maharashtra

The Jaina caves in Maharashtra belong to the Digambar sect. These are excavated primarily in western Maharashtra, clustered in Nasik district, though a few sites are also found in Marathwada and northern Maharashtra (Figure 1).Pale in Pune district is the only early example of a Jaina cave in this region, while the rest can be dated to the period during 6th through 14th-15th centuries CE, with most emerging during 9th through 14th centuries.

Architecturally, these caves are similar to contemporary Buddhist and Brāhmaṇical caves. The 6th-century caves at Dhāraṇi in Osmanabad district resemble Buddhist *caitya-vihāras* found at Ajanta in terms of the ground plan, pillar ornamentation and the treatment of the main icon in the shrine. The Jaina caves at Ellora are akin to the Brāhmaṇical caves of Kailāsa and Lankēśvara in terms of façade treatment, types of pillars and doorways, ground plan and use of Draviḍa mode of architecture. Similarly, the late caves of 12th-13th centuries at Ankai-Tankai and Tringalwadi follow contemporary temple architecture of the region as evident in the treatment of plinth, pillar, façade, and ceiling. However, a large number of these caves such as those found at Bhamer, Chandor, Mohida, Chambhara Lena and Mangi-Tungi are plain rooms with a large number of icons. The iconographic program focuses primarily on the Jina figures; while the later caves also display a range of subsidiary deities such as *yakśa-yakśi* pair of Sarvānubhūti-Ambikā; *yakśi*s Cakrēśvarī and Padmāvati; Sarasvati and Kṣētrapāla. A large number of monk figures are depicted at Mangi-Tungi. Thus, with the exception of a few ornate caves at Ellora, Ankai-Tankai, and Tringalwadi, most of the Jaina caves in Maharashtra are architecturally very simple, with the profusion of icons instead. In some of the sites such as Ankai-Tankai and Tringalwadi, loose icons must have been installed as attested by almost absence of rock-cut icons and finds of a number of loose icons from the vicinity (Shah 2008).

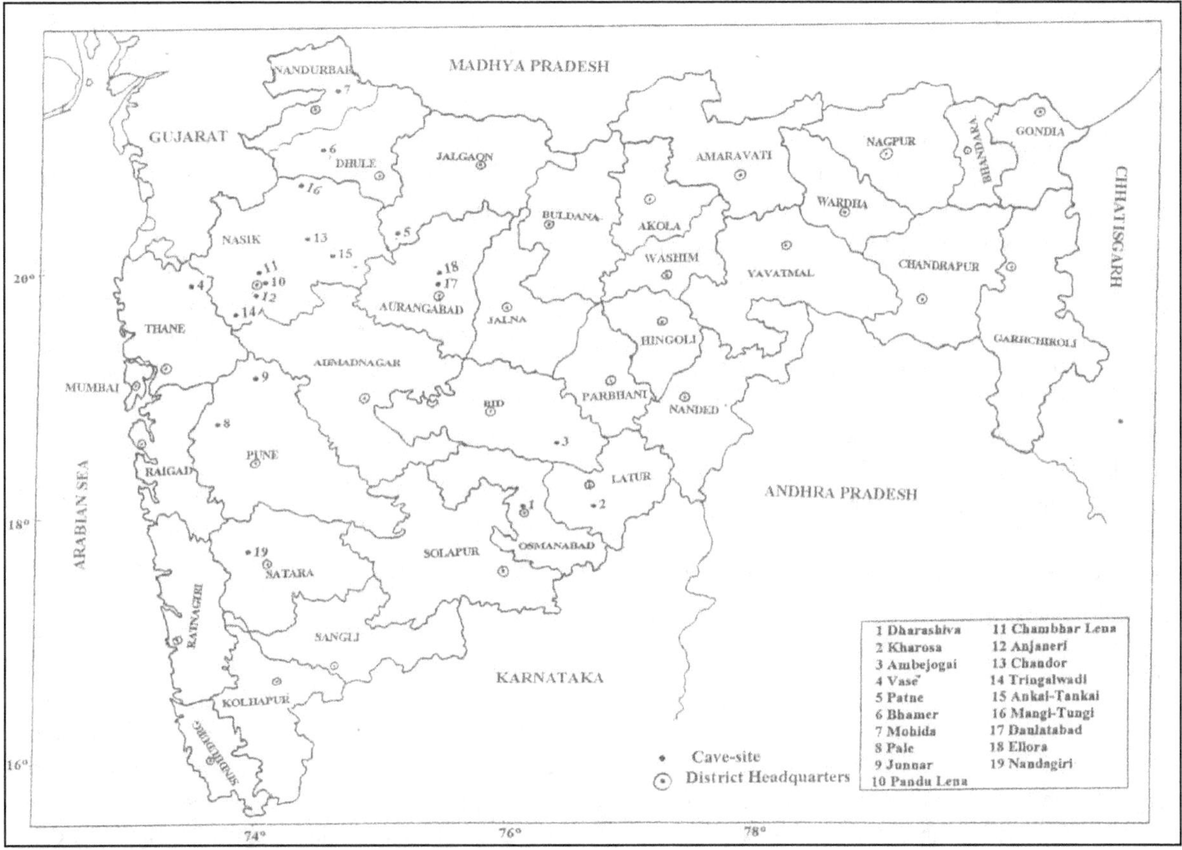

Fig. 1: *Location of Jaina Caves in Maharashtra*

It should be pointed out that the tradition of cave architecture had almost died out in this region after the 9th century CE and was replaced with structural temples. However, Jainas continued to excavate caves and add rock-cut icons on the bare surfaces of hills at least till 14th-15th century CE.

Patronage

The nature and late date of most of these caves throw up a few interesting questions about the issue of patronage such as who were the patrons of these caves? Were the caves patronized by the community in general or by individual donors? What types of donations are recorded in epigraphic sources? In the absence of epigraphic records, is it possible to identify individual donations by examining architectural and iconographic patterns? What were the motives of the donors in patronizing these caves?

I) Epigraphic Evidence

Unfortunately, there are not many inscriptions available. The epigraphic evidence consists of a few fragmentary and mostly illegible inscriptions on the bases of icons, cave walls, pillars or doorways. These are from the caves at Pale, Ellora, Ankai-Tankai, Tringalwadi, Mangi-Tungi, and Mohida.

a) Pale: The cave in a hill close to the village of Pale, near Kamshet, is a plain room with a cistern. Above the cistern is a two-line Brahmi inscription that records the donation of the cave and a cistern by one *Indarkhita* (*Indrakhita*). The inscription begins with the invocation '*Namō arhaṃtānaṃ*' and is dated to 1st century BCE on palaeographic grounds. Since no contemporary Buddhist cave carries any invocation and such an invocation is known to be typically Jaina, the cave is considered to belong to Jaina faith (Sankalia and Gokhale 1969: 167-168).

b) Ellora: The most famous and ornate Jaina caves of the region are at Ellora, dated to 9th century CE on stylistic grounds (Shah 2008: 124-126). These caves, at the northern end of the hill range, though considered to be five excavations and numbered 30 to 34, are clusters of about 26 independent caves. There are six more caves excavated on the other side of the same hill during the 12th-13th century CE (Pereira 1977). Of these, J13, J15 (in the courtyard of Cave 32 or Indra Sabha) and J25 (Cave 33 or Jagannath Sabha) have furnished a few short inscriptions, engraved below icons. The author, in this paper, has followed the numbering of the caves proposed by Jose Pereira in *Monolithis Jinas*.

Outside Cave J13, on the veranda wall of J15, there are two large standing icons of Jinas, facing each other. Below one of these, there is an inscription in old Nagari characters. It reads, "*Śrī Sōhila brahmacārinaḥ Śāntibhaṭṭāraka pratimēyaṃ*", meaning "the image of *Śāntibhaṭṭāraka* (made by) *Sōhila*, a *brahmacāri*" (Burgess and Indraji 1881: 98) (Figure 2).

On one of the pillars in the unfinished hall of the lower storey of Indra Sabha (J15), there is a large standing figure of a Jina with a seated figure of a male devotee on each side. Of these, the figure on the right wears a necklace with hair tied in a bun above the head and a beard. Below this image is an inscription, which says "*Śrī Nāgavarmma krita pratimā*" meaning "(This) image (is) made by Sri *Nāgavarmma*" (Burgess and Indraji 1881: 98) (Figure 3).

On the hall pillars of J25, on opposing faces, there are two identical images, each with a small standing figure of Jina flanked by six male and five female devotees. There is a Kannada inscription under each figure, demarcated by lines. These appear to be names of each of the devotee. Some of the names like *Naganadi, Achabe, Silabe* can be read (Gopal 1969: 285-286, No. 85 & 86) (Figures 4 & 5).

The only detailed inscription available at the site is from the Yadava period icon carved on the other face of the same hill. This icon on the rock face is about five metres high colossus of Pārśvanātha. It consists of a seated figure of Pārśvanātha flanked by *Yakṣa* Dharanēndra and *Yakṣi* Padmāvati and seated figure of a devotee (Figure 6). There is a five-lined Dēvanagari inscription on the cushion on which Pārśvanātha is shown seated. It records the donation of the icon by one Cakrēśvara from Vardhanapura. It reads:

Hail, in the year 1156 of the famous *Śaka* era, in the year (*of the Bṛhaspati cycle*) called Jaya. In *Śrī(va)rdhanapura* was born Ranugi……his son (*was*) Galugi [Mhalugi] (whose) wife (was) Svarna (dear) also to the world.

From those two sprang four sons, Cakrēśvara and the rest. Cakrēśvara was chief among them excelling through the virtue of liberality.

He gave, on the hill that is frequented by *Cāranas*, a monument of Pārśvanātha, and by

(this act of) liberality (he made) an oblation of his *karma*.

Many huge images of the lordly Jinas he made, and converted the *Cāraṅādri* thereby into a holy *tīrtha*, just as Bharata (made) Mount Kailāśa (*a tīrtha*).

The unique image of faith, of firm and pure convictions, kind, constant to his faithful wife, resembling the tree of paradise (in liberality), Cakrēśvara becomes a protector of the pure faith, a fifth Vasudēva. Phalguna 3, Wednesday." (Burgess and Indraji 1881: 98-99).

c) Ankai-Tankai: The 12th-century caves on the connecting ridge of the twin hills of Ankai-Tankai near Manmad in the Nasik district are architecturally some of the finest Jaina caves of the region, though with minimum icons carved *in situ*. Of these, Cave VI carries a beautifully carved doorway to the shrine. Interestingly, this doorway is not rock-cut but is structural, made of loose stone slabs (Figure 7). On the *staṃbha śākhā* of this doorway, there is a male figure on the right jamb (Figure 8) and a couple on the left jamb (Figure 9). The male figures, with beard and hair tied in large buns, stand with hands in *anjalimudrā*, while the female has her right hand in a sort of *varadamudrā* and her left hand on the hip. Under each of these figures, there is an inscription in Dēvanagari, probably the names of these figures as they appear to be important devotees or donors. The same figures are also repeated in the central compartment above the lintel. The inscriptions are not legible (Shah 2008: 185-86).

d) Tringalwadi: The Jaina cave at the base of the hill fort of Tringalwadi, about 10 km from Igatpuri in the Nasik district, is a fine example of cave-architecture, though much in ruins now. Like Ankai-Tankai, this cave is also architecturally quite decorative, while the only *in situ* icon is the image of Ṛshabhanātha, carved on the back wall of the shrine. On the cushion of this image, there is a two-line Dēvanagari inscription, which unfortunately is not very clear. It mentions the *Śaka* year 1266 (1344 CE) and Mūla Sangha (Burgess 1877: 20).

e) Mangi-Tungi: The only site that furnishes a substantial number of inscriptions is Mangi-Tungi, though most of these are of much later date and record only the names of monks represented in sculptures. Mangi and Tungi are the twin peaks on

Fig. 2: Image of Śāntinātha made by Sohila, J13, Ellora

Fig. 4: Devotee/Donor figures with inscription in Kannada, on the pillar in J25, Ellora

Fig. 3: Jina image made by Nāgavarmma, on the hall pillar, J15, Ellora

Fig. 5: Devotee/Donor figures with inscription in Kannada, on the opposite pillar in J25, Ellora

Fig. 6: Colossal image of Pārśvanātha donated by Cakrēśvara, J27, Ellora

Fig. 8: Male devotee/donor, Shrine doorway, Cave VI, Ankai-Tankai

Fig. 7: Structural shrine doorway, Cave VI, Ankai-Tankai

Fig. 9: Couple devotee/donor, Shrine doorway, Cave VI, Ankai-Tankai

the western border of Nasik district, where a few simple caves have been excavated with a multitude of icons during 9th through 14th-15th centuries CE. A large number of icons are carved directly on the rock-face of these peculiarly-shaped, bare peaks that are distinctly visible in the landscape for some distance. The Mangi peak has four caves containing 140 icons and around 135 icons on the rock-face, while the Tungi peak has two caves with 26 icons and eight icons on the rock-face (Shah 2008: 238-252).

Of the caves, those on the Tungi peak do not contain any inscriptions, while there are a few inscriptions in the caves on the Mangi peak. A number of icons, mainly of the monks, in Ādinātha Guphā and Śāntinātha Guphā, carry individual names of the monks in almost modern Dēvanagari. These appear to have been written much later than the icons, but probably recording memory of older tradition (Shah 2008: 241-46). There are two, long inscriptions, which are historically important. The Sanskrit inscription in Adinatha Guphā refers to some *ācārya*s and also some other well-known people, which are not clear. The inscription in Śāntinātha Guphā is very important. It refers to the monks of *Sarasvati gachha, balātkāra gaṇa,* and *śrī kunkundācārya anvaya*, possibly represented in the panel above. There is a reference to Chiniyaraja Viramsena, Pradhanasena, Kanaksena, and their wives. Viramsena was the Rathod king of Mulher, a fort nearby. The region around Baglan was ruled by Raṣṭrōdha or Rathod dynasty from Rajputana from 1297 CE. As per their historical account written by the poet Rudra in 1596 CE, a total of 54 rulers of the family ruled the area. The area was annexed by Aurangzeb in 1637 CE. There are as many as three kings called Vīrasēna, the third, thirty-sixth and forty-fourth, of this dynasty (Balsekar and Bhamre 2006: 88-90). As the date in the inscription is not legible, it is not clear which Viramsena is referred to in this inscription.

Of the inscriptions from other Jaina caves of the region, those below the shrine icon in Cave I at Mohida and on the veranda pillar in Cave IV at Ankai-Tankai, though long, are difficult to read. There is a trace of an inscription below one of the Jina icons at Bhamer but is almost illegible. Similarly, the inscription below one of the male devotees in J30 at Ellora can also not be read. There was an inscription on the veranda wall of the cave at Tringalwadi but cannot be traced now (Shah 2008).

II) Who were the patrons?

The epigraphic evidence reveals only a few names such as Indrakhita, Sohila, Nāgavarmma, and Cakrēśvara as patrons. Of these, nothing much is known about any of them, except Cakrēśvara, who donated the colossus of Pārśvanātha at Ellora in the 13th century CE. He provides his genealogy and also proclaims his own intentions in making this religious donation. He was the native of Śrīvardhanapura, which has been identified with ancient Nandivardhana, modern-day Nagardhan near Ramtek in Nagpur district. Some scholars also identify it with Shrivardhan in Raigad district (Bakker 1990: Note 22, 77). He appears to have been a devout Jaina, who claims to have made many such donations and turned the Cāranādri (hill in which the caves are excavated) into a holy *tirtha*. He compares his religious acts with those of Bharata, son of the first *Tīrthaṃkara* Ṛshabhanātha, who is believed to have built numerous *stupa*s and shrines on Mount Kailash (Shah 1987). One of the loose icons found from the lower caves of Ellora contains an inscription dated to 1247 CE and records the donation of the image by a native of Vardhanapura (Burgess and Indraji 1881: 98). It is quite possible that the donor of this particular icon was also Cakrēśvara as he claims to have donated many Jina icons on the same hill.

Donor Figures

Interestingly, a few 'devotee' figures can be identified as donors at a number of sites even though there are no donative inscriptions available except a few label inscriptions.

Such donor figures with inscriptions can be seen at Ellora and Ankai-Tankai. Sohila and Nāgavarmma are clearly depicted in the panels as devotees at Ellora (See Figures 2 & 3). Nāgavarmma is shown wearing a necklace with a beard and hair tied in a bun above the head. He must have been a devout *śrāvaka*, who donated a large Jina icon on the hall pillar of the unfinished lower storey of Indra Sabha or J15. Sohila, who donated the image of 16th*Tīrthaṃkara*Śāntinātha at Ellora, was probably an ascetic or a young novice as he calls himself '*brahmacāri*'. This '*brahmacāri*' is apparently the devotee depicted in the panel kneeling beside the Jina with his hands in *anjalimudrā*. He is shown as a youth wearing a short lower garment; an *uttariya* draped across the shoulders and shaved head. His '*brahmacāri*' status is emphasized by his attire, plain head and lack of ornaments.

The male-female figures with individual names in Kannada in small panels on the pillars in J25 at Ellora could also be donors or relatives of a donor. The male figures are shown with right hands on knees, while the females are in *anjalimudrā* and all are shown seated. There are no traces of garments or ornaments on any of the figures. The names written below are demarcated by lines to indicate the individual name of the figure above. Some of the names can be read as Naganandi, Achabe, and Silabe in both cases representing the same individuals in both the panels on the pillars facing each other. The panel consists of a seated figure of Jina flanked by Sarvānubhūti-Ambikā with another small, standing figure of Jina flanked by male-female devotees/donors in question below (See Figures 4 & 5). Both the panels are identical and were obviously donated by the same donor/s, probably depicting his family as devotees. These panels also have a water chute and a small pit cut in the floor in front of them, probably for collecting the water used in worship ritual. There is another identical panel on the damaged front wall of the veranda of the same cave

(Figure 10). This also must have been donated by the same donor/s, though no inscription can be traced here.

The devotees with label inscriptions on the *staṃbha śākhā* of the shrine doorway of Cave VI at Ankai-Tankai are also obviously donors, who appear to have donated this beautifully carved structural doorway. The male on the right jamb and the couple on the left are fully decked with males wearing beards and hair tied in large buns on sides (See Figures 8 & 9). These figures are repeated in the central compartment above the lintel, occupying the same position, male to right and couple to left, but here all three are seated with hands in *anjalimudrā*. Unfortunately, the label inscriptions are too indistinct to read.

On one of the pillars in J25, a small standing figure of Pārśvanātha is carved, flanked by his *yakṣi* Padmāvati and a large, male devotee to left. This devotee was probably a monk as he is shown wearing a thin lower garment and no ornaments. His hands are in *anjalimudrā*, while on his right hand hangs a *kamaṇḍalu*. There is a two-line inscription in Kannada below this panel, which has not been deciphered (Figure 11). There is a water chute

Fig. 10: Panel with devotee/donor figures as in the panels on pillars, J25, Ellora

leading to a small pit cut in the floor in front of the icon, probably to collect the water used in the ritual. Even though the inscription has not been read, it is possible that the devotee is meant to be either a donor or an important monk, probably preceptor of the donor.

Some of the other devotee figures without any inscriptions can also be identified as donors. The large figure of a male devotee near the icon of Cakrēśvarī in J20A at Ellora appears to be the donor, as indicated by his placement in a separate niche and size of the figure, though it does not carry any inscription. This icon is placed in a small, almost independent room leading to the veranda of J20 from J18 or the upper storey of Indra Sabha. The 'devotee' is shown seated, facing the icon of Cakrēśvarī with hands in *anjalimudrā*. He is depicted wearing a rich costume and jewellery (Figure 12). The independent nature of the icon, its placement at a significant location in the cave and the way this devotee figure is depicted indicate that he was the donor of the icon of Cakrēśvarī.

A panel depicting the penance of Bāhubali outside J14 at Ellora shows a seated devotee couple with hands in *anjalimudrā*, which could be donors as such figures do not feature in the regular iconographic format of Bāhubali's penance and are not found in any of the other Bāhubali panels at Ellora (Figure 13).

A few of such devotee figures in the lower tier of images in the halls of Caves I and II at Mohida could also be donors of particular icons. These devotee figures, male or couples are shown standing with hands in *anjalimudrā* below Jina icons (Figure 14).

It appears that the donors were devout *śrāvaka*-s or householders and possibly monks in some cases. In a few cases, the donors not only patronized the icons but also solicited permanent presence before the Jinas/deities by portraying themselves as devotees. The variations and marked distinction in the depiction of these donor figures indicate that these were meant to represent specific individuals even though it is argued that Indian art predominantly depicts a standardized form in the portrait sculptures (Desai 1990: 22). They must have hailed from nearby towns and were obviously affluent as most of them are depicted richly decked. The recorded epigraphic and sculptural evidence suggests that only male devotees made donations, while the women are found represented as the partners of men in the depiction of couples.

III) Types of donations

It appears that most of the inscriptions in the Jaina caves record donations of individual icons rather than the entire cave. The only record of donation of the cave along with the cistern is from Pale near Pune. The other inscriptions record the donation of individual icons with perhaps the exception of the shrine doorway of Cave VI at Ankai-Tankai. Even in the absence of inscriptions, there are indications that individual donors contributed mostly with donations of icons rather than doorways, pillars or any other architectural components.

Most of the Jaina caves appear to have been community efforts, probably supervised by the monastery or a lay organization of trustees as many of these caves are well-planned, symmetrical edifices. Since no donative inscription is found at any of the sites except at Pale, it would appear that the donors made common donations towards the excavation of a cave, which were utilized by the monastery or an organization of the lay community. Unlike early Buddhist monuments, where the donations of different architectural components such as pillars, *tōraṇa*s or the railings in a cave or *stupa* were individually recorded down in accompanying inscriptions; the Jaina caves record only the donation of Jina icons. The nature and arrangement of icons in a few caves indicate that some of these were independent donations and did not form part of the original plan of the cave, even though there are no donative inscriptions available. This feature is quite evident at Ellora. These independent donations are carved mostly on pillars and pilasters or any space available that would catch the attention of the visitor. Apart from their placements, the nature of the icons also indicates that they were independent donations. It is to be noted that most of these icons carry individual pair of *yakṣa-yakṣi*, a feature not noticed in most of the Jina icons at Ellora since a single pair of *yakṣa-yakṣi* was carved in a cave. Some of these independent donations, as mentioned above, have arrangements made for worship ritual in the form of a water chute and pit cut in the floor. A few of such icons are carved within a pavilion with *phaṃsana* roof. It appears that the Jina figures in the lower tier in the hall of J21 were independent donations as although the lower tier is quite uniform, it does not tally with the size and nature of the icons in the upper tier (Figure 15). Almost all the Jina figures in the lower tier have individual pair of

Fig. 11: Jina icons with undeciphered inscription in Kannada, on the hall pillar, J25, Ellora

Fig. 13: Penance of Bāhubali with devotee/donor couple, J14, Ellora

Fig. 12: Devotee/Donor figure bowing down to Cakrēśvarī, J20A, Ellora

Fig. 15: Asymmetrical panels of Jina icons, Hall of J21, Ellora

Fig. 14: Devotee/Donor figures, Cave I, Mohida

Fig. 16: Jina figure within a shrine with *śālā śikhara* and accompanied by *yakṣa-yakṣī*, J21, Ellora

Fig. 17: Haphazard arrangement of Jina figures, Hall of J3, Ellora

yakṣa-yakṣi, while one of the Jina figures is placed within a shrine with *śālā śikhara* (Figure 16). This kind of haphazard arrangement of icons is noticed in a few other caves at Ellora, clearly suggesting that these icons were donated by individual donors at the available spaces on the walls of the caves (Figure 17). The caves at Bhamer, Chandor, Anjaneri, and Mangi-Tungi also point at similar patterns. The asymmetrical arrangement of Jina icons of varying sizes and depiction of more than one figure of a few *yakṣis* such as Ambika, especially at Chandor, indicate that these were independent donations by individual donors. The size and placement of icons obviously depended on the resources of the donors. In the case of Ankai-Tankai and Tringalwadi, where mostly loose icons were installed, it is possible that the icons were patronized by individual donors; while the caves were excavated through community donations.

Probably, different such monastic establishments or community organizations were operative, which explains why the lower storey of Cave 32 or Indra Sabha at Ellora was left unfinished. This cave, planned as a two-storied edifice with a monolithic *sarvatōbhadra* shrine, *mānastaṃbha* and a large figure of an elephant in the courtyard, is one of the most elaborate Jaina caves of the region. The upper storey or J18 is the finest cave with intricately carved pillars, doorways and ceiling decorations; beautifully rendered icons; and elaborately painted ceilings. The *sarvatōbhadra* shrine, *mānastaṃbha,* and elephant figure are also complete. However, the lower storey or J15 is left unfinished with veranda completed and hall roughly laid out. The side portions of the hall and the antechamber are left unfinished, though the shrine is complete with the main icon of Jina on the back wall. Thus, the cave was clearly consecrated and under worship. There are no other icons in the cave. It is difficult to explain why this cave was not finished if it was patronized by the community. Possibly, the resources were exhausted and other community organizations were more interested in initiating their own caves than completing a half-finished cave. The main icon in the shrine was worshipped and the hall was frequented by the devotees as Nāgavarmma donated the large figure on one of the pillars of this incomplete hall.

IV) Piety

The simple architecture and a wealth of icons with a predominance of Jina figures in most of the Jaina caves of the region seem to indicate focused interests and limited resources of the donors. The patrons were clearly interested in earning religious merit by donating the icons of Jinas. The patrons also appear to be more interested in donating icons at the site, which were celebrated as *tīrtha*s and were considered to be more sacred than the others. Many of the Jaina cave-sites emerged as *tīrtha*s and were frequented by pilgrims from far off regions. Nāgavarmma, Naganandi, Silabe, Achabe and Cakrēśvara were obviously pilgrims to Ellora. Cakrēśvara clearly mentions that he was from Śrīvardhanapura, a distance of almost 550 km. He also specifies that by making this and many such donations, he had turned the site into a holy *tīrtha* and had become the protector of Jainism. Ellora had emerged as a Jaina *tirtha* as evident from a few texts. While a number of texts refer to Ellora, specific reference to the Jaina caves is from a Marathi Jaina text, '*Jaṃbusvāmi caritra*', which refers to Yarulanagara as one of the *tīrtha*s, the main icon being Dharanēndra-Padmāvati-Pārśvanātha (Akkole 1968: 192-193). This obviously refers to the colossus of Pārśvanātha donated by Cakrēśvara. This icon was in worship even in the late 17th century CE as Muni Shilavijaya, mentions Ellora caves as built by Viśvakarmā (Premi 1956a: 465). A large number of pilgrims' records at Mangi-Tungi reveal that the site was considered to be a Jaina *tīrtha* and was visited regularly by the pilgrims, as it is today. There are a number of Jaina texts, which refer to the site as a Jaina *tīrtha*. The earliest reference to the site is in the 13th century Sanskrit text, '*Nirvāṇabhakti*', dealing with the Digambar *tīrtha*s (Premi and Jaina 1939: 182). Here Tungigiri is referred to as the place from where Bālabhadras attained liberation (Premi 1956a: 434). '*Tīrthācanacandrikā*' of Guṇabhadra (ca. 1575 CE) refers to the site as 'Tungigiri', along with a number of other Digambar *tīrtha*s (Premi 1956a: 424 Footnote 1). Muni Shilavijaya mentions Tungigiri along with Ellora caves. (Premi 1956b: 465). Viśvanātha, in his text, refers to Tungigiri, along with other Jaina *tīrtha*s such as Girnar, Śatruñjaya, Champapuri, Pavapuri, Hastinapur, etc. The site is mentioned as the *nirvana* place of *Bālabhadras*-s and *Siddha*-s and a place, where all disease, hardships and worries disappear. Viśvanātha's date is not determined, but he belongs to a relatively modern period (Premi 1956a: 435-436, Footnote 1). It is possible that Viramsena, the Rathod king of Muller, or some of the important dignitaries associated with him made donations here. This site is peculiar in depicting mostly Jina icons and figures of monks on the rock-face with very little architectural embellishment.

The sacred nature of some of these cave-sites also explains why Jainas continued to make donations to caves as late as 14th-15th century CE even when the structural architecture had become the more popular form of religious architecture. Clearly, the donors focused on donating Jina icons on the hills/caves considered to be *tirtha*s and believed to be associated with holy figures, as a way of earning more religious merit. The simple architectural features of most of these caves could mean that the larger share of patronage was spent on the structural temples erected in the midst of towns, which were more frequently visited.

Conclusion

The lack of enough epigraphic sources makes it very difficult to reconstruct the patronage patterns to the Jaina caves of Maharashtra, which were excavated during the period of 1st century BCE to 14th-15th century CE. The handful available inscriptions predominantly record the individual donation of icons with the exception of donation of the cave in one case. Other inscriptions record individual names, which were most probably donors as indicated by their representation as devotees in the said sculptural panels. Such representation interestingly suggests that a structural doorway to the shrine of a cave at Ankai-Tankai could have been donated by a couple and a man, most probably family members. Architecturally decorative, and well-planned, symmetrical caves at the sites such as Ellora, Ankai-Tankai and Tringalwadi seem to suggest that the excavation of a cave was undertaken by community, either a monastic organization or a trust of lay followers by pooling in common resources; while the individual donors patronized the Jina icons or images of other deities. Such a trend can also be confirmed by the distinct depictions of many devotee figures that can be clearly identified as donor figures; and independent nature of some of the icons with a separate pair of *yakśa-yakśi*, depiction within independent shrine like relief, and eye-catching placements in the cave. Most of the other caves are architecturally simple structures, just rooms in many cases, with a predominance of icons. The haphazard arrangement of icons in varying sizes in such caves and multiple representations of the same deity, especially *yakśis* such as Ambika in a single cave, seem to reinforce the assumption that many of these icons were independent donations. Even in the case of a few well-planned caves such as those at Ellora, there are clear indications that a few icons were patronized by individual donors as the placement and size of these icons do not match with the overall sculptural pattern of the cave.

This obvious focus on the donation of an icon was clearly tied to the issue of religious merit. Moreover, most of such donations can be identified at sites such as Ellora and Mangi-Tungi, which were considered to be *tirtha*s. This added to the significance of such donations. In a few cases, donors also immortalized their donations by representing themselves as devotees in the donated panels, both claiming long-lasting fame as well as a permanent presence before the deity. However, most of the donors still remain unknown to us.

References

Akkole, Subhashchandra 1968 *Prachin Marathi Jaina Sahitya* (in Marathi), Nagpur-Pune: Suvichar Prakashan Mandala

Bakker Hans 1990 Ramtek: An Ancient Centre of Visnu Devotion in Maharashtra in Hans Bakker ed. *The History of Sacred Places as reflected in Traditional Literature*, Leiden: E. J. Brill, pp. 62-85

Balsekar Dilip P and S. J. Bhamre 2006 *Khandesh Faruqui Gharane: Itihas va Nani* (in Marathi), Mumbai: Indian Institute of Research in Numismatic Studies

Burgess, J. 1877 *Antiquities of the talukas of Parner, Sangamner, Ankole and Koparguam- with Revised Lists of Remains in the Ahemadnagar, Nasik, Puna, Thana and Kala'dgi Zilla*, Archaeological Survey of Western India, No. VI, Bombay: Government Central Press

Burgess, J. and Bhagwanlal Indraji 1881 *Inscriptions from the Cave Temples of Western India*, Archaeological Survey of Western India, Bombay: Government Central Press

Desai Dēvangana 1990 Social Dimensions of Art in Early India, *Social Scientist*, Volume 18, No 3, pp. 3-32

Gopal, B. R. (Ed) 1969 *Karnatak Inscriptions Series*, Vol. V, Dharwar: Kannada Research Institute

Pereira, J. 1977 *Monolithic Jinas*, Delhi: Motilal Banarsidass

Premi, Nathuram and Jaina Hiralal 1939 *Hamare Tirthakshetra* (in Hindi), *Jaina Siddhanta Bhaskara*, Vol. 5, pp. 179-203

Premi, Nathuram 1956a *Hamare Tirthakshetra* in *Jaina Sahitya and Itihas* (in Hindi), Second Edition, pp. 422-451, Bombay: Hindi Grantha Ratnakar Ltd

Premi, Nathuram 1956b *Dakṣiṇa ke Tirthakshetra* in *Jaina Sahitya Aur Itihas* (in Hindi), Second edition, pp. 452-467, Bombay: Hindi Grantha Ratnakar

Sankalia, H. D. and Gokhale Shobhana 1969 A Brahmi Inscription from Pale, *Epigraphia Indica*, Vol. XXXVIII, pp. 167-168

Shah, U. P. 1987 *Jaina Rupa-Mandana*, Delhi: Abhinav Publications

Shah Viraj 2008 *Jaina Rock-cut Caves in Western India*, New Delhi: Agam Kala Prakashan

संघंशरणंगच्छामि:Understanding the Role and Control of Monastery through the Inscriptions in the Buddhist Cave Temples of Maharashtra

Abhijit Dandekar, Deccan College Post-Graduate and Research Institute, Pune

Abstract

The present paper takes a review of the donatory inscriptions in the Buddhist cave temples of Maharashtra. It seeks to record the changing pattern of donors and their donations. It attempts to corroborate the same with the change/development in the architecture of the Caityas in order to demonstrate the increasing dominance of the monastic establishments over the lay worshippers resulting in the alienation of the Buddha from laity over time.

Introduction

Soon after the introduction of Buddhism in the Deccan, the Western Ghats witnessed a hectic activity of excavation of caves which were initially meant for the monks to reside during the heavy monsoons and subsequently got transformed into monasteries and seats of learning. As Buddhism gained popularity, especially amongst the mercantile communities this activity was undertaken on a much larger scale with the addition of a lot of paintings and sculptures. Indeed, it is not a mere exaggeration when the '*Sēṭhi* Bhūtapāla from Vaijayanti', probably the main sponsor of the cave complex at Karle, states (LL 1087) that the rock-mansion that he completed was excellent in the entire '*Jambudvīpa*'.

This patronage by the mercantile community and later on by the royal families such as the Sātavāhanas, the Kṣaharatas, the Mahābhōjas and the Kāṇabhōjas to name a few, was one of the main reasons behind the spread of the Buddhist monastic establishments in the Western Deccan. The donative and eulogistic inscriptions on the walls of these caves are a testimony to the overwhelming support of the elite and masses that the monastic order received during the early centuries of Common Era in the Western Deccan. Present paper analyses the 'text' and the 'context' of these inscriptions. It looks not at only the changing pattern of donations, but also at that of the donors and the donees. It tries to build a narrative around these patterns to locate the monastic order and its changing role along the years. Though the paper is about the inscriptions, it is not a survey of inscriptions. Only those inscriptions have been taken into consideration which bear importance as regards understanding the nature of the monastic order. The emphasis of this paper is more on the epigraphical data than the texts. The primary reason behind this standpoint is, as Schopen (1997: 56) states, the inscriptional evidence has distinct advantages. First it predates the datable literary sources; and more importantly, it tells us what the Buddhist people, laity or monks actually did, as against what is prescribed in the texts. This standpoint also takes a diversion from other Buddhist studies where the textual reference is considered primary and thus sacrosanct when juxtaposed against the archaeological or epigraphical evidence. In other words, "… Such a procedure has, of course, placed archaeology and epigraphy in a very awkward position. If then, archaeology and epigraphy are to be in the service of a "history" base on written sources of this kind, then they are going to have to "support and amplify" something that very probably did not exist: they are going to have to sit quietly in the corner spinning cloth for the emperor's new clothes." (Schopen, 1991).

The inscriptions under the purview of this paper belong to the early centuries of Common Era. They are the Hīnayānic inscriptions, barring one from Kuḍā which records a gift of a *Śākyabhikṣu*, a phenomenon commonly recorded in the inscriptions as Ajanta. The inscription from Kuḍā is cited only as an example of personal wealth accumulation of monks. The issue of the *Śākyabhikṣu* is not taken into consideration since the primary aim of this article is to trace the evolution of the tradition of donations and the entry of the *saṃgha* into these economic activities. Secondly, the phenomenon of *Śākyabhikṣu* has been dealt with by many scholars (Schopen 1979, Cohen 2000, Cousins 2003) and it would be unnecessary repetition of the debate. It may also be pointed out at this juncture that this paper does not attempt to set up any chronology on the basis of either the palaeography or the content of the inscriptions. Neither does it intend to look at the inscriptions in a chronological sequence. It only attempts to understand the nature of the monastic order as revealed through them. This paper accepts the chronology proposed by Prof. Nagaraju (1981) merely as a backdrop against which the changing pattern can be highlighted. It does not aim to enter the labyrinth of the debate over the chronology of these cave complexes.

The Inscriptions

Almost all the cave complexes bear at least one inscription barring only one cave complex, i.e. the Tulja group of caves at Junnar which has no inscription reported so far. Conspicuously, this cave complex happens to be one of the earliest cave complexes in the Western Deccan.

Contemporary or of slightly later date is the Bhaje group of caves. It has some of the earliest donative inscriptions. An inscription on one of the beams in the Caitya cave (IAR 1955-56: 29) records a donation by one Dhamabhaga. Another inscription on the entrance of a cell in cave no. 6 mentions a donation by a lady named 'Badha', wife of a ploughman (LL 1084; Burgess and Indraji 1881: 25). The third one is of a person Nadasava, resident of Bhogavati (LL 1078). All these inscriptions are written in low relief and are very difficult to spot. The donors also do not mention the intent of their donations.

At Bedsa we see the mention of the 'status' of the donor. An inscription on the door of one of the cells mentions the donation of Pusanaka, son of a *Sēṭhi* Ananda from Nasik (LL 1109). Here, though the inscription is inscribed in an inconspicuous manner, nevertheless mentions a merchant as the donor.

At Junnar, in all the groups, and especially in the Manmodi group there are a number of donations (LL 1162, 1164, 1165, 1166, 1167) which are of perpetual endowment (*akṣayanivi*) type. They are in the form of fields. Some of them are done to the Aparājitā *saṃgha* (LL 1158, 1163). Most of these donations are by the big merchants (*sēṭhi*), householders (*gahapati*) or their sons/relatives. A couple of donations, though not of this nature, are also by courtiers or ministers or persons of royal families (LL 1174). The 'catchment area' also

seems to have been fairly large as we have donations coming from as far as Bharukaccha (LL 1169) or modern Bharuch in the Gujarat state.

At Karle, not only there are donations for the monks, but also by the monks. For example, an inscription in the veranda of the Caitya cave records a donation by *bhadanta* Indradēva of (images of) elephants and railings (LL 1089). Another inscription (LL 1101) above the pair of figures on the extreme right of the veranda records gift of the *mithuna* (the couple) by *bhadanta* Bhadasama. There is another important phenomenon of converting a pillar into a memorial recorded in two inscriptions (LL 1094, 1095) and this is done by a preacher (*bhāṇaka*) Satimita of Dharmōttariya *saṃgha* (Dandekar and Pradhan 2014). There are some more inscriptions in the same cave (LL 1098, 1104) which record gifts/donations given by nuns or their mothers.

Another interesting observation about the inscriptions at Karle is donations to the Mahāsaṃghikas. It appears that a separate *lēṇa* (cave no. XV) was excavated for them. The inscription (LL 1106) in the cave mentions the gift by Harapharana, son of Setapharana as the sole or special property of the *saṃgha*. Another inscription, that of Mahārathī Sōmadēva (LL 1100), inscribed in the veranda of the Caitya cave mentions donation of a village for the repairs of the monastery. The name of the *saṃgha* is 'Valuraka *Saṃgha*'. Another inscription in the same cave (LL 1099) records donation of the village Karajaka to the monks of four quarters by Uṣavadāta, son-in-law of the Kṣaharata king Nāhāpaṇa. One more inscription (LL 1105) 'prepared' by Śivakhadaguta as per the orders of the king (name of the king is obliterated in the inscription. However, Mirashi (1981: 28-31) speculates it to be Gautamiputra Sātakarṇi) mentions the endowed land as '*Bhikkhuhala*' or Monk's Land. This endowment was attached with certain immunities probably giving the monastic order a perpetual right over the endowment.

At Nasik, this phenomenon of donations to a specific *saṃgha* gets further highlighted. The left and the back walls of the veranda of the cave no 3 bear four inscriptions of the Sātavāhana dynasty (LL 1123, 1124, 1125, 1126) which elaborate not only on the grant of lands but also specify certain immunities such as barring entry to the royal servants or magisterial functionary, ban on digging for salt attached with the grant of the land. This cave appears to have been the residence of a specific monastic order of the

Bhadrāyaniya sect. They enjoyed regular donations by the Sātavāhana kings. Not only did the kings donate villages, but there were amendments in these gifts also. These gifts of lands, as can be interpreted through these inscriptions, appears to be the perpetual property of the Bhadrāyaniyas.

Uṣavadāta, the rival of the Sātavāhanas also made handsome donations to the *Catudisasa Bhikhusaṃgha* (*Saṃgha* s of four quarters) as evident from his inscriptions in cave no. 10 (LL 1131, 1133, 1135). He donated a cave and also made specific investments in two guilds the interest of which was to be given to the monastery (LL 1133). These were definitely very elaborate arrangements for the maintenance of the *saṃgha* over a long period.

Apart from these major donations/gifts there were many other such gifts by other laity such as gift of a 4 celled cave by a merchant Vīra (LL 1127) or by another merchant Rāmaṇaka by a perpetual endowment of 100 *paṇas* for the monks' robes or *civara* (LL 1139) or endowment of a field by one Dhamanadi (LL 1130), the produce of which would provide for the clothes of the monks. A slightly later inscription in cave no. 10 during the time of Ābhira king Madhariputra Ishvarasena (LL 1137) also mentions a perpetual endowment for the provision of medicines to the sick monks dwelling in the monastery through investments in different guilds.

Such donative inscriptions are found in the Kuḍā cave complex also. Most of the donations are either by members associated with the royal family or by professionals such as doctors or caravanners who gave meritorious gifts to the monastery as recorded in their inscriptions (LL 1037, 1045 1048, 1049, 1053, 1054, 1058, 1065, 1066). In addition, there are many donations by the monks themselves. A late, but nevertheless noteworthy inscription is that of a *Śākyabhikṣu* Saṃghadēva (LL 1047) who has not only donated an image of Buddha but also has made investments in a field, the interest of which probably went to the upkeep of the monastery. This inscription thus reveals that the monks not only possessed personal wealth but also were involved in complex economic activities.

At Kanheri such inscriptions related to the *saṃgha* are many. Cave no. 3, for example, has a very elaborate inscription of the time of Yajñaśrī Sātakarṇi regarding the ownership of the cave (LL 987). It gives details of people involved in its excavation. One monk Bodhika also acted as an overseer in the project. There are records of laity giving handsome donations to the monastic order (LL 988, 998). In addition, there are individual gifts and endowments on behalf of the monks/nuns made in the name of the *saṃgha* (LL 1006, 1020, 1027) further highlighting their private possessions.

Discussion

The overall picture that emerges through these donative inscriptions is very interesting. One observes that the monks who were the donees at one time, have themselves become donors. Interestingly all these practices of accumulation of wealth and private property are not sanctioned by the early canons. The *Vinaya* categorically prescribes a *Nissaggiya Pācittya* to the monks and nuns involved either in the transaction/receiving/accumulation of gold/silver/cash or in various kinds of buying and selling (Saṅkrityayana 1935: 19-20; Rhys Davids and Oldenberg 2003: 27). These rules, however, appear to have been neglected by the monastic order in practice though. An example of this comes from Kanheri where one of the inscriptions cited above (LL 1066; Gokhale 1991: 88) mentions a perpetual endowment of 200 *kārṣāpaṇas* in addition to other gifts by a nun, thus clearly flouting the rules. Another text, the *Mūlasarvastivāda Vinaya*, gives such liberties to the members of the monastic order as regards economic transactions (Schopen 1994). This was probably done to sanctify such activities and hence many rules and regulations were amended, modified and even changed to suit the prevalent practices in the order. Monks were allowed to act as venture capitalists profit of such investment would, of course, go to the *saṃgha*. Though the text is dated to the period later than the inscriptions discussed above, there is a scope to believe that because such practices were in vogue, there was a need of a text to sanctify such actions.

Ivan Strenski (1983) terms such behaviour of the *saṃgha* as 'domestication'. He argues that this process of domestication begins when certain relationships are established between the *saṃgha* and the laity. He further identifies five salient areas of domesticating relationships, viz. residential, ritual, social, political and economic. When it is said that the *saṃgha* is 'domesticated' it should mean that it has established a relationship with the lay society in one or more of these five (or more) senses. A careful look at the inscriptions in the rock-cut caves of the Western Deccan stands testimony to the complex and multi-layered relationship between the *saṃgha* and the laity. Hence one can say that the *saṃgha* was 'domesticated' right since its inception in this region. This inevitable process was probably envisaged by the Buddha and hence strict rules were made in order to maintain the sanctity and purity of the order. In spite of this, probably owing to the growing dependence of the laity on the monastic for the 'transfer of merit' and to fulfil their duty of 'filial piety' the *saṃgha* and in turn the members of the *saṃgha* became much powerful and slowly the entire mechanism of worship went into their hands thus further distancing the laity away from the Buddha.

References

Burgess, Jas and Pandit Bhagwanlal Indraji 1881. *Inscriptions from the Cave Temples of Western India, with Descriptive Notes, & c.* Bombay: Archaeological Survey of western India.

Cohen, Richard S. 2000. Kinsmen of the Son: Śakyabhikṣus and the Institutionalization of the Bodhisattva Ideal, *History of Religions* 40 (1): 1-31.

Cousins, L.S. 2003. Sākiyabhikkhu/Sākyabhikkhu/Śākyabhikṣu: A Mistaken Link to the Mahāyāna? Saṃbhāṣā 23: 1-27

Gokhale, Shobhana 1991. *Kanheri Inscriptions*. Pune: Deccan College Post Graduate and Research Institute.

IAR: *Indian Archaeology: A Review* 1955-56. New Delhi: Archaeological Survey of India.

Lüders, H. 1912. A List of Inscriptions from the Earliest Times to about A.D. 400 with the Exception of those of Asoka, *EI* X, Appendix.

Nagaraju, S. 1981. *Buddhist Architecture of Western India (C. 250 B.C.—C. A.D. 300)*. Delhi: Agam Kala Prakashan.

Rhys Davids, T.W. and Hermann Oldenberg (Tr) 2003 (reprint). *Vinaya Texts*. Delhi: Motilal Banarsidass Publishers Private Limited.

Sankrityayana, Rahul (Tr) 1935. *Vinaya Pitaka* (Hindi) Sarnath: Mahabodhi Sabha.

Schopen, Gregory 1979. Mahāyāna in Indian Inscriptions, *Indo-Iranian Journal* 21: 1-19.

Schopen, Gregory 1991. Archaeology and Protestant Presuppositions in the Study of Indian Buddhism, *Archaeology of Religions* 31 (1): 1-23.

Schopen, Gregory 1994. Doing Business for the Lord: Lending on Interest and Written Loan Contracts in the Mūlasarvastivāda-vinaya, *Journal of the American Oriental Society* 114(4): 527-554.

Schopen, Gregory 1997. *Bones, Stones and Buddhist Monks*. Ann Arbor: Michigan University

Strenski, Ivan 1983. On Generalized Exchange and the Domestication of the Sangha, *Man*, New Series 18 (3): 463-477.

Early Historic Caves of Maharashtra and Sātavāhana Patronage: A Case Study

Smita Haldar, University of Calcutta, Kolkata

Abstract

The early historic phase in the Deccan begins sometime around the 2nd century BCE and extends up to the 3rd century CE. Early historic Deccan witnessed the emergence of a newly developed architecture in the form of rock-cut cave temples, especially occupied by the Buddhist monks in the western part of the territory in the Western Ghats. The tradition of making donations or giving gifts was an integral part of Indian culture at least from the Vedic period if not earlier. It is evident from the early literature that gift-giving or dāna was related to religious rituals or symbolism. The earliest references to d n come from the dāna-stuti hymns of Ṛg Veda. Professor Romila Thapar has shown that the dāna was also a form of exchange in ancient India. However, "the purpose of the dāna in the Ṛgvēdic times was different from what it was to become in later times". During the reign of the Mauryas, the Indian sub-continent had witnessed for the first time the donation of rock-cut caves when the Barabar caves were donated to the Ājīvikas by Aśōka and then by his grandson Daśaratha in Nagarjuni hills. Both the Barabar and Nagarjuni caves were pure royal donations to a religious sect i.e. the Ājīvikas, probably to enable them to perform their death-rituals. At a later period, the donation of caves or part of caves to religious sects became a trend in western Deccan and in the post-Mauryan period common people too started to take part in such donations besides the royal personalities. There are hundreds of rock-cut caves in western Deccan. Donations of which are documented on the stones. In the Deccan, this cave architecture has mainly been developed during the Sātavāhana period and there are several important sites in the Sātavāhana territory which bear the cave dwellings and inscriptions. The analysis of the inscriptions often helps us to understand a certain pattern of donation. The weather-worn stones are not well preserved always; neither do the epigraphs always speak of entire events. Thus, in this article, we would understand the pattern of patronage and socio-political condition of the Sātavāhana period in the light of the donation of these caves. Often taking specific sites as a case study at the same time we would also like to produce an overview of the patronage to rock-cut architecture by the Sātavāhana rulers.

Introduction

The first ever hewn rock-cut caves in India have been built far from the Deccan at the Barabar and Nagarjuni hills (Image 1, 1A) in Bihar, under Mauryan royal patronage, but the main concentration of these architectural activities was in the western part of the country. Early historic Deccan (c. 2nd century BCE – 3rd century CE) witnessed the emergence of a newly developed architecture in the form of rock-cut cave temples, especially occupied by Buddhist monks in the western part of the territory. In this phase, the rock-cut cave building became a major architectural activity in the Deccan. Most of the rock-cut caves are concentrated in western Deccan, especially in Maharashtra[25]. All these rock-cut caves are situated in strategic locations on the way to the ghats, like Nasik (Pāṇḍuleṇā) cave cluster located close to the two passes i.e. Sherghat and Talghat, Junnar, one of the vibrant sites with several caves was located near the Naneghat, Daryaghat and Malshejghat, the Pune caves near the passes of Bhorghat and Tahminighat and so on. Thus, the sites and their passage to the sea and hinterland though these passes were almost a network. The massive extension of this architecture was based on donations from royal houses and common people. The tradition of making donations or giving gifts was an integral part of Indian culture at least from the Vedic

---

[25]Major early rock-cut cave sites of Maharashtra are – Pāṇḍuleṇā, Karhad, Kuda, Kol, Mahad, Ajanta, Pitalkhora, Bedsa, Bhaje, Amba-Ambika, Bhimashankara, Bhutleni, Lenyadri, Shivneri, Tuljaleni, Naneghat, Karla, Shelarwadi, Kanheri, Ambivale, Karad, Kōṇḍaṇē, Kondivaṭē, Nadsur, Pale etc. There are also some less known and unnamed caves situated in the Western Ghats.

period if not earlier[26]. We have many literary and archaeological pieces of evidence indicating such donations. It is evident from early literary records that gift-giving or dāna was

---

[26] 2Earliest reference to dāna comes from dāna-stuti hymns of R̥g Veda (VI.63.9; V.27; V.30.12-14; VI.47; VIII.1.33; VIII.5.37, VIII.6.47

Figure 53: A) Caves at Barabar (above) B) Caves at Nagarjuni (below)

related to religious rituals or symbolism[27]. The earliest references to dāna come from the dāna-stuti hymns of Ṛg Veda. Romila Thapar has shown that the dāna was also a form of exchange in ancient India[28]. However, "the purpose of the dāna in the Ṛgvēdic age was different from what it was to become in later times"[29]. During the time of the Mauryas, the Indian sub-continent witnessed for the first time the donation of rock-cut caves[30]. At a later period, the donation of caves or parts of caves to different religious sects became a trend in western Deccan. In the post-Mauryan period, common people too started to take part in such donations along with the royal houses. In the Deccan, this cave architecture mainly developed during the reign of the Sātavāhanas and there are several important sites in the Sātavāhana territory which bear evidence of cave donations and dedicatory inscriptions. The analysis of the inscriptions often helps us to understand a certain pattern of donation.

The cave temples of western India and their association with the first indigenous ruling family of Deccan (i.e. the Sātavāhanas) have attracted scholars for the last two centuries. Publications related to various aspects of these rock-cut cave temples – the art and architecture, inscriptions, socio-economic factors

---

[27]Romila Thapar, "Dāna and Dakṣiṇā as Forms of Exchange", Cultural Pasts: Essays in Early Indian History, Oxford University Press, 2000, p. 521.

[28]Thapar, ibid.

[29]Thapar, ibid, p.524

[30]The Barabar caves were donated to the Ājīvikas by Aśōka and then by his grandson Daśaratha in Nagarjuni hills. For details see Basu Majumdar, Barabar and Nagarjuni: Biography of the Twin Sites, K.P.J.R.I., in press (2015).

and so on which have been considered as milestones have been consulted for the present study[31]. Here we would like to deal with the issue of royal patronage under the Sātavāhanas to the cave sites in Maharashtra and the study will be carried a critical analysis of the epigraphic literature.

There are two different types of references regarding the Sātavāhanas – one is the records of royal donations by the Sātavāhanas or by some officers of the dynasty, and the other consists of indirect references, in which the Sātavāhanas are mentioned as the ruling power. There are about seven cave inscriptions in the first category, while the second group consists of nine cave inscriptions in Maharashtra[32]. However, while the caves in the Western Ghats have religious affiliation especially with Buddhism or Jainism, the cave-site at Naneghat is totally different in character. This will be discussed separately later.

Cave architecture flourished in the Deccan during the realm of the Sātavāhanas, but only a few important sites bear records of Sātavāhana patronage. These sites are –Nasik, Naneghat, Karla, and Kanheri. There are hundreds of cave temples in western Deccan, where there are several sites which do not bear any Sātavāhana inscription or inscriptions that mention them. Thus, we do not know whether the Sātavāhanas had played an important role as a patron in such cave complexes as Junnar or Kuḍā, etc.

Available records show that the Buddhist cave temples started receiving patronage from the Sātavāhana royal house from the time of Kṛṣṇa, the second king, according to the Purāṇas and the tradition continued till the time of the later Sātavāhana kings like Vāsiṣṭhīputra Puḷumāvi. The presence of the relief of King Simuka along with other Sātavāhana kings in the Mahāvihāra of Kanaganahalli also indicates that the

Sātavāhanas were one of the important patrons of Buddhist architectural activities. However, here we have confined our study to the rock-cut cave temples of Maharashtra, particularly the sites which bear the Sātavāhana epigraphs. It is worth mentioning here that apart from Naneghat, Sātavāhana royal records have only been found from three sites, i.e. Nasik, Karla, and Kanheri. A detailed study of these epigraphs provides us with a pattern of donation.

Nasik (Pāṇḍuleṇā)

Pāṇḍuleṇā or Pāṇḍavalēṇī (Image 2), one of the important rock-cut cave temples of western India, is situated in Nasik, on the trade route coming from the coastal land of western India and going towards central India. At present, it is located on the Nasik-Bombay highway and about 8km. south-west of the Nasik Town. This site consists of twenty-seven inscriptions in twenty-four caves of the early historic period. The Nasik cave group is the most important among the western Indian cave temples, as this place bears evidence of some of the early records of land donation in the sub-continent, as well as the earliest Sātavāhana epigraph of the time of Kṛṣṇa, the second Sātavāhana king, according to the Purāṇic list.

The inscriptions from Pāṇḍuleṇā portray an interesting pattern in the case of donation. The records provide us with lists of donors belonging to varied backgrounds and social strata; these include Śakas and Yavanas, women, Buddhist ascetics, common people along with the Sātavāhanas and the Kṣaharatas. This is the only cave site in western India where we get the praśastis of Gautamīputra Sātakarni.

Four inscriptions from Nasik mention the Sātavāhana kings and family members as donors, while another one records the donation by an official of the

---

[31]These are the Report on the Buddhist Cave Temples and Their Inscriptions and Memorandum on The Buddhist Caves at Junnar by J. Burgess, Buddhist Architecture of Western India (c. 250 B.C. – C. A.D.) by S. Nagaraju, Early Buddhist Rock Temples A Chronological Studies by Vidya Dehejia, Sātavāhana Art by M.K. Dhavalikar, The Caves at Aurangabad Early Buddhist Tantric Art in India by Berkson, Buddhist Monks and Monasteries of India: Their History and Their Contribution to Indian Culture by Sukumar Dutt, Kanheri Inscriptions, Lord of Dakshinapatha Coins, Trade and Trade-Centres Under the Sātavāhanas by Shobhana Gokhale, The History and Inscriptions of the Sātavāhanas and the Western Ksatrapas by Mirashi, Monastery and Guild Commerce Under the Sātavāhanas by Ray, Buddhist Cave Temples of India by Wauchope, Stories in Stone: Historical Caves of Mumbai by Suraj A. Pandit and Arun Narayanan etc. There are many important edited volumes that also contribute to this study like Living Rock Buddhist, Hindu and Jaina Cave Temples in the Western Deccan, The Age of the Sātavāhanas in two volumes and a number of PhD thesis done by scholars from different institutions on this area, like the thesis by Manjiri Thuse, or the one done by Suresh Jadav, the research work of Shailendra Bhandare etc.

[32]One inscription is not clear

Figure 54: Pāṇḍavalēṇī at Nasik

Sātavāhanas – the officer-in-charge of the Śramaṇas at Nasik, in the reign of king Kṛṣṇa. A fragmentary inscription mentions Dhaṇama, a Kuṭumbika, who along with his family members, donated there during the reign of Vāsiṣṭhiputra sāmi siri Pulumāi, while another fragmentary inscription during the reign of the same king does not bear the name of the donor or any other detail at present. Another inscription also refers to the Sātavāhanas as the ruling power – the donor, a Mahāsenāpatnī, (wife of Mahāsenāpati), donated a lēṇa there during the reign of king Gautamīputra Śrī Yajña Sātakarṇi. An interesting inscription comes from Pāṇḍuleṇā, which bears the name of Mahāhakusiri, who was the grandfather of the donor Bhaṭapālikā. However, it is not certain whether this Mahāhakusiri was identical with homonymous member of Sātavāhana family mentioned in the Naneghat inscription, but the affiliation of both the father and husband of Bhaṭapālikā with the important royal office somehow indicate towards the importance

of the family of Mahāhakusiri and it seems that he could have been a member of the royal house.

Pāṇḍuleṇā bears five inscriptions of the Śaka Uṣabhadatta and his wife Dakṣamitrā. The inscriptions of Uṣabhadatta mention his donations at various places while recording the donation at Pāṇḍuleṇā. At Triraśmī hill (i.e. Pāṇḍuleṇā cave) he donated 2 caves, a field, 8000 stems of coconut trees, cisterns and money (3000 + 70000 kārṣāpaṇa) while Dakṣamitrā, his wife, donated two cells. One inscription of Uṣabhadatta does not enlighten us about the donation by him at the mountain of Triraśmī, as the inscription is badly preserved. However, the record of his donation at other places has been reconstructed by Senart[33]. Besides the inscriptions of Uṣabhadatta, there are two inscriptions of a writer of Śaka origin named Vudhika and one inscription of a Yavana named Indrāgnidatta with his son Dharmarakṣita. Lēkhaka Vudhika, son of Viṣṇudattā had hailed from Daśapura and donated a

---

[33]EI, Vol. VIII, p. 86.

cave and two cisterns, among which one cistern was donated on behalf of his parents. Indrāgnidatta, son of Yavana Dharmadēva and his son Dharmarakṣita, had hailed from Dātāmiti (Dattāmitrī) and donated a cave and a caityagṛha inside the cave along with three cisterns. In this inscription, Indrāgnidatta is mentioned as a northerner. There is another inscription that mentions a writer. It records the donation of a lēṇa by Rāmaṇaka, son of writer Sivamita. The name Rāmaṇaka is also known from another inscription at the same locale, but this second Rāmaṇaka was the son of Velīdāta and he belonged to a community (nekama = nigama) who donated a cave along with 100 kārṣāpaṇa as a perpetual endowment. We have another inscription that refers to a negama – the inscription of Vīra and his family- who donated four lēṇas. Vīra was a member of the gahapati community (Gahapati - Nyegamaṃ). Interestingly, a fisherman (dāsaka) and a person of the upāsika community of Cētikas named Mugudāsa, along with their family too donated lēṇas at Pāṇḍuleṇā. However, we do not know whether these two Mugudāsas were identical or not. This name is also known from the Kuḍā cave inscription, but these two persons were not identical, as the person from Kuḍā was a mālākāra by profession[34]. The same inscription that refers to Mugudāsa as a member of upāsika negama, also bears another name of an upāsika-putra Dhamanandin who donated a kṣētra. There are two more inscriptions which record donations by religious persons – one is the record of donation of a cave by Mamma an upāsikā and the other of the donation of a lēṇa by Tāpasini, a pavaitā and aṃtevāsini of bhayaṃta Savvasa. There is another inscription recording the donation by the village of Dhambhika of Nasik people. Another inscription mentions the name of Nadāsiri as the donor of rail pattern and a Yakṣa.

Excavations of a cave by the officer in charge of the Śramaṇas at Nasik under the Sātavāhana king Kṛṣṇa[35], indicate that the site of Pāṇḍuleṇā was still in making during the early phase of Sātavāhana rule and the process was ongoing till the later phase of their rule, at least up to the realm of Yajñaśrī Sātakarṇi but it is interesting to note that there is no other Sātavāhana donation before Gautamīputra Sātakarṇi. Only the name of Mahāhakusiri[36] is mentioned as the donor's grand-father among early Sātavāhanas (if we consider him as a Sātavāhana family member at all). One inscription tells us that the cave lay incomplete for many years after its creation by the ascetic Bopaki, and then it was donated by a Mahāsenāpatnī Vāsu, wife of Mahāsenāpati Bhavagōpa of Kauśika gotra in the seventh regnal year of king Gautamiputra Śrī Yajña Sātakarṇi[37]. Another Mahāsenāpati is known from another inscription there – Mahāsenāpati Medhuna, who had written down the deed of a donation which was verbally ordered by the king to Sivakhandila, the officer at Gōvardhana in the 22nd regnal year of Vāsiṣṭhīputra Śrī Puḷumāvi[38]. However, the word Mahāsenāpati is also known from numismatic evidence of early historic Deccan and especially from Andhra Pradesh. Coins of the Mahāsenāpatis have been unearthed at Kotalingala along with that of the Mahātalavāras, which bear the symbol of svastikā and horse on the obverse, respectively[39]. Kondapur also yielded svastikā type coins of the Mahāsenāpatis and of the Mahāgāmikas. Interestingly the Mahāsenāpati coins from Kondapur bear arrow and thunderbolt, the royal emblem of the Śaka Kṣatrapa Kṣaharata Nahapāna on the reverse, while at least one coin bears Ujjain symbol, - the royal emblem of the Sātavāhanas on its reverse[40]. This definitely reveals the political alliances between the Mahāsenāpatis and the Śakas or Mahāsenāpatis and the Sātavāhanas. Thus, it seems that Mahāsenāpati Medhuna and Mahāsenāpati Bhavagōpa were not the commanders-in-chief of the army of the Sātavāhanas, but that they belonged to the

---

[34]J. Burgess, Archaeological Survey of Western India, Vol. 4, p. 88

[35]EI, Vol. VIII, p. 93

[36]EI, Vol. VIII, p. 91

[37]EI, Vol. VIII, p. 94

[38]EI, Vol. VIII, p. 65ff

[39]Unpublished Ph.D. thesis by Shailendra Bhandare
[40]Unpublished Ph.D. thesis by Shailendra Bhandare

Mahāsenāpati families of Deccan. Another evidence of the presence of a Mahāsenāpati in the state system comes from early historic Chhattisgarh. The Kirari wooden pillar inscription[41] from Chhattisgarh reflects the region witnessed secondary state formation by c. 2nd century CE[42]. However, this Mahāsenāpati is an administrative post and not in any way related to the family of Mahāsenāpatis found from Deccan.

It is interesting to note that all inscriptions of the Sātavāhanas at Pāṇḍuleṇā have recorded the data on the land donation, along with other information, while Uṣabhadatta refers mainly to the donation of money and stems of coconut trees, besides the donation of land. The inscriptions point to an active relation of Uṣabhadatta with the guilds of Nasik.

Gautamiputra, in his eighteenth regnal year, donated 200 nivartanas of land, which was previously enjoyed by Uṣabhadatta in the village of western Kakhadi; but after 6 years of the donation, he had to make a donation again of another piece of land from the royal estate to the same monks in his 24th regnal year, as the village donated previously was neither tilled nor inhabited (…ca kheta …kasate so ca gāmo na vasati evaṃ)[43]. The inscription shows that the village of Western Kakhadi was not inhabited and did not produce any crop. Thus, the monks probably made a re-application to the royal office and they had been donated a new land from the royal field in exchange for the gift land.

This somehow indicates towards a process of agricultural expansion by the state where the state tried to cultivate a fallow land by donating it. However, it is hard to believe that a land which was previously enjoyed by Uṣabhadatta was a fallow land and uninhabited, thus, it seems that the impact of the war between the Śakas and the Sātavāhanas, which is described in the famous Nasik inscription of Gautamī Balaśrī, was so devastating that after almost 6 years of donation, the land still remained untilled and the village remained uninhabited. It is noteworthy that the land from rājakaṃ kheta i.e. the royal field was donated by Gautamiputra Sātakarṇi along with his mother (rājamātu), who was the Mahādevī[44]. It suggests that the position of Gautamī Balaśrī, mother of Sātakarṇi[45], in the royal house was one of strength, for which reason Sātakarṇi had to mention her name while donating royal land.

The importance of Gautamī Balaśrī in the Sātavāhana family is also reflected in her own inscription at Pāṇḍuleṇā which was incised during the realm of her grand-son Vāsiṣṭhīputra Puḷumāvi. In this inscription Gautamī Balaśrī donated a village named Pisājipadaka on the south-west side of mount Tiraṇhu[46] along with an excellent lēṇa in the 19th year of Vāsiṣṭhīputra Puḷumāvi, but in the subsequent inscription which is documented in the 22nd regnal year of Vāsiṣṭhīputra Puḷumāvi, the name of this previously donated village is mentioned as Sudisaṇa or Sudasaṇa which had been

---

[41]Susmita Basu Majumdar and Shivkant Bajpai, Select Early Historic Inscriptions: Epigraphic Perspectives on the Ancient Past of Chhattisgarh, 2015, pp. 48ff.

[42]The inscription shows a hierarchy both in the territorial units and in the administrative post. The inscription starts with a reference of nagara-rakṣis or the persons in-charge of the town and it ends with the reference of a Kumāra or prince. Other administrative posts which mentions in the inscription are senāpati or commander in-chief, pratihāra or door keepers, gaṇaka or accountant, bhāṇḍagārika or officer in-charge of Granary, hastipaka or officer-in-charge of elephants, gomāṇḍalika or the officer-in-charge of cows, yānasāla=āyudhadharika or the officer –in-charge of carriage and weapons used in war, mahāsenāpati etc. The presence of the senāpati and Mahāsenāpati definitely shows a hierarchy in the rank system. If we take this Mahāsenāpati as a member of the Mahāsenāpati family of Deccan, then it seems that the professional hierarchy or professional identity transformed into their social identity or vis-à-vis. The presence of the hastyāroha or elephant riders, aśvāroha or horse riders, pādamulika or infantry, rathika or charioteer along with the posts like yānasāla=āyudhadharika, senāpati, Mahāsenāpati, hastipaka etc. show the presence of a well-uniformed army. The inscription also refers to many professionals like the dhāvaka or runners, gahapati or land lord, saugandhika or perfumer, lekhahāraka or letter/notification bearer etc. which also indicates towards a well-stratified state system. This inscription could be one of the important inscriptions of early historic period which shows the result of the transformation period in which the Deccan was going through during the time of the pre-Sātavāhanas. These evidences strongly support to the concept of B.D. Chattopadhyaya's emerging locality and locality nuclei. The inscriptions of the Sātavāhanas and that of the Uṣabhadatta indicate towards the emergence of the localities under the local chiefs. Gōvardhana was such a locality nucleus, which was previously ruled by Uṣabhadatta, during the realm of the Sātavāhanas under which a locality of the Mahāsenāpatis was related. However, the name of the locality of the Mahāsenāpatis is not certain in the inscriptions.

[43]EI., vol. 8, p. 73

[44]ibid.

[45]The famous inscription of queen Balaśrī from the same place tells us king Sātakarṇi was her son

[46]EI, Vol. 8, p. 60ff.

exchanged with another village named Sāmalipada. Due to the dearth of data, it is difficult to understand whether the village of Pisājipadaka or Paiśācipadraka and Sudasaṇa (Sudarśaṇa) are identical or there is the absence of data revealing the grant of Sudasaṇa. In the latter case, we have to assume that the lēṇa under discussion was so important that it received more than one village for subsistence that too royal in nature[47].

At Pāṇḍuleṇā, there are fourteen inscriptions among twenty-seven, which refer to the donation of common people at the site. The site enjoyed donations till the post- Sātavāhana phase at least up to the Ābhira rule.

Naneghat

In Pune district, there are many rock-cut cave temples like Karla, Bhaje, Bedsa, Bhandara, Shelarwadi, Patan, Shivneri, Lenyadri, Amba-Ambika, Bhimashankar, Bhutleni, Naneghat, etc. The caves of Pune district have been divided into two groups by the present author[48] the Pune group and the Junnar group. The first cluster i.e. the Pune group, has about 100 excavations hewn into different hills, consists of the caves are located on the way to Bhorghat and Tahminighat near Pune city. This cluster consists of the cave sites of Karla, Bhaje, Bedsa, Shelarwadi etc. The second cluster i.e. the Junnar group lead to the passes of Naneghat, Malshejghat and Daryaghat. Junnar is the largest rock-cut cave centre in western India with

---

[47]There is no doubt that the second inscription of Vāsiṣṭhīputra Puḷumāvi mentions about the gift in exchange of the previous village donated by Gautamī Balaśrī. As the day, year and the donees mentioned in his inscription of 22nd regnal year are same in both the inscriptions it speaks of a single donation. If we consider the translation of the inscriptions by Senart, analysis of these two inscriptions makes the possibility of both the villages being the same because of the mention of the date but still it is a question to ponder upon why one village was mentioned in two different names in two inscriptions in the same location both the inscriptions being royal in character. However, a fresh look at the first inscription suggests a different reading of it. It seems that the name of the donated village was not Pisājipadaka rather the name is absent in the first inscription and the inscription informs us that the village was situated within the Pisājipadaka or Paiśācipadraka towards the south-west of the mountain of Tiraṇhu (...dadāti gāma Tiraṇhupavatasa aparadakhiṇapase Pisājipadakaṁ...). The word Paiśācipadraka may suggest that the village was located in that padraka or the locality was inhabited by the people who spoke Paiśāci-Prākṛta. Thus, from the second inscription we may reconstruct the name of the village which was donated by Queen Gautamī Balaśrī as Sudisaṇa. It also helps us to know the hierarchy of the administrative units like grāma > padraka> āhara.

[48]In the paper entitled "Donation Pattern of Early Historic Rock Cut Caves in Pune: Gleanings from Epigraphs" presented in the 75th session of IHC, 2014.

Figure 55: Statue gallery at Naneghat

about 250 excavations in different hills, consisting the cave sites of Lenyadri, Shivneri, Tuljaleni, Amba-Ambika, Bhimashankar, Naneghat, etc.

Naneghat caves (Image 3) are situated on the Naneghat pass itself (Image 3A) not very far from the ancient settlement of Junnar in Pune district. Almost all the excavations are unfinished here except the main cave, along with some water cisterns. The contents of this cave have drawn the attention of scholars since the publication of the inscriptions of Naneghat by Sykes in 1837 in the 4th volume of the Journal of the Royal Asiatic Society. Walls of Naneghat main cave are full of inscriptions of early century BCE and bear fragmentary parts of the statues of the royal family i.e. of the Sātavāhanas. This is the first archaeological finding of an indigenous statue gallery or Pratimā-gṛha in the sub-continent.

Bhāsa, the litterateur, recorded the tradition of making Pratimāgṛha[49] in ancient India in his Pratimā-nāṭakam, based on the story of the Rāmāyaṇa. The third aṅka of the nāṭaka gives a detailed description of pratimāgṛha. The play had been named Pratima-nāṭakam after the pratimāgṛha. Though the words pratimā-gṛha always reminds us of the Pratimā-nāṭakam first, there are a few archaeological sites elsewhere in the subcontinent too, which bear proof of the existence of pratimāgṛha or its remnants. The tradition of making pratimāgṛha in the sub-continent goes back to the reign of the Kuṣāṇas. The significant archaeological findings of the Kuṣāṇa dēvakulas from Mat and Surkh-kotal bear such evidence of the erection of royal statue galleries. At a later period, we come to know from the Rabatak inscription that the Kuṣāṇas ordered the erection of another shrine or pratimāgṛha at the site of Rabatak

---

[49]The part of the pratimāgṛha discussed here is originally published in Bengali by the present author in the proceedings of the annual conference of Pashchim Banga Itihas Samsad, 2015

like that of the one at Mat[50]. So far as the early

Figure 3A: Naneghat pass

historic pratimāgṛhas are concerned, in Indian sub-continent, the prime focus on them came from the Kuṣāṇas. The Kuṣāṇa rulers both the dead and living along with some of the deities remain enshrined in the dēvakulas built or renovated during the time from Vima Kadphises up to the reign of Huviṣka. This tradition of enshrining the living ruler in the pratimāgṛha, however, is absent in the Pratimā-nāṭakam by Bhāsa, as the play clearly mentions that only deceased persons had been enshrined in the pratimāgṛha. In reality, the Kuṣāṇas deified themselves not only in the dēvakulas but the endeavour is also reflected in their coins and inscriptions. In the above-mentioned play, the priest of the pratimāgṛha, which is decorated as a temple and higher even than royal palaces, was quite concerned that no Brāhmaṇa should bow in front of the statues. The play also clearly suggests that wayfarers could go

there without any restriction or permission from the gatekeepers and pay their respect in the pratimāgṛha without saluting[51].

The period of Bhāsa is debatable, but scholars are unanimous on the point that he definitely belonged to the pre-Kālidāsa period. Whatever the period of Bhāsa may have been, it is clear that the concept of pratimāgṛha was very much present in Indian tradition, although there were some primary disparities between the Indian concept and that of the Kuṣāṇas. However, it is clear from archaeological evidence presented by the memorial pillar, memorial inscriptions, and other memorial architectures of Indian sub-continent, that the tradition of the commemoration of a dead person was widely exercised.

During the early historic period apart from the Kuṣāṇas, the Sātavāhanas could also claim the credit of building the statue-gallery which is situated at Naneghat in the Pune district. The location of the cave on the gate-way to Junnar from Konkan coastal land is significant. This strategic location of the cave site at Naneghat should be taken into consideration. The large cell is situated at the entry point from the coastal area in the Western Ghats to the mainland. The cave bears the traces of nine statues. However, all the statues at the gallery have been lost or destroyed deliberately. At present only the feet of these figures remain (Image 4) and the image inscriptions bear the identity of the statues which are as follows[52] –

Sl. No.	Inscription	Image(s) of
1.	Rāyā Simuka-Sātavāhano Sirimāto	King Simuka
2.	Devi-Nāyanikāya raño ca siri Sātakānino	Queen Nāganikā King Sātakarṇi
3.	Kumāro Bhāya.... (Bhāyala?)[53]	Prince Bhāya...
4.	Mahārathi Tranakayiro	Mahārathī

---

[50]Nicholas Sims-Williams & Joe Cribb, „A New Bactrian Inscription of Kanishka the Great", Silk Road Art and Archaeology 4,1995/96, pp. 75-142.

[51]Kumudranjan Ray ed., Bhasa's Pratima-Natakam, Calcutta, 1942, p.247

[52]last two image inscriptions are too corroded to read

[53]J. Burgess, Archaeological Survey of Western India, Vol. 5, p. 59-74.

		Tranakayiro
5.	Kumāro Hakusiri	Prince Hakusiri
6.	Kumāro Sātavāhano	Prince Sātavāhana
7.	Corroded	Unidentified
8.	Corroded	Unidentified

Figure 56: Fragmentary parts of statues at Naneghat.

Thus, Naneghat does not bear the general characteristics of the other contemporary western Indian cave temples or cave sites. Unlike the western Indian caves, the purpose of excavating the cave at this place was more political than religious. Besides the image inscriptions, the left and right walls of the cave are full of large inscriptions, but unfortunately, important parts of the large inscriptions have been lost at present. However, we are not going into a detailed study of the statues or about the role of the gallery in this paper. The purpose of inscribing the large inscription on the wall is not clear as it is not well preserved. However, the inscription starts with obeisance to various Brāhmaṇical gods and refers to various meritorious acts and the performance of many

Vedic sacrifices.

It is well known from both the Sātavāhana and Śaka inscriptions that the rulers were keen to express their activities relating to the Brāhmaṇical religion, though also made regular donations to Buddhists which were also recorded. At Pāṇḍuleṇā, Sātakarṇi has been mentioned as ekabāhmana and follower of Vedic rituals. It is probably because of the necessity of legitimizing of power that he did not dare to ignore the role of the Buddhist monasteries in economic life. On the other hand, rulers had to maintain good relations with the followers of the Brāhmaṇical religion, who constituted the majority in the sub-continent. However, regarding the cave site of Naneghat, it seems that it had probably been built as a part of royal policy. The formation of the site was thus dependent on the royal treasury, but the reason behind the unfinished caves at Naneghat is not clear. If we look at another inscription on a cistern near the large cave at Naneghat, we come to know that the cistern was donated by a person named Goviṃdadāsa of Sopara.

Karla

Figure 57: Wooden chatra at Karla

The site of Karla is situated near Lonavala on the old Bombay-Pune highway. This is one of the earliest rock-cut cave temples which is bearing the original wooden chatrāvali (Image 5) on the stūpa of main caitya hall. There are almost fifty inscriptions in the Pune group of cave temples[54]. Karla has received the largest donations among the rock-cut cave temples of Pune, though it has only 16 excavations at the site.

---

[54]Almost all the fifty inscriptions are donative in nature except the Bhaje votive stūpa-inscriptions which do not refer to any donation.

Among these fifty inscriptions, thirty-six come from Karla and the rest from the other sites. It is interesting to note that the maximum numbers of donations at Karla have come from the people of Dhenukākaṭa who have donated thirteen pillars, one cell, and two façades. The occupation and socio-cultural background of these people are also interesting. There was a gahapati, a hālaka, a gaṃdhika, a vaḍhaki, a vāniya-putra, a gharini and five Yavanas[55] who had hailed from Dhenukākaṭa. One inscription refers to a gāma of vāniya in Dhenukākaṭa too. The analysis of the inscriptions shows that Dhenukākaṭa was an important trade centre at that time and was also famous for its craftsmanship. Besides this, it had a good communication with the Pune region and especially with Karla. Reference to Dhenukākaṭa in Shelarwadi also suggests of a network and that the connection was retained at least till 3rd century CE if not later.

The site bears the inscriptions of the Śakas and the Sātavāhanas, along with those of the common people and Mahārathīs; but it is interesting to note that all the inscriptions of the Sātavāhanas are records of land donations. There are only three land grants among these thirty-six inscriptions, all being royal donations. One of which was a record of the donation of a village named Karajika by Uṣabhadatta, the son of Diṇika, and the son-in-law of the Śaka king Nahapāna[56]. This is the only donation by Uṣabhadatta or by any representative of Kṣaharata Nahapāna. In this inscription too, the trend of recording previous pious works done by Uṣabhadatta has been followed as seen previously in the case of Pāṇḍuleṇā. The inscription shows the ancient name of the site of Karla as Valūraka. There is another inscription from Karla which records the donation of the same village i.e. Karajika (here the name is recorded as Karajaka)[57]. However, the weather-worn part of the inscription does not allow us to read the name of the king, but according to scholars, this is a Sātavāhana inscription issued during the time (in the 14th regnal year) of Vāsiṣṭhīputra Puḷumāvi[58]. The inscription is very similar to that of the Nasik (Pāṇḍuleṇā) inscription (no. 3) of Vāsiṣṭhīputra Puḷumāvi. The king verbally commanded the minister-in-charge (amacha i.e. Amātya) at Māmāḷa to donate the village of Karajaka, which is situated on the northern road in the Māmālahāra, for the support of the Mahāsaṃghikas of Valūraka caves. It is interesting to note that the previous inscription of Uṣabhadatta states that he donated this land to all sects who were dwelling in the caves of Valūraka, without any discrimination. There is epigraphic evidence at Karla which refers to the Sātavāhanas as the ruling power and records the donation for the Mahāsaṃghikas. The inscription tells us about the donation of a nine celled (navagabha) Maṇḍapa by upāsaka Harapharaṇa, a Sovasaka, son of Setapharaṇa, hailing from Abulāma in the 24th regnal year of Vāsiṣṭhīputra Śrī Puḷumāvi.

Another record of land donation which refers to the site as Valūraka is present at Karla. The inscription refers to Mahārathi Vāsiṣṭhīputra Sōmadēva as the donor of a village. He had donated a village to the Valūraka-saṃgha of Valūraka caves[59] in the 7th regnal year of the Sātavāhana king Vāsiṣṭhiputra Sāmi Siri Puḷumāvi. The inscription also mentions that he (i.e. Sōmadēva) was the son of Mahārathi Kośikīputra Mitradēva of the Okhaḷakiyas. A pillar inscription from the same site tells us that Mitadēvanaka, who had hailed from Dhenukākaṭa, was the son of Uṣabhadatta[60]. If this Mitadēvanaka of that pillar inscription and Mitadēva of the land grant are identical, then the inscriptions of Karla show a hereditary control of the family of Uṣabhadatta over that region and that the family of Uṣabhadatta hailed

---

[55]There is a donation by Dhammayavana but it is not clear what does the word exactly express.
[56]EI, Vol. 7, p.57-58.

[57]The name of the village Karajaka or Karajika probably came after the name of Karanja tree (a kind of timber tree) which is available abundantly in this region of Deccan. The tree is also referred in an inscription from Junnar which informs us that 12 nivartanas land in the direction of Karanja plantation (karajabhati) in the village of Valāhakā was donated to the monastery. The place might be identified with a modern village of Junnar named Karanjale which is situated near Malsejghat towards the north-west of Junnar.

[58]EI, vol. 7. p. 66
[59]These three inscriptions clearly show that there was more than one community of the Buddhist monks. Among them one of the communities was the Mahāsaṃghikas and the other was known as the Valūraka-saṃgha.
[60]EI, Vol.7, p. 49

from Dheṇukākaṭa. At the time of Nahapāna, Uṣabhadatta was probably in-charge of Pune region and this could be one major reason for the large number of donations to Karla by the people of Dheṇukākaṭa.

Thus, it seems that the excavations of the Karla caityagṛha had started during the reign of Nahapāna, under the supervision of Uṣabhadatta and after the defeat of the Kṣaharatas by Gautamīputra Sātakarṇi the region came under the Sātavāhanas and the family of Uṣabhadatta had probably been sent back to Dheṇukākaṭa region as a sub-ordinate Mahāraṭhī power.

Among the cave sites of Pune, Karla has the most ornate caityagṛha. One of the inscriptions from Karla itself claimed that the caityagṛha of Karla is the most beautiful in Jambudvīpa[61]. Bhūtapāla, the sēṭhi residing at Vaijayanti had completed that selāghara or the rock-mansion. Senart rightly indicates that though there are several inscriptions as records of the pillars of the hall, the honour of having completed this hall goes to Bhūtapāla, as the inscription mentions it.

The most magnificent part of the architecture of Karla is its huge lion pillar (Siha-thabhō) (Image 6) in front of the main caityagṛha. It was donated by a Mahāraṭhī Gotiputra Agimitraṇaka. However, we do not know to which Mahāraṭhī family[62] he belonged.

Figure 58: Lion pillar (Siha-thabhō) in front of the main caitya hall

The donation pattern at Karla is distinctly visible from a critical analysis of its inscriptions, the architectural pattern and also the miniature sculptures found on the pillars. All these reflect that initially the architectural inlay was first planned and then decided which part of the architectural component will be funded by Mahāraṭhī Gotiputra Agimitraṇaka. One of the pillars (No. _ in the right side) of the caityagṛha bears the replica of the lion pillar along with a stūpa and another pillar which is probably a dharmacakra pillar[63](Image 7).

---

[61]The Bedsa main caityagṛha has a similar type of plan like Karla but unfortunately it is unfinished which is probably because of lack of donations.

[62]Interestingly the cave sites of Pune tell us about some more mahārathis and Mahābhōjas like, Mahāraṭhi Kosikiputa Vinhudata in Bhaje, Mahābhoya bālikā Mahādevi Mahāraṭhiṇi Sāmadinikā in Bedsa, Mahāraṭhi Vāsiṣṭhiputra Sōmadeva, son of Kosikiputa Mitadeva in Karla etc.

[63]It is hard to conclude whether the part of the dharmacakra has been destroyed now or it was a relic pillar.

Figure 59: Symbols on a pillar at Karla

Figure 60: Pillar from Kōṇḍaṇē

Two of the three symbols are identifiable – one is a symbolic representation of the lion pillar gifted by Agnimitraṇaka and another is that of the stūpa, the main stūpa in the Karla cave. It is hard to interpret the third symbol i.e. the dharmacakra on a pillar. The location of the lion pillar itself suggests that there was one more pillar in front of the entrance of the Caityagṛha, probably on the right side where the temple of Dēvī Ēkavirā is situated at present. It is noteworthy that a pillar in the main caityagṛha of Kōṇḍaṇē also bears a symbol of a stūpa (Image 8), and though the main stūpa has been destroyed, it seems that it represents the original structure of the main stūpa. However, we do not know who the donor of that pillar was, but in case of Karle, it seems that either the whole combination of symbolic donations i.e. the stūpa and two pillars have been funded by Mahārathī Agnimitraṇaka or it shows the basic plan of the caitya architecture.

Besides the royal patronage by which the major works were initiated, we find that there are other patrons to the whole sites. Sihadata, the gaṃdhika (perfumer) hailed from Dheṇukākaṭa and donated a gharamukha or façade. One inscription refers to a Vardhaki (carpenter) Sāmi, the son of Veṇuvāsa from Dheṇukākaṭa, who donated labour and expertise and built the gigantic facade of the cave (opening of the cave) (Image 9).

Figure 61: Facade of the main cave at Karla donated by a Vardhaki (carpenter)

There is another inscription in the main caityagṛha, which refers to the donation of a pillar by Somilaṇaka who had also hailed from Dheṇukākaṭa. The name of the donor in the previous pillar inscription which records the donation of the opening of the cave has been read as Sāmileṇa by S. Nagaraju in his book. If we take the reading of Nagaraju into consideration, the person named Somilaṇaka and the person named Sāmileṇa might be identical. Later on, the rest of the architecture was completed with the help of community patronage and as and when the funding was available the work on the site progressed. This is distinctly visible from the inscriptions which mention about the donations of individual pillars by individual donors who hailed mostly from Dheṇukākaṭa and we have a maximum number of donors hailing from Dheṇukākaṭa as mentioned earlier.

Another splendid part of the architecture of Karla caitya hall is the elephants in the veranda. The elephants along with the vēdikā (Image 10) had been donated by thēra bhayaṃta Iṃdadēva.

Figure 62: Elephants in the veranda at Karla.

The important part of donations at the site of Karle is the donation of the relic-pillar (Image 11) in the main caityagṛha. There are two different inscriptions with almost the same content but the first one was deliberately effaced probably during the time of engraving the second one. The unusual part of the 1st inscription is that Sātimita has been introduced as the

husband of Nadi (Nandī) while the 2nd inscription does not mention her name, rather it says that it was "sasariro thabhō". We should keep in mind that the term is not only "sariro thabhō". Keeping the point in mind, it seems that Sātimita had donated an amount for the construction of the pillar and in the meantime, he passed away. So, the engraver records his name as the husband of Nadi who was executing the formalities on behalf of her husband, but probably before his death, it was a wish of her husband to keep the ashes in the pillar. Therefore, it appears that a fresh inscription had been engraved with the term "sasariro thabhō" instead of the previous one. Basically, it was a pillar containing the relics of the Bhayaṃta, the Bhāṇaka of the Dharmōttariya sect Svātimitra of Sopara[64]. However, the relic pillar has a round floral design on it. There is a hole in the centre of the floral design. This hole contained the relics of Sātimita. We have a similar kind of hole on a pillar in Bhaje (Image 12).

Figure 63: the relic-pillar (sasariro thabhō)

---

[64]Another inscription from Junnar refers to a nunnery that was built for the nuns of the Dharmōttariya sect. Burgess, ibid

Figure 64: A pillar at Bhaje

It has a floral design with a hole but there is no inscription related to the pillar. The cave at Bedsa also has similar floral designs along with some other symbols on a pillar, but the hole or the relic chamber is absent there (Image 13).

Figure 65: Pillars from Bedsa

So, it seems that almost a particular amount of money, which was almost fixed for a pillar, seemed affordable and also would have matched the financial status of a trader and it is more or less the traders who funded the pillars at Karla. But most of the pillars do not bear inscriptions which reflect that it was partially accomplished with the funding of an individual or was made with the collective funding of many. So, it does not have the name of a single donor and it all came up through the community patronage. At Karla when we do the patronage analysis it seems that the accomplishment of the whole project was through community patronage and the initiation was through the help of the royal patronage. Some of the parts were also provided by the people who had worked on the site as in the case of carpenter Sāmi who, we assume, might have received the contract of finishing the woodwork inside the cave and towards the completion of his work he also planned to donate a portion which is mentioned in one of the inscriptions. The inscription was engraved on a pillar as it was not possible to engrave it in the open space or on the woods.

Kanheri

Kanheri (Image 14) or ancient Kṛṣṇagiri is situated near Borivali, a suburb of metropolitan Bombay. More than a hundred caves have been excavated at the site, which bears 58 inscriptions, along with 5 Pahlavi inscriptions and about 27 epitaphs[65]. In this paper, we shall discuss only the inscriptions of the early historic period (i.e. c. 2nd century BCE – c. 3rd Century CE). No Sātavāhana inscriptions have been found at Kanheri. A few inscriptions only refer to them as the

---

[65]Gokhale, S., Kanheri Inscriptions, Deccan College Post Graduate and Research Institute, Pune, 1991.

ruling power and all of them are of the time of the later Sātavāhana rulers. The names of the Sātavāhana rulers which come from the site are - Gautamiputra Śrī Yajñaśrī Sātakarṇi and Vāsiṣṭhīputra Sātakarṇi.

Two brothers Gajasēna and Gajamita, excavated the caitya during the reign of Gautamiputra (Yajna)Sātakarṇi. Aṇadaputa upāsaka Aparēṇu, together with

Figure 66: Kanheri - a rock-cut cave

his family[66] donated a cave and a hall in the mountain Kaṇhasela i.e. Kanheri. He had also donated 200 kārṣāpaṇa, bearing a monthly interest of 1 kārṣāpaṇa, and half a share of the produce of the field at Magalasthāna, from which the community would give 1/16th share for clothing. The donation had been made in the 16th regnal year of the king Svāmī Gautamiputra Śrī Yajñaśrī Sātakarṇi. The inscription indicates that Aparēṇu possessed the field together with another unnamed partner and donated his share of produce. Magalasthāna has been identified with Magathane near Kanheri by Gokhale. According to her, the name Juvāriṇikā derives from the place name Jorwe, near Nasik and she hailed from Jorwe.

Sāteraka, the confidential minister of Vāsiṣṭhīputra Sātakarṇi (?) donated a water-cistern (Pāniyabhājanaṃ). The inscription refers to the queen of the illustrious Vāsiṣṭhīputra Sātakarṇi, (daughter of the Mahākṣatrapa Rudra), descended from the Kārddamaka race. This is a supportive inscription that indicates matrimonial alliances between the

Sātavāhanas and the Śakas.

The site had goldsmith, Vaṇika (Merchant), confidential minister, upāsaka, Amātya (minister), Kamāra (blacksmith), Sēṭhi, gahapati, maṇikāra (Jewellers), Bhojiki, nun, etc. for a long-time span, from almost the early century CE to 11th century CE. Receipt of donations viz. his wife, Ānadamātu (i.e. his grand-mother) Juvāriṇikā[67], her son Ānada, his (Ānada's) daughters-in-law, wives of Ānada (data has been lost as the part is not readable) Dhamadevī etc. suggests that the Buddhist vihāra at Kanheri survived as an active institution for more than a thousand years.

Kanheri also bears the records of people coming from different places of the subcontinent. An inscription of the early part of the 2nd century CE from Kanheri records the donation of a sata (satra) by a person named Nākaṇaka, hailing from Nasik.

Sāmidata (Svāmidatta) a goldsmith from Kaliyaṇa (Kalyan), along with a community of ascetics (Saṃgha) and lay-brothers (_) donated cisterns (Paniyaka). Another person from Kalyan (Kaliṇa)

---

[66] viz. his wife, Ānadamātu (i.e. his grand-mother) Juvāriṇikā, her son Ānada, his (Ānada's) daughters-in-law, wives of Ānada (data has been lost as the part is not readable) Dhamadevī etc.

[67] Gokhale, Kanheri Inscription, p. 52.

named Punavasu, the son of a trader Chita also donated a cistern.

An interesting inscription from cave no. 3, informs us about gifts bestowed at other places by the donor, besides that of Kanheri. The fragmentary inscription prevents efforts at reading all the data clearly, but it talks about some addition to the caitya at Kanheri; a perpetual endowment was given, but the details have been lost. In Sopārakāhāra or the district of Sopara three (cells?) were added to some building; In the Ambālikāvihāra situated at Kalyan, a caitya, a hall of reception (upathānasālā) and cells for monks (ovaraka) were built; At Paithan a caityagṛha and thirteen cells for the monks (ovaraka terasa) together with an akṣayanivi were given. The inscription also informs us that in the Taluka of Paithan called Rājatalāka a meditation room (kuṭi) and a residential room (koḍhi) were erected at the vihāra of Sevuju and a monastery was built and endowed with a perpetual grant. Such generous gifts by the donor were made for his own benefit (puñatha)[68]. We do not know the name of the donor, but according to Gokhale, the letters of the inscription are bold and similar to those of the inscriptions of Nahapāna. The whole record of the gifts given to the Buddhist monks and monasteries certainly suggests that the donor must have been a rich person, probably belonging to a royal house. Besides the palaeography of the inscription, if we compare the trend of recording other donations in an inscription, which is also well known from the inscriptions of Uṣabhadatta at Pāṇḍuleṇā, we may assume that the inscription was of either Nahapāna or his son-in-law Uṣabhadatta.

Another inscription from Kanheri refers to Kalyan as well as to the Ambālikāvihāra – a 3rd-century inscription records that Lavanikā[69] the wife of gahapati sēthi Acala, the son of Upāsaka Nandaṇa of Kalyan donated a cave (leṇi), a cistern for drinking water (pānipapoḍhi) along with a cistern for bathing (nhāṇapoḍhi). The inscription also records that she gifted a perpetual endowment of 300 kārṣāpaṇas for the monks residing at Ambālikāvihāra at Kalyan, for distribution of old clothes. Ambālikāvihāra is identified with the cave site of Ambivale by Gokhale[70].

Yet another inscription mentions Ambālikāvihāra at Kanheri and interestingly the donor Upāsaka Sivadata again hailed from Kalyan. This fragmentary inscription records the donation of a lēṇa at the hill of Kaṇhasele (i.e. Kanheri) by Upāsaka Sivadata of Kalyan for the Bhikhusaṃgha. The next part of the inscription has been lost. It seems that the inscription is talking about a perpetual endowment (Akṣayanivi) of 100 kārṣāpaṇa to the Bhikhusaṃgha and about a donation of civarikas (clothes) and also about 300 kārṣāpaṇa to the Ambālikāvihāra.

Another early historic inscription from the site says that Sivapālitanikā, wife of the goldsmith (Hēraṇika) Dhamaṇaka, donated a stūpa of the thēra bhadanta Dharmapāla. The name Dhamaṇaka is also known from another inscription from the same site i.e. Kanheri, who was the son of Hēraṇika Rohiṇimita and hailed from Cemulika, modern Chaul in Raigad district in Maharashtra. He had donated a pathway (Patho). It seems that the Dhamaṇaka in of both these inscriptions was identical. Another inscription of the same period (c. 2nd century CE) from Kanheri, mentions a person named Sulasadata, who was also the son of a goldsmith (Hēraṇika) Rohiṇimitra and hailed from Cemula, modern Chaul in Raigad district in Maharashtra. It seems that Dhamaṇaka and Sulasadata were siblings. The term Hēraṇika is also known from an inscription of Junnar which mentions Sulasadata as Heraṇikaputa hailing from Kalyan. Sulasadata of Kanheri and Sulasadata of Junnar might not be the same person, as the places they had hailed from are different, but what is interesting is the link with the goldsmith in both the cases. Another person named Sivaputa had hailed from Cemulaka i.e. modern Chaul and donated a cave. The inscription is of c. 3rd century CE and written in an ornamental style, which is different from the rest of the Kanheri inscriptions. There are two more inscriptions which refer to the donation of patho, one is by Nada (Nanda), a blacksmith hailing from Kalyan and the other of a person who had hailed from Cemula.

A Pōḍhi was donated at Kanheri by Sāmika, a lay

---

[68]

[69]According to Gokhale, the name Lavanikā may derive from the place name of Lona which is mentioned in Śīlahāra records too – king Aparāditya made a grant in favour of god Loṇādiya. Another king Mallikārjuna repaired the garden at Lona, modern Lonad, situated on the left bank of the river Ulhas.

[70]Shobhana Gokhale, Kanheri Inscriptions, p. 101.

worshiper (upāsaka) of Sopara and belonging to Soparaga Negama. Bhadanta Sama had made some donation there, but that part of the inscription has been lost. Another fragmentary inscription of the later part of c. 2nd century CE mentions a nun as the donor. An inscription in mixed Prākṛt and Saṃskṛt, in mixed Brāhmi letters of c. the 3rd century and earlier forms, informs us about the donation of a cave and a water cistern for the benefit of the Bhadrāyaṇiyas. The name of the donor has been lost, but it states that the name of the donor's mother was Nandinikā. The same inscription also informs that his wife and Dāmilā donated a cell. The name Dāmilā is also known from other inscriptions of Kanheri – one inscription says that Dāmilā who hailed from Kalyan was a Bhojiki of the Aparānta, while another informs us that she was a Bhikkhuni, but interestingly this Dāmilā had also hailed from Kalyan and donated a cave and cistern like the previous one. However, we do not know whether these three Dāmilā are identical or not, but it seems that the two latter ones are the same. Probably the Bhojaki became a nun at a later time. Whatever the relation of these Dāmilās may have been, it is interesting to note that the presence of a Bhojaki at Aparānta is significant, as we know that the Mahābhōjas were the ruling power of the Konkan area.

An inscription records a donation of a Chetaṃ (khetaṃ? = Kṣetraṃ). According to Shobhana Gokhale, the name of the donor was Muṇḍapāla, who was the son of upāsaka Viṇhumita, and his wife and children. She also mentions that the name is quite unusual and probably related to the Munda tribe, but the point to be noted is that there is no word or expression that suggests that Muṇḍapāla was the son of upāsaka Viṇhumita; rather, the name of the donor should be upāsaka Viṇhumita who belonged to the community (negama) of the Muṇḍapāla (Sidhaṃ upāsakasa viṇhumitasa negamasa Muṇḍapālasa) and he had hailed from Soparaka (Sopara)[71]

Budhaka, the son of Sivamita of Dhama_ community along with his family of Kalyan had donated a cave, a cistern, benches, a chair, and a flight of stairs. He also

had donated 16 kārṣāpaṇas, the interest from which would meet the expenses to buy clothes, a small amount for alms bowl, one kārṣāpaṇa for shoes, etc. and the rest for repairing of the cave. The person also donated a monastery at Kalyan in the Gandharikābhami. According to Gokhale, Gandharikābhami (Gandhārikābhramī) was a colony of the people of Gandhāra.

A pavajita or ascetic Ānada (the brother of the teacher ācarya bhadanta Vīra), along with all his kin, donated a cave and twenty kārṣāpaṇas for clothes (from the interest of those twenty kārṣāpaṇas).

An interesting inscription comes from the Kanheri complex. It records the donation of a dam (Talāka) by a sēṭhi Puṇaka hailing from Sopara. The inscription is written in mid-2nd-century Brāhmi scripts, which is palaeographically very close to those of the time of Vāśiṣṭhīputra Puḷumāvi. This is the earliest reference to dam construction in Maharashtra. The person Puṇaka and Buddhist legendary figure Purṇa are identical[72]. However, we have another instance of the donation of (khaṇitaṃ) a dam or taḷāka in the 8th regnal year of the Sātavāhana king Siri Puḷumāvi in the janapada of Sātavāhani-hāra, belonging to the Mahāsenāpati Khaṃdanāka (Skandanāga) by a gahapati, a resident of the village Vepuraka belonging to the gāmika Kumāradata[73].

A cave and a water cistern had been donated by Poṇakisaṇā along with her sister and brothers who entered into monkhood. A perpetual endowment of 200 kārṣāpaṇa was also given, of which 1/16th share was for clothes and a value of 1 kārṣāpaṇa had to be given to each monk in the „right" season. A cave and a cistern along with money (100 kārṣāpaṇas) were also given by Kaṇha, a pupil of the thēra bhadanta Hālaka. Sāpā, daughter of Upāsaka Yasakulapiya Dhamaṇaka and pupil of the thēra bhadata Bodhika came here from Dheṇukākaṭa with her sister Ratinikā and donated a cave, cistern and some money.

Isipāla donated a cave and a cistern in the memory of his parents. He had also gifted a field in the village of

---

[71]Translation by Gokhale: "The inscription records a permanent gift of a field by the merchant Muṇḍapāla the son of Upāsaka Viṇhumita, along with his wife and children." (Kanheri Inscription, p. 75)

New Translation: Sridham (I) Upāsaka Viṇhumita of the community (negama) of Muṇḍapāla of Soparaka has donated a permanent gift of chetak (field) along with his wife (kuṭubini) and son.
[72]Shobhana Gokhale, Kanheri Inscriptions, p. 86
[73]Interestingly no metronymic is used and Puḷumāvi is mentioned as „Raño Sātavahanānaṃ'; EI, Vol. 14, p.155.

Saphāu[74]. The inscription gives a detailed division of this perpetual endowment - 1/12th share should be given to the ascetics, who were living for four months, for clothes in the hot season (one kārṣāpaṇa each month). With the remaining amount, minor repairs had to be done in the Maṇḍapa (porch) and pravāḍa (windows). The donor Isipāla hailed from Kalyan (Kaliaṇaka) and according to Gokhale's translation, he was the son of merchant Golaṇaka. However, the presence of the word negama before the word golaṇakaputasa and also before Kalianakasa may suggest that Isipāla was a member of the community of golaṇakaputras and of the community of Kalyan, though the meaning of golaṇakaputras is not clear.

There is another inscription which tells us about the negama of Kalyan – a 3rd century CE inscription of the time of Māḍharīputra Svāmi Sakasena (in the 8th regnal year), which records a donation of a lēṇa by a member of the community of the gahapatis, the son of Veṇhunaṃdi[75]- a member of Kalyan community. There is another inscription in the same cave where the previous inscription is recorded. This inscription also belongs to the same family of Veṇhunaṃdi, but unfortunately, this too is fragmentary like the previous one. It records the donation of a cave[76] by Hālaṇikā, the wife of the previous donor (daughter-in-law of Veṇhunaṃdi).

A second century CE fragmentary inscription from Kanheri tells us about the local ruling elite classes of Deccan. The donor Nāgamūlanikā was the daughter of a great king (mahārāja) and daughter of a Mahābhoji. However, the name of the king is not given or has been lost at present, but the title Mahābhoji for her mother and Mahābhōja for her brother ahija Dhēṇaseṇa, suggests that the king belonged to a Mahābhōja family of Deccan and to be more specific probably of Konkan[77]. The inscription also reveals that Nāgamūlanikā was the wife of a Mahāraṭhi and mother of the Khandanāgaśataka. The inscription does not allow us to know anything more about this Mahāraṭhi family.

An interesting inscription comes from Kanheri, which is written in Brāhmi similar to those of Nahapāna's inscriptions. The inscription records donations of a lēṇa and a pōḍhi and a perpetual endowment by an ascetic (Pavajita) Mitanaka, a pupil of …pāla. The inscription is unique, as it refers to the word nivāṇāsa (Nirvāṇāśā). It is the only inscription which records the wish of the donor for final liberation[78].

There are several small inscriptions which are donative in nature. These record the donation of caves, cisterns or any other parts of the rock-cut temples like vēdikā, patho, etc., along with money as a perpetual endowment, at times. The nature of the donors were traders, manikāra, etc. An inscription from cave no. 99, which was the cave of the thēra bhadanta Mitabhūti at Kanheri, refers to the name of the cave as Sāgarapaloganaṃ. The location of the cave itself is befitting, as a fine view of the Bassein creek and sea beyond is visible from there.

There are only 25 inscriptions of the early historic period which refers to the place from where the donors had hailed. At Kanheri, maximum numbers of donors were from Kalyan. Twelve out of these twenty-five inscriptions mention the name of Kalyan as donors" residential place while one person had hailed from Nasik, five donors from Cemula or Chaul, four from Sopara and one from Dhenukākaṭa.

However, any discussion on the cave temples of Maharashtra will be incomplete if the vibrant site of Junnar is left out. It is the largest rock-cut cave temple site of western India. As the site does not bear any inscription of the Sātavāhanas or any other contemporary ruling family except an inscription of the Amātya of Nahapāna and another one of the wives of Isamulānanda, we shall discuss the cave site very briefly in this article.

Junnar

Junnar is situated on the midway to Pune from Nasik on the right bank of the river Kukadi (Image 15). The

---

[74]Modern Saphale near Virar
[75]The name of the donor has been lost at present. The name ends with ti.

[76]Second room attached to the larger one
[77]A Mahābhōja family of Konkan is well known from the cave inscriptions of Kuda. There are some numismatic evidences too issued by the Mahābhōjas in the Konkan area. However, we do not know whether Nāgamūlanikā and her brother belonged to the same family but at least two localities ruled by the Mahābhōjas and the Mahārathīs can be traced by the inscription.

[78]Gokhale, p. 136

region is not far from the three passes of Western Ghats – the Naneghat, the Malshej Ghat and the

Figure 67: The River Kukadi at Junnar

Figure 68A: Lenyadri, Junnar

Figure 16B: Shivneri, Junnar

Figure 16C: Manmodi, Junnar

Figure 16D: Tuljaleni, Junnar

Daryaghat which links Junnar with the coastal land easily and connect the port-cities like Chaul, Kalyan, Sopara, and Bharuch with the chief market towns like Ujjain, Paithan, and Ter.

Junnar group has the largest concentration of Buddhist rock-cut caves in Western India. There are more than two-hundred-fifty rock-cut caves scattered in the hills encompassing the town within a radius of eight km. on the ancient route to Paithan from Kalyan (Image 16A, 16B, 16C, 16D). There are forty-one inscriptions from Junnar among which nine come from Shivneri, twenty-six from Manmodi and rest of the six inscriptions from Lenyadri or Ganesh Leni. These inscriptions from Junnar are donative in nature and associated with the Buddhist vihāras of the region. Unlike Pune or Nasik, Junnar has land grants from common people and not from any royal house. Lands are mentioned to have been donated in thirteen inscriptions, from a minimum of 2 nivartanas to a maximum of 26 nivartanas. All the donated lands are measured in the unit of nivatana (i.e. nivartanas) except two which were measured in Karṣa and hala respectively. Unfortunately, most of the inscriptions recording these grants are damaged or incomplete and hence it is difficult to make out the donor.

It is interesting that though Junnar was within the domain of the Sātavāhanas and located near their principal port of Kalyan, it does not bear any inscription of the Sātavāhanas; rather the largest donation of land in Junnar was made by a person of Śaka origin named Aduthuma. He donated 60 nivartanas of land out of approximately 111 nivartanas. It is interesting to note that one of the inscriptions mentions a piece of land of 2 nivartanas with a row of mango trees, donated by a two-wheel cart owner Vachedukasa. The mention of the mango tree is significant as Junnar is still famous for its production of mangoes both in abundance and quality (Image 17).

Inscriptions from Junnar show a different type of donation pattern. Junnar has got only two donations from any person related to the royal houses - Ayama the āmatya of king Nahapāṇa donated a Pōḍhi and a maṇḍapa and Naḍabālikā Nāḍika, wife of Isimulasāmi donated a Pōḍhi. The person Isimulasāmi, could be identified with the locality chief, whose coins are available under the name of Kumāra Isimula or Vāśiṣṭhīputra Isimula in this region.

The inscriptions of Junnar reflect the presence of five

Figure 17: Mango and mango trees at Junnar

guilds – the guild of Konācikas[79], the guild of basakaras (bamboo-workers), a guild of Kasakaras (the braziers), the guild of suvarnakāras (goldsmiths) and of Dhanikaseniya[80]. To denote guild the word seniya has been used in the inscriptions. Two of the inscriptions mention the term negama or nigama to denote an association or community but unfortunately one of the inscriptions is damaged and does not allow us to understand the nature of this negama. Other one is Dhamma-nigama which is related to some kind of religious association. Interestingly, one inscription from Karla also refers to the same name i.e. Dhamma, but the term is Dhammayavana, which could be the name of a person of Yavana origin. However, the nature of this particular negama is not clear.

A very interesting donation comes forth from an inscription which mentions an akṣayanivi or a perpetual endowment for the construction of a lēṇa, a cistern and a nunnery by Giribhuti, a Pativadhaka. The term Pativadhaka probably means a reporter or a spy (Prativedaka). This nunnery was built for the nuns of the Dharmottariya sect and it is significant that it is situated in the nagara, though the fragmentary part of the inscription does not allow us to identify the nagara. Two brothers Buddhamitra and Buddharakshita who are mentioned as lankudiyas and sons of Asasama donated two cells. These brothers are said to have hailed from Bhrigukachcha or Broach. The mention of the timber tree of Karanjaka also indicates the economic activities based on wood. An interesting pillar inscription comes from Junnar, which mentions that the donor of the pillar was a nun of a Raṭhi family and the highest bidder. However, we do not know what kind of bidding she could have been involved in? We also find the donation of a Bhojana maṇḍapa - donated by a Yavana to the saṃgha and a lēṇa given to Kapichita saṃgha (the ancient Lenyadri) by Sivabhuti the son of Samara, an upāsaka.

Junnar was one of the vibrant localities of the Deccan, where the scope of systematic archaeological excavation is limited, as the present town of Junnar is situated on the ancient settlement-area. The strategic location of Junnar was one of the principal causes of a continuous struggle between two major powers of

early historic Deccan – The Sātavāhanas and the Western Kṣatrapas, which is well attested by the numismatic evidence of the region. However, in this article we are trying to trace the donation pattern of the cave sites under the Sātavāhanas, thus this context is irrelevant here.

From the above discussion, a distinct political contestation among the Śakas and the Sātavāhanas is also reflected in the donations and religious patronage. We have noticed that even in the land donations made by the Sātavāhanas, at the places where land previously was donated by the Śaka rulers and especially by Uṣabhadatta, the son-in-law of Nahapāna. There are two cases one at Karla and the other at Nasik. Apart from this it also is distinct from the epigraphs that the Sātavāhanas who belonged to the Brāhmaṇical sect and were upholders of varṇa jāti order made donations to the Buddhist monasteries a part of the royal policy. However, we do not know the reason why the largest centre of Buddhist rock-cut temples in western India i.e. Junnar does not bear any royal land grant although there are about 13 records of land donations, but if we look at the Buddhist monasteries of that period almost all of them have been built by community patronage from different social and economic backgrounds and not by the particular royal house alone. However, the pattern of donation at any Buddhist site by the Sātavāhanas indicates a political contest between the two powers – the Śakas and the Sātavāhanas on one hand, and the support for the Mahāsaṃghikas on the other. Probably it became a necessity to donate to the flourishing Buddhist monasteries to get legitimacy and support and to regain the power of the Sātavāhana family in western Deccan. Thus, the policy of gift giving to the rock-cut temples and especially the land grants to the Buddhist monasteries by the Sātavāhanas has been noticed at a later phase, mainly during the reign of Gautamiputra Sātakarṇi and his successors. One more point deserves mention here, that a comparison between the land grants of the Sātavāhanas and the Śakas shows that the Sātavāhana grants were more specific about the documentation of grants than the Śakas. However, at the sites discussed above, there is not a single inscription directly issued by the Śaka king

---

[79]Aḍuthuma is mentioned as an upāsaka or lay worshiper belonging to Konāchika śreni. However, we do not know what the meaning is of the word Konācikas.

[80]Scholars take this as corn-dealer but as the term Dhānya means paddy, thus we would say it paddy-dealers.

Nahapāna. It is very clear that the part of Western Deccan was being enjoyed by his son-in-law Uṣabhadatta and the territory was not in his direct control. The inscriptions of the Sātavāhanas, especially those of Gautamīputra Sātakarṇi, indicate the presence of a secondary state formation, where there were several administrative officers performing their official duties along those of the state. Presence of the Mahāsenāpatis as subordinates of the Sātavāhanas is also an interesting point in the formation of the political power structure in the then Deccan. The epigraphs also reveal that common people usually donated cisterns in the rock-cut temples as the donation of cisterns was considered as a pious act and making of a cistern was also needed a small amount of money.

A few donations have come from the local ruling authorities like the Mahārathīs or Mahābhōjas but the maintenance and regular activities of the large vihāras were mainly dependent on royal donations of land and money. However, the larger picture emerges as an act of community patronage which helped in shaping up of the rock-cut Buddhist monuments and monasteries of western Deccan into major religious institutions.

Acknowledgements

I would like to show my gratitude to my mentor Dr. Susmita Basu Majumdar, Associate Professor of the Dept. of A.I.H.C., the University of Calcutta for her guidance. I am indebted to Prof. Ranabir Chakravarti and Dr. Manjiri Bhalerao for their suggestions. I would like to show my gratitude to my teacher, Mrs. Kesara Mukherjee for her endless support. I am thankful to Mr. Atul Arun Kajale, Ms. Chandrima Das and Mr. Sunil Kale for accompanying me to the many sites of Maharashtra. Thanks also to the library staff of my own campus library of The University of Calcutta, Kolkata who have been very helpful; The Deccan College, Pune; The Asiatic Society, Kolkata; CASTEI, Kolkata, etc. Last but not least I am thankful to the organizer of the international seminar for inviting me to the seminar and giving me the opportunity to present this paper.

Bibliography

Basu Majumdar, S. and Bajpai, S., Select Early Historic Inscriptions: Epigraphic Perspectives on the Ancient Past of Chhattisgarh, Shatakshi Prakashan, 2015.

__________ Barabar and Nagarjuni: Biography of the Twin Sites, K.P.J.R.I., in press (2015).

Berkson, C., The Caves at Aurangabad Early Buddhist Tantric Art in India, Mapin International Inc., New York, 1986.

Bhandare, S., Ph.D. Thesis 'Historical Analysis of the Sātavāhana Era: A Study of Coins' (in two parts), submitted to the University of Mumbai.

Brancaccio, P. ed. Living Rock Buddhist, Hindu and Jaina Cave Temples in the Western Deccan, Marg, 2013.

Burgess, J., Memorandum on The Buddhist Caves at Junnar and Translations of three Inscriptions from Badami, Pattadakal and Aiholli, Bombay, 1874.

__________, Report on the Buddhist Cave Temples and Their Inscriptions: Supplementary to the Volume on 'The Cave Temples of India', ASI, 1883, 1994 (Rep.)

Chattopadhyaya, B.D., „Transition to Early Historical Phase in the Deccan: A Note", Studying Early India, New Delhi, 2004.

Dehejia, V., Early Buddhist Rock Temples A Chronological Studies, Thames and Hudson, London, 1972.Dhavalikar, M.K., Sātavāhana Art, Sharada Publishing House, Delhi, 2004

Dutt. S., Buddhist Monks and Monasteries of India: Their History and Their Contribution to Indian Culture, George Allen and Unwin Ltd., London, 1962.

Gokhale, S., Kanheri Inscriptions, Deccan College Post Graduate and Research Institute, Pune, 1991.

__________ Lord of Dakshinapatha Coins, Trade and Trade-Centres Under the Sātavāhanas, Reesha Books International, Mumbai, 1999.

Halder, S., „Bharatiya Upamahadeshe „Pratima-griha": Adi-aitihasik Dakshinatye er Gurutva", Itihas Anusandhan, Vol. 29, Pashchimbanga Itihas Samsad, Kolkata, 2015. (In Bengali)

__________ „Lekha o Mudrātattver Aloke Kura Rajavamsha", Itihas Anusandhan, Vol. 28, Pashchimbanga Itihas Samsad, Kolkata, 2014, pp.135-142. (In Bengali)

Jadhav, S. V., Ph.D. Thesis „Rock-Cut Cave Temples at Junnar An Integrated Study', submitted to the Dept. of Archaeology, Deccan College, Pune.

Mirashi, V. V., The History and Inscriptions of the Sātavāhanas and the Western Ksatrapas, Maharashtra State Board for Literature and Culture, Bombay, 1981.

Nagaraju, S. Buddhist Architecture of Western India (c. 250 B.C. – C. A.D. 300), Agam Kala Prakashan, Delhi, 1981.

Pandit, Suraj A., and Narayanan, A., Stories in Stone: Historical Caves of Mumbai, INSTUCEN Trust, Mumbai, 2013.

Ray, H. P., Monastery and Guild Commerce under the Sātavāhanas, Oxford University Press, Delhi, 1986.

Ray, K. ed., Bhasa's Pratima-Natakam, Calcutta, 1942

Senart, E., „The Inscriptions in the Cave at Nasik", Epigraphia Indica, Vol. VIII, pp. 59ff.

_______ „The Inscriptions in the Caves at Karle", Epigraphia Indica, Vol. VII, pp. 47ff.

Shastry, A.M. ed., The Age of the Sātavāhanas, Vol. I and II, Aryan Books International, New Delhi, 1999.

Thapar, R., "Dāna and Dakṣiṇā as Forms of Exchange", Cultural Pasts: Essays in Early Indian History, Oxford University Press, 2000.

Thuse, M., Ph.D. Thesis „Buddhist Caves at Nasik – An Analytical Study", submitted to the Dept. of Archaeology, Deccan College, Pune.

Wauchope, R.S., Buddhist Cave Temples of India, New Delhi, 1981.

Williams, N. S., and Cribb, J., „A New Bactrian Inscription of Kanishka the Great", Silk Road Art and Archaeology 4,1995/96, pp. 75-142.

Table 1: Donation pattern at Pāṇḍuleṇā

S. No.	Personal Name	Occupation/ Identity	Hailing from	Donation of	Purpose of donation/ inscription	Other Information
1.						In the 6th year of Vāśiṣṭhīputra Puḷumāvi
2.	Gotamiputo Siri Sadakaṇi	lord of Benākaṭaka of Govadhana		200 nivartanas Ajakāla field in the village of western Kakhaḍi	To the Tekirasi ascetics i.e. the monks of Triraśmī hill	In the 18th regnal year of Gotamiputo Siri Sadakaṇi. Previously enjoyed by Uṣabhadatta Verbally ordered by the king from Vijayaskandavar of Vaijayanti Commanded to Viṇhupālita, the officer at Gōvardhana Written down by Sivaguta Kept by Mahāsāmiyas Deed executed by Tāpasa
3.	Raño Gotamiputo Sātakaṇi and Mahādevī rājamātu			100 nivartanas land at the end of the town(nagarasīme) in the royal field		In the 24th regnal year of Gotamiputo Sātakaṇi Verbally ordered by the king to Sāmaka, the officer at Gōvardhana

No.	Donor	Status	Gift	Purpose	Remarks
			(rājakaṃ kheta)		Written down by doorkeeper Loṭā Deed executed by Sujīvin
4.	Queen Gautamī Balaśrī		An excellent lēṇa village Pisājipadaka on the south-west side of mount Tiraṇhu	To the saṃgha of the Bhadrāyaṇiyas	In the 19th year of Vāsiṣṭhīputra Puḷumāvi Prasasti of Gautamiputa Sātakarṇi, king of Asika, Asaka, Muḷaka, Suraṭha, Kukura, Aparanta, Anūpa, Vidhava, Ākarāvanti Lord of the mountains Vindhya, Chavata, Pāricāta, Sahya, Kāṇhagiri, Maca, Siriṭana, Malaya, Mahendra, Seṭagiri, Cakora. Destroyed the Śaka-Yavana-Palhavas Rooted out the Khakharata Race Restored the glory of the Sātavāhanas
5.	Vāsiṣṭhīputra Śrī Puḷumāvi	Lord of Navanara	In exchange for the gift of the village of Sudisaṇa on the southern road(dakhiṇam age) in Govadhanāhara, the village of Sāmalipada on the eastern road in Govadhanāhara	Dhanakaṭasamana The Bhadrāyaniyas dwelling in the queen's cave to produce a perpetual rent for the care of the cave.	In the 22nd regnal year of Vāsiṣṭhīputra Śrī Puḷumāvi Verbally ordered by the king to Sivakhandila, the officer at Gōvardhana Written down by Mahāsenāpati Medhuna
6.	Vīra Naṃdasiri Purisadattā	Gahapati-Nyegamaṃ Wife of Vīra Daughter of Vīra	lēṇa lēṇa lēṇa	For the universal Saṃgha	Total of four cells
7.	Tāpasini	Pavayitā and aṃtevāsini of Bhayaṃta Savvasa	lēṇa	For the universal Saṃgha	

8.	Mugudāsa along with his family	A fisherman(dāsaka)	Leṇa		From Kuḍā, we find another person with the same name – Mugudāsa but of a different profession – Mālākāra
9.	Mugudāsa along with his family Dhamanandin	Of the Upāsika community of Cētikas Son of upāsaka Bodhiguta	Leṇa A field (kheta) in western Kaṇhahini (aparilīya Kaṇhahiniya)	To provide clothes for the ascetics of the lēṇa	
10.	Uṣabhadatta	Son of Dīnīka and son-in-law of Kṣaharata Kṣatrapa king Nahapāna	A cave and cisterns in the Triraśmī hill at Gōvardhana A field bought at the hand of the Brāhmaṇa Aśvibhūti, son of Vārāhī for the price of 4000 Kārṣāpaṇa which belonged to his father, on the town towards the north-western side.	Inspired by true religion To procure food for all monks without distinction dwelling in his cave	the donation of three hundred thousand cows, money, tīrthas on the river Barnes. 16 villages to the Brahmanas, Arrangement of food of one hundred thousand brahmanas for the year Eight wives to the brahmanas at the religious tīrtha of Prabhas Shelter of a quadrangular rest house at Bharukaccha, Daśāpura, Gōvardhana, and Sopāraga, Wells, tanks, gardens, free ferries by boats on the Ibā, Pārādā, Damaṇa, Tāpī, Karabenā, Dāhanukā, shelters for meeting and gratuitous distribution of water on both banks of the rivers. Thirty-two thousand stems of coconut trees at the village Nānaṃgola to the congregation of Carakas at Pīṃḍītakāvḍa, Gōvardhana, Suvarṇamukha, and Rāmatīrtha in Sorpāraga By order of the lord (i.e. Nahapāna?) he went to release the chief of Uttamabhadras from the Mālayas,
11.	Dakṣamitrā	Wife of Uṣabhadatta, Daughter of Kṣaharata kṣatrapa king	lēṇa		

		Nahapāna				
12.	Uṣabhadatta	Son of Dīnīka and son-in – law of Kṣaharata Kṣatrapa king Nahapāna		A cave The perpetual endowment of3000 kāhāpaṇas 8000 stems of coconut trees at the village of Chikhalapadra in Kāpura dist. 70000 Kārṣāpaṇas =2000 suvarṇas	To the Saṃgha To buy clothes (from the 2000 kārṣāpaṇas) and for outside life (kuśaṇa) (from1000 Kārṣāpaṇas) for all monks (20 in number) of any sect dwelling in his cave from the interest of the money (3000 kārṣāpaṇas)	In the year 42 The money will be invested in the guilds dwelling at Gōvardhana – 2000 in a weavers' guild with the interest one pratika (monthly) for a hundred 1000 in another weavers' guild with the interest of three-quarters of a paḍika (monthly) for the hundred All this has been proclaimed and registered at the town's hall at the record office according to the custom In the year 41 In the year 45 (each 35 making a Suvarṇa)
13.	Dakṣamitrā	Daughter of Kṣaharata kṣatrapa king Nahapāna, Wife of Uṣabhadatta		Cell (ovarako)		
14.	Uṣabhadāta	Śaka Son of Dīnīka, Son – in – law of Kṣaharata kṣatrapa king Nahapana				One-hundred –thousand holy Brahmanas dine [the whole year round] at……. chechiñña, at the town of Dāhanūkā, at Kekāpura, ……at Anugāmi, at Ujeni, at Sākhā
						Three-hundred-thousand cows to the Brahmanas 16 villages to the holy gods and Brahmanas Money and a tīrtha in the Barṇasā river
15.	Viṣṇudatā	Śākāni (Śākānikā?) Upāsika Mother of		Perpetual endowment	To provide medicines to the monks of chāturdiśabhikshu	In the 9th regnal year of Ābhīra king Māḍharipura Īśvarasena son of Śivadata Ābhīra Money invested in the guild of

		Gaṇāpaka Viśvavarma, wife of Gaṇāpaka Rebhila and daughter of Śakāgnivarmma (Agnivarmma – the Śaka)			saṃgha in the Vihāra on the Triraśmiparvata	Gōvardhana– 1000 kārṣāpaṇas to the guild of Kularikas 2000 to the guild of Odayantrikas 500 to the guild of …… …… to the guild of oil millers
16.	Rāmaṇaka	Son of writer Sivamita		lēṇa		
17.	Rāmaṇaka	Son of Velīdāta of nekama	Chhākalepa	A cave 100 kārṣāpaṇas (Akṣayanivi)	twelve kārṣāpaṇas as cloth money is to be given to the ascetics of the (cave?)	
18.	Indrāgnidatta With his son Dharmarakṣita	Son of Yavana Dharmadēva	A native of the northern country Inhabitant of Dātāmiti (Dattāmitrī)	A cave on the mountain Tiraṇhu A caityagṛha inside the cave and (three) cisterns	For the sake of his parents For the worship of all Buddhas Has been made over to the community of the monks from the four points of horizons	
19.	Bhaṭapālikā	Grand-daughter of Mahāhakusiri, Daughter of the royal officer Arahalaya, Wife of the royal officer Agiyataṇaka of the treasure Office, Mother of Kapaṇaṇaka	Calisīlaṇa	caityagṛha at the mount Tiraṇhu		
20.	Village of Dhambhika of the Nasik people					
21.	Nadāsiri and……			Rail pattern and a Yakṣa		

No.						
22.	this cave has been caused to be made by the officer in charge of the Śramaṇas at Nasik			Cave		Under king Kṛṣṇa of the Sātavāhana family
23.	Mahāsenāpatnī Vāsu	Wife of Kosika Mahāsenāpati Bhavagōpa		lēṇa	To the universal saṃgha	7th regnal year of king Gautamiputra Śrī Yajña Sātakarṇi
24.	Dhaṇama together with his father mother and….	Kuṭuṃbika				2nd regnal year of king Vāsiṣṭhiputra sāmi siri Pulumāi
25.	Śaka Dāmacika Vudhika	Lēkhaka Son of Viṣṇudattā	Daśapura	A cave and two cisterns		The cistern with a small opening was on behalf of his parents.
26.	Śaka Dāmacika Vudhika	leghaka		About the above cistern		
27.	Mammā	Upāsikā		A cave		

Table 2: Donation pattern at Karla

Donations of	Karla
Elephant and Vēdikā	elephants and a vēdikā by Thēra bhayaṃta Indadēva
gabho/lena	One by Pavaita Budharakhita
Gharamukha	One by Sihadata, a gaṃdhika (perfumer) hailing from Dheṇukākaṭa One by Sāmila/Sāmi, a carpenter (Vaḍhaki) son of Veṇuvāsa, hailing from Dheṇukākaṭa made the Façade[81].
Land or village	A village (Karajiko gāmo) by Uṣabhadāta, son of Diṇika, son-in-law of Nahapāna A village by Mahāraṭhi Vāsiṣṭhiputra Sōmadēva, son of Kosikiputa Mitadēva given to the Vāluraka saṃgha of Vāluraka caves A village named Karajaka in Māmālahāra by king
lēṇa and *Pōḍhi*	One by a lady pupil? of bhayata….
Lion pillar	One by Mahāraṭhi Gotiputra Agimitraṇaka
Mithuna figures	Two pairs by Bhadasama (Bhadraśarman) a bhikkhu

---

[81]Now the inscription is mostly covered by mortar.

Multiple celled Maṇḍapa	One nine celled (navagabha) Maṇḍapa by Upāsaka Harapharaṇa, a Sovasaka, son of Setapharaṇa, from Abulāma. Mother of Budharakhita was also a donor.
Pillar	One by Bhāyilā, mother of Gahata (Gṛhasta) Mahādēvaṇaka One by Sihadhaya, a Yavana from Dhenukākaṭa One by Dhammayavana from Dhenukākaṭa One by Mitadēvaṇaka, son of Usabhadata from Dhenukākaṭa One by Yavana Viṭasagatāna from Umehanākaṭa One by upāsaka Dhamula of Gonekāka One by the Vaniya gāma of Dhenukākaṭa One by Yavana Dhamadhaya from Dhenukākaṭa One by Rohamita from Dhenukākaṭa for Agila, a resident of Culapeṭu One by Yavana Culayakha from Dhenukākaṭa One by Yavana Sihadhaya from Dhenukākaṭa One by Somilanaka from Dhenukākaṭa One by Isalaka, son of Gola-vāniya from Dhenukākaṭa One by Yavana Yasavadhana from Dhenukākaṭa One by Mahamatā – a gharini (Gṛhinī?) from Dhenukākaṭa One Dhamadevī, a relation of the Gahapati Aseka from Dhenukākaṭa
Pōḍhi	One by a nun (?)
Relic Pillar	by Sātimita, a bhayaṃta, husband of Nadi[82], abhāṇaka of Dhamutariyas, with his wife? From Sopāraka
Selāghara	By Sēṭhi Bhūtapāla from Vejayanti
Vēdikā	One by Asāḍhamitā, Bhikhuṇi One by the mother of …. samaṇā One by Koḍi, a nun, mother of Ghuṇika and made by Naṃdika One by ____________ maṇayūtā

Table 3: Sātavāhana Patronage

Inscription from	Donated by	Hailing from	Donated for	Donated to	Donation of	In the reign of	Regnal Year
Pāṇḍuleṇā (Direct patronage)	Made by Śramaṇa-Mahāmātya at Nasik				Cave	Rājan Kaṇha	
Pāṇḍuleṇā (Indirect patronage)	Vāsiṭiputa Ānaṃda. The foreman of King Sātakarṇi					Siri Sātakarṇi	

____

[82]Nadi was bhānaka, the aṃtevasi of There Atula, a Bhayata of Dhamutarariya Samānatha

Pāṇḍuleṇā (Direct Patronage)	Bhaṭapālikā, daughter of Rājāmātya Arahalaya, Grand-daughter of Hakusiri, wife of theRājāmātya and Bhāṇḍāgārika Agiyataṇaka and mother of Kapanaṇaka				Caitya cave on the Trirasmi hill	
Pāṇḍuleṇā (Direct Patronage)	Gautamīputra Sātakarṇi	Brief details Issued from the victorious camp of Gōvardhana, Sātakarṇi – lord of Benākaṭaka The land was previously owned by Uṣabhadatta Order given orally Safely preserved by Mahāsvāmikas	The mendicant monks	Field of 200Nivartana in the village of western Kakhaḍi	Gautamīputra Sātakarṇi	18th
Karle (Direct patronage)		The land was previously donated by Uṣabhadatta Ordered orally Issued from a victorious camp	The Mahāsaṃghika monks of Valuraka caves	Village Karajaka		14th
Pāṇḍuleṇā (Direct patronage)	Gautamīputra Sātakarṇi and his motherQueenMahādevī	Previously donated village Kakhaḍi was not cultivated	The mendicant monks dwelling in the cave given by the Sātavāhanas in Trirasmi hill	100 nivartanas land in the royal field[83]	Gautamīputra Sātakarṇi	24th
Pāṇḍuleṇā (indirect patronage)	Kuṭuṃbika Dhaṇama with his parents and his sister			Cave	Vāsiṣṭhiputra Siri Puḷumayi	2nd

---

[83]Royal field - rājakaṁ kheta

		Too corroded		The community of Buddhist monks and the Buddha	Cistern	Vāsiṣṭhiputra Siri Puḷumayi	5th
Karle (Indirect patronage)	The female disciple of bhadanta….and their śrāvikā sisters						
Pāṇḍuleṇā (not clear)	-	-	-	-	-	Raño Vāsiṣṭhiputra Siri Puḷumayi	6th
Karle (Indirect patronage)	Mahāraṭhī Vāśiṣṭhīputra Sōmadēva, son of Mahāraṭhī Kośikīputra Mitadēva			The community of monks at Valūraka to keep the caves at Valūraka in repair.	A village	Vāsiṣṭhiputra Siri Puḷumayi	7th
Pāṇḍuleṇā (Direct patronage)	Gautamī Balaśrī, mother of King of Kings Siri Sātakarṇi		The sake of the establishment of the cave	The saṃgha of monks	Cave	Raño Vāsiṣṭhiputra Siri Puḷumayi	19th
Pāṇḍuleṇā (Direct patronage)	Vāsiṣṭhiputra Siri Puḷumayi			To the Bhadrāyaṇiyas of Queen's cave	Village	Raño Vāsiṣṭhiputra Siri Puḷumayi	22nd
Karle (Indirect patronage)	Upāsaka Harapharaṇa, son of Setapharana, a Sovasaka,	Abulāmā		To the Mahāsaṃghikas	Nine-celled Maṇḍapa	Vāsiṣṭhiputra Siri Puḷumayi	24th
Naneghat (Indirect patronage)	Gahapati Damaghoṣa	Kāmavana			Cistern on the Śvetagiri hill	Vāsiṣṭhiputra Sātakarṇi/ Caturpana Sātakarṇi[84]	13th
Kanheri (Indirect patronage)	Khatiya brothers Gajasēna and Gajamitra				Caitya hall	Gautamīputra Yajñaśrī Sātakarṇi	
Kanheri (Indirect patronage)	Confidential Minister Sāteraka of queen of Vāsiṣṭhīputra Śrī Sātakarṇi and daughter of Kardamaka King				Cistern	Vāsiṣṭhīputra Śrī Sātakarṇi	

[84]Nagaraju, op.cit, p.346

	Rudradāman					
Kanheri (Indirect patronage)	Aparēṇu, son of Ānanda together with his family Mother of Ānanda with her family members	Kalyan		A cave A cave and a hall 200 kāṣāpaṇa Half a share of	Gautamīputra Yajñaśrī Sātakarṇi	16th

Donation pattern at Junnar

Donations of	Shivneri	Manmodi (Bhimashankara, Amba-Ambika, Bhutleni)	Lenyadri
Caityagṛha (Cetiyaghara)	By Virasena, a Gahapatipamugha of Dhammanigama Isipālita, son of Ugaha, with his family		by Sulasādata, Son ofHeraṇika of Kalyan by Ānada, son of UpāsakaTāpasa and grandson of Upāsaka Kapila
Cell (gabho/lena)		2 cells by two brothers Buddhamitra and Buddharakshita, lankudiyas, sons of Asasama, from Bhrigukachcha	
Cell and cistern (lēṇa and Pōḍhi)	A cistern and probably a cave by …. thbhutiṇaka By Patibadhaka Giribhūti, son of Savagiriyasa of the Apaguriyas with his wife Sivapālaṇikā		by Sivabhūti, son of Upāsaka Sāmara for the saṃgha of Kapicita
Cash for Cell, cistern and Nunnery	Some Kārṣāpaṇas by Patibadhaka Giribhūtisakhuyāru, son of Savagiriyasa of the Apaguriyas for a cave and a cistern and a		

	nunnery in the town		
Upaṭhana (Reception room)	By Mudhakiya Mala and Golakiya Ānada		
Cistern (Pōḍhi)	Two cisterns by Yavana Irila of the Gatā country	by Sivabhūti, son of Sivasama by Kumiyā, mother of Sulasā by Sulasā, daughter of Kumiyā Krami Yajnaputa to the Arya saṃgha	by Saghaka, a suvarṇakāra, son of Kulira of Kalyan by Lachiṇika, wife of Torika and Naḍabālikā Nāḍika, wife of Isimulasāmi
Façade(gharamukha/ghar amugha/Gabhodara)		By Yavana Chaṃda	

Land or village		In the village of Mahāveja 26nivartanas to the assembly of Apājita	
		In front of the hill Mānamukuḍa 3 nivartanas…	
		The Town in front of …. mountain…. nivartanas	
		12 nivatana in Valahaka village and …. nivatanas in Seuraka village For Karajabhati By The guild of bamboo workers (Vasakara) And The guild of the braziers (Kasakara)	
		20 nivatanas in Vadalika near karanja tree	
		9 nivatanas in Kataputaka near the banyan tree	
		By Aduthuma a Saka an upāsaka of the guild of Konacikas2 nivartanas with a row of mango trees, donated by a two-wheel cart owner Vachedukasa	
		By Palapa 15 nivatanas in Puvanada village in the hand of Payogoka of Aparājitā Sect	
		By Sārasavaṇṇa, the dyer (Vaṇakara) 4 hala land to the Gṛghravihāra for the sake of a pānasālā hailing from Kāka	
		By a suvarnakaraseni 16 nivartanas of land in the village Danagra of coarse land along with grazing land and the king's share of grains.	
		Half karṣa land in the	

		village Paṇakavaṇya to the Sāṃmitiya sect to meet the expenses of sandals	
		A field in the village Madahata to the Gṛdhravihāra. The artisans of the cave have a 5%share in the meritorious gift	
		A trader of Dāmaṇadeśa – 8nivartanas of land to meet the rice and beans to the assemblage of Kākaputiyas	

Oil for lamps		In the same inscriptions of land donation in Madahata village	
Multiple celled cave		One 5-celled cave by …………	Seven celled cave and Pōḍhi by Dhaṃñikaseṇi
Pōḍhi and Maṇḍapa		One Pōḍhi and a Maṇḍapa by Ayama of Vacca gotra, Āmātya of Raño Mahākhatapasa Sāmi Nahapāṇa	
Bhojaṇa-maṭapa (Refectory)	Yavana Chiṭa of the Gatā country		
Pillar		By the son of Kesu, a Coppersmith (tabake) A Nun of Rathi family, the Highest bidder, hailing from Aparānta	
Uncertain donations		Virabhuti, of negama of Upāsaka, son of Stamata? Gahapati Srivatsa son of Sanity – gahapati, with his wife (bitiyikāya) with his family? (Cave?) Gahapati Nanda and his family? Isipālita, son of Upāsaka Ugāha, with his son	

Later Brāhmaṇical Caves of Maharashtra

Arvind Jamkhedkar, Chairman, ICHR, New Delhi & Chancellor, Deccan College PGRI, Pune

Abstract

Ferguson and Burgess, when they wrote on the Brāhmaṇical caves in Western India did not know about the Śaiva caves (at Devlane in the vicinity of Bhandak, in Chandrapur Dist., at Salbardi in Amraoti Dist., and those at Palsambe in Kolhapur Dist.) and Vaishnava caves (at Bhandak, and at Bhatala in the vicinity of Warora in the same Dist., and those at Shiur in Nanded Dist.) in Maharashtra. It is again a matter of guess as to why both don't take into consideration the Udaigiri caves, of Gupta period, in the vicinity of Vidisha. They, of course, do make a statement that the antiquity of the Śaiva caves can go back to the fourth cent. C.E.

They seem to make a very important observation regarding the development of the Brāhmaṇical caves. Both of them are sure that the architects imitated the form of the Later Buddhist Vihāra for fashioning their caves at Ellora, Elephanta, and other sites initially. It is only later that they are able to develop a rock-temple form of their own. It is also observed that instead of painting the wall faces, as at Ajanta, they decorated the interior as also exterior with relief sculptures and panels; and that quite successfully.

For lack of Inscriptional evidence, in contrast with the Buddhist caves, it was found difficult to date precisely the Brāhmaṇical caves. They thought that the rock-cut activity in the Brāhmaṇical phase covered a period of 300 years, from circa 500 to 800 C. E. Later researches showed that the activity continued even in post-Krishna Rāṣṭrakūṭa period up to Yadava/Śīlahāra period also. There was a refinement of the earlier chronology, first by Spink (1967), and then by Soundararajan (1981). With new evidence coming forth, there is a need to give attention afresh to this problem.

It was first Stella Kramrisch who gave the key to understand the iconographic scheme in the Śaiva caves, with her article on Cave 1 at Elephanta. This was further developed and elaborated by Collins in his erudite monograph on the same cave. With better documentation and study of these caves by Soundararajan, the Śaiva caves will have to be studied in detail, from the iconographic point of view. For this, the evidence from structural temples of the Badami Cālukya, and if possible, of the Vākāṭakas also will have to be taken into consideration.

Introduction

When James Fergusson wrote the introduction to his magnum opus, Cave Temples of India in 1880, he discussed many issues concerning the rock-cut cave architecture in India. Some of these issues were as follows:

(i) the origin of rock-cut cave architecture in India;

(ii) the place of Buddhist rock-cut cave architecture in that of India as a whole,

(iii) the other schools of rock-cut cave architecture with a different religious affiliation, and their relationship with the Buddhist rock-cut cave architecture, especially in Western India;

(iv) the various factors that are to be taken into consideration, such as

    a. Chronology

    b. Religion

    c. History, and

    d. Ethnography

while understanding the developments of architecture in a given region or country. Fergusson was quite sure that the tradition of cutting rock to create a religious or secular monument must have been developed by Indians due to their contacts with the Greeks, or the Indo-Greeks that made their presence felt in the North-West-Frontier-Region of India, even before the advent of Alexander the Great. It is known that the earliest attempts of Indians in secular or religious architecture were more in brick-and timber; it is only the Greeks and Romans and other earlier civilizations of the old world that chose stone for sculpture and monumental architecture. It was the Achaemenid Iranians, who created their funeral monuments on the slopes of the hills near

Behistun. The influence of Classical Persian art on the Ashokan pillars is quite evident, and therefore it was not unexpected that Fergusson should trace the origin of the Barabar caves near Bodhgaya to the Indian contact with the Hellenistic art in India. Fergusson was a pioneer in the study of rock-cut cave architecture in India, in the sense that he studied this variety of architecture in India on a pan Indian basis in collaboration with James Burgess and wrote a complete volume on the subject. There were earlier attempts made by scholars of both Indian and European origin, but the comprehensive way and the depth and seriousness with which these two art historians worked on rock-cut cave architecture was unprecedented as their later works would show. For both Fergusson and Burgess, the work on Rock-cut-Temples of India (1880) was just a beginning of their studies in Indian Architecture. Later on, Fergusson very extensively wrote on Indian Art and Architecture and the writings left a deep imprint on the future works in the subject. J. Burgess in his later years concentrated more on built architecture. What was more significant in the case of Fergusson was his very original standpoint that the Buddhist Rock Cut Architecture was, what he called 'true' Architecture and very forceful arguments he put forth in support of his observation regarding the rock-cut architecture of the Buddhist, especially in the Deccan. While emphasizing the importance of the Buddhist architecture of the Deccan, which was in a very large number, and covered a span of more than 1000 years (roughly from 2nd cent. BCE to 8th cent. CE). The early Buddhist settlements and sites for monumental architecture of the Buddhist in the north were known to the world of scholars, mainly through the pioneering efforts of the first director of the Archaeological Survey of India viz. (Sir) Alexander Cunningham and his very industrious assistants, like Beglar and Carlyle. But to trace the history of the Buddhist architecture in north India was a huge and enormous task involving excavations and explorations over vast areas which would consume a very long span of time. The task was made very easy because of the very much imperishable and long-surviving evidence in the form of the rock-cut shrines of the Deccan. Fergusson had his own reasons to believe-and rightly so-that the Buddhist rock-cut architecture was 'true' architecture. This in a way went on to prove that in ancient India there was an artistic tradition of producing true architecture. Such a statement was very much necessary in contemporary times, as the sculptural art of India was being criticised as 'monstrous'. According to the current European view, Indians were very capable in craftsmanship; but lacking in artistic imagination. Another very important feature of Fergusson's art historical approach was his aesthetics, which emphasized the usefulness of the work of art and its own natural growth from the artistic point of view. He very firmly believed that no 'true' architecture imitated blindly other artistic traditions. This is very well reflected in his approach of taking into consideration the four important factors that shape the development of art and architecture of a given group of people in a specified area where they are located. He very seriously dealt with the known Indian chronology as understood from the Vedic, Puranic and Buddhist tradition, the place and the year of death of the Buddha in the same tradition; and later on, while dealing with the spread of Buddhism took into consideration the Ceylonese accounts such as that like in Mahāvaṃsa. He also takes into consideration the history of the Sātavāhanas and the Śaka-Kṣatrapas, as also that of Kharvēla of Mahameghavahana Dynasty. His observations about ethnology and ancient ethnic groups of India are quite interesting and amusing. Apparently, he has not given any weight age to the role of the Austro-Asiatic group of people and their languages that form a language family by itself. He rather overemphasised the importance of the Dravidian group of people, their languages and the role played by them in the origin and spread of Shaivism. He also suspected that probably this ethnic group, which had a Mediterranean origin, had left its vestiges in the north in the form of the Brahui dialect in Baluchistan, had a role perhaps to play in the origin and spread of Vaishnavism also. Based on his observations of both, languages and the ethnic tradition of people, Fergusson chose to make an observation that the South Indian architecture was different from that in North because of the particular ethnic characteristics. In fact, Burgess went on a step ahead and proclaimed that the North Indian Temple Architecture especially of Western India is distinct from the architecture of the rest of India because of the ethnic groups (like the Huna-s and Gurjara-s) that came from central Asia and had a distinct ethnic characteristic. We need not comment much on both these views as the early South Indian Buddhist art and architecture is inspired by that from the Deccan, Central India and that in the Gangetic Doab; and the traditions whether artistic or religious, usually tend to remain orthodox in the South.

I

One of the most important observations made by Fergusson in the case of the Rock Cut Architecture of the Hindus is that the Brāhmaṇical rock-cut architecture is not 'true' like its precedent, the Buddhist Architecture; it is imitative (of the Buddhist architecture) and does not serve the purpose for which it was created. According to him the Brāhmaṇical architecture as illustrated in the caves of Mandapeshwar, Jogeshwari, and Elephanta simply imitate the plan of the earlier Buddhist caves as at Ajanta and Aurangabad. Similarly, Fergusson does not have any idea whether for the Hindu monks (like the Pāśupata-s) it was necessary to live in a cave temple. All these Brāhmaṇical caves do not have any aesthetic appeal also. However, he compliments the architects of the Brāhmaṇical caves in that, even if they somewhat discontinued the tradition of narrative mural paintings on the wall faces and replaced these with sculptures in relief, they used the device in a very effective manner as shown by examples in caves no. 15 and 16 ant Ellora. He however hardly compliments the monolithic creation of a temple in the form of the Kailas at Ellora. In fact, he sees the great creation as an aesthetic failure because it is situated as though in a pit or a ditch.

There seems to be a shift in paradigm when we come to the next phase of studies in the Rock Cut cave architecture of the Deccan, when in the 60s of the last centuries (to be precise in 1967) Walter Spink took a review of the important stages of the rock-cut activities in the Deccan in a complete number of Marg dedicated to the art from 5th Cent. to the 10th Cent. He tried to show that there was something like continuity in the rock-cut creations of the Deccan regarding the plan of caves, doorways, ceilings, the pillar forms, different human forms and decorative elements. Scholars have been all the time aware that there was a decrease both in terms of sites and volume in the creation of the rock-cut Buddhist caves in the last phase. These were created on the trade routes; especially those starting from the seaports on the coastal strip of Konkan to various commercial and trading centres on the plateau to places of political importance such as Ter, Junnar, and Paithan. The patronage of these caves was with the prosperous trade merchants and the other sections of the society. With the disruptions in the international trade on the silk route, so many sites in

the north decline and perish. With the fall of the Gupta and Vakataka empire's the patronage of Buddhism was immensely affected. In fact, according to Walter Spink with the fall of the empire of Hariśēna all Buddhist Rock Cut activities seems to have come to a standstill. And the centre of the power of in the Deccan seems to have shifted from Vidarbha (Vatsagulma is the same as Washim in Western Vidarbha) to Badami in the southern Deccan. According to Spink, because of this loss of patronage, the artists from Ajanta and surrounding area shifted from Washim-Aurangabad area to Mandapeshwar, Jogeshwari (near Kanheri), and Elephanta, and from there to Badami in the southern Deccan, from where they seem to have found their way back to Ellora. Dynasty-wise, the artists got attracted first to regions controlled by the early Kalacūri-s (who also controlled the Konkan area) and from there, after the rise of the Western Cālukyas; they found patronage with them at Badami, and in the latter half of the 8th cent. AD., they came back to Ellora under the Rāṣṭrakūṭa-s of Paithan. It is significant that Spink prefers not to comment on the observations made by Fergusson regarding the imitative character of the Brāhmaṇical caves or their deficiency in aesthetic appeal.

II

Around this time only, K. V. Soundararajan took up the work of surveying the non-Buddhist, especially the Brāhmaṇical cave architecture of the Deccan. He not only covered the specimens created by the Western Cālukyas at Badami and the surrounding regions but for the first time took a fresh survey of those caves completed under the patronage of the Eastern Cālukyas and some of those which had escaped the attention of Fergusson and Burgess (such as the caves at Bokardhan). While explaining his stand, he emphasized the need of studying the Brāhmaṇical rock-cut architecture of the Deccan especially in the context of the contribution of the Western Cālukyas and the vigorous patronage that they provided for the emergence of the structural Nāgara and Drāviḍa temple architecture. Because of his observations, regarding especially the pillar forms and stylistic development in sculpture, Soundara Rajan firmly believes that the post-Vakataka rock-cut architecture of the Deccan in the early period was essentially Cālukya; and the one that followed as is known is obviously a creation under the Rāṣṭrakūṭa patronage. Whether the rock-cut architecture that came up in northern Deccan was fully Cālukya or not can be a matter of debate, but his sumptuous monograph on the Brāhmaṇical architecture of the Deccan is definitely a big contribution because of the detailed descriptions, and plans of monuments made afresh under the temple survey scheme of the ASI. Another significant feature of the work of the learned scholar is the awareness about the Śaiva and Vaiṣṇava agamic traditions that received a significant visual expression in the post-Vakataka art of the northern and southern Deccan. Soundararajan not only gives a very detailed iconographic description of the Śaiva and Vaiṣṇava divinities but very clearly suggests their affiliation with the iconographic forms that are prevalent and seen in the structural temples on the contemporary period with a clear agamic affiliation. For example, he refers to the five faces of Sadāśiva in the Pāśupata tradition and their appearance in the cave art as at Elephanta and those at Ellora (caves no. 17 to 23, and those in the Ganesha-lena group). However, the real correspondence between the philosophical thought, its expression in visual form in the Brāhmaṇical caves was very well demonstrated in a very crystal-clear form by Stella Kramrisch in a very seminal article written by her in the 4th volume of Ancient India. She very clearly showed that threefold representation of Śiva in the form of a Śivaliṅga, in a separate sarvatōbhadra shrine, his representation in the back wall as Sadāśiva, and the eight narrative scenes in relief rendered on the wall faces of the cave complex give clear expression to the aniconic para-śiva, to the aniconic-iconic Sadāśiva and the manifestations of the Maheshvara as explained in the Pāśupata-sutra-s. This was further substantiated by the studies of C. D. Collins (1988, Iconography and Ritual of Śiva at Elephanta) of the caves at Elephanta giving various details how the cave was constructed keeping in view the ritualistic prescription and conduct code of a sādhaka in the Pāśupata tradition. From the review of the work done by the above mentioned three scholars (Soundararajan, Stella Kramrisch, and Collins), it becomes very clear that the caves as at Mandapeshwar, Jogeshvari, Elephanta and cave no. 29 at Ellora were created with the specific objective of serving a ritualistic purpose and spiritual practice of the Pāśupata monks; the caves were definitely not executed as part of the blind imitative activity as pre-supposed by Fergusson. They had a definite plan that served a purpose. Similarly, with a detailed study done of the Pāśupata caves at Ankai-Tankai, Takali Dhokeshwar (Ahemadnagar district), Mahur

(Nanded district), and Ellora, it becomes very clear that after the decline of the Buddhist Mahāyāna tradition, the Śaiva Pāśupata tradition emerged as a vigorous religious force in the spiritual life of the Deccan. In fact, the studies done by Suraj Pandit very clearly show the rivalry that existed between Buddhists and the Śaiva-s in order to get patronage and donations from the people.

III

With the discovery of a new set of antiquities in Vidarbha area, which dated definitely from the Vakataka period, the studies in Vakataka art and architecture received a completely new dimension. This was mainly prompted because of the accidental discovery of images with Śaiva and Vaiṣṇava affiliation at the site of Mandhal (about 75km from and) in the vicinity of Nagpur. The excavation revealed also the association of this place with donations that were given by Pravarsena II (c. 415 to 450 CE) and Pṛthvīṣena II (c.470 to 475 CE). A copperplate attributed to Pravarsena-s father Rudrasena II (c. 390 to 395CE) was also discovered in a field nearby in the same village. An Iconographic analysis and interpretation of the śākta, śaiva and vaiṣnava images has shown that these images had definitely an agamic affiliation (viz. Pāśupata and Sātvata/ Pāncarātra). This also again was a reminder of the narrative panels from the Parandhama Ashram of a Vinobaji at Paunar, which illustrated scenes from the life of Kṛṣna and Dāśarathi Rāma. The Vakatakas had a long tradition of devotion to Śiva, as clearly shown by their attribute Paramamāheśvara. Similarly, both Rudrasena II and his wife Prabhāvatiguptā bear the title paramabhāgavata. The inscription of Prabhāvatiguptā usually opened with a Sātvata devotional expression: 'Jitam Bhagavatā Puruṣeṇa!' There is also evidence from another set of copperplates that makes a reference to a sātvata establishment (maṭhikā) that existed at Vatsagulma. All these pieces of evidence very clearly showed that there existed in the Vakataka realm religious establishments and structures connected with Pāśupata and Pāncarātra sects. So, among the religious structures, some must have belonged to Pāśupata and Pāncarātra patrons. The Vakataka structures revealed or discovered at Ramtek include two caves-one of them (viz. the Gupta Rama Cave) was with an image of Viṣṇu and the other which was a cave-cum-structural temple enshrined a Śivaliṅga. The latter must have been for the use of a Pāśupata

Sādhaka. A visit to the twin caves at Patur (district Washim) gives a rough idea of the plan of a Pāśupata cave. Whereas one cave enshrined a Śivaliṅga, the other provided for an image of Pārvatī in penance. In the one that enshrined a Śivaliṅga, there was a slab that carried seven images in a group; these were probably of the seven mothers whose images form an invariable part of an iconographic scheme of a Pāśupata cave. The observation is very well substantiated by caves no. 21, 22, and 23 at Ellora. In cave no. 21 there is a complete narration of incident involving the wedding of Śaiva with Pārvatī, including the penance of Parvati. In the veranda opposite to this, are depicted the Seven Mothers.

A visit to the cave complex at Salabardi (district Amravati) brought to light a sculptural frieze depicting Umā-maheśvara as also Lakulīśa. In the vicinity of Bhandak/ Bhadravati (district Chandrapur) is a complex of caves affiliated to Buddhism, śhaivism, and Vaishnavism. Whereas the cave enshrining Narasiṃha image is a dwarf cave measuring hardly a meter and half sq; the cave near Gaurala lake though bigger is of very moderate proportions. Inside, it provides seven sockets for structural images, obliviously for the seven Mothers. There is a depiction of a Śivaliṅga on the face of the outer wall. This obliviously was a Pāśupata establishment. Another set of caves in a village called Dēvalane not far from Bandhak, provides for the residence of Pāśupata sādhaka-s, with one cell enshrined with a Śivaliṅga. A small sculpture inside of the doorframe of a female figure and an inscription in shell characters clearly show that the establishment is of the Vakataka period.

The very recent discovery of a group of 10 caves at Katalgaon-Javade (District Ratnagiri) in the vicinity of Lanje was reported first (2015) by Anjay Dhanawade. This was followed by an article (2016) by Anita Rane-Kothare in the Research Journal of the CSMVS, and still another by Gopal Joge, Abhijit Dandekar, Anjay Dhanawade, Shrikant Ganvir and Hemant Dalavi (2018) in the JRASSL (New Series). The discovery is indeed very significant because of the date of the caves and the images, as also their location in the Coastal Konkan. Here we would not like to go into details of the iconographic features of these images but would like to point out the importance of the iconographic forms of the concerned images and the themes connected with them. In their detailed article Gopal Joge and others

inform us that the images identified are as follows:

Nāgapuruṣa in cave no. 1 (fig. 7a and 7b)

Kevala-Nṛsiṃha in cave no. 3 (fig. 11a and 11b)

Kaliyādamana in cave no. 4 (fig. 12)

Kārtikeya, along with two attendant figures on his either side, probably Brahmā and Viṣṇu in cave no. 6 (fig. 14a and 14b; 15, 16)

Viṣṇu in cave no. 7, along with Gaṇeśa of a later period, and gaṇa-s (fig. 18a and 18b)

Brahmā or Sadāśiva in cave no. 8 (fig. 21a and 21b)

Śiva and Pārvatī riding a bull, and Gangāvataraṇa in cave no. 9 (fig. 25a, 25b, and 26a, 26b recp.)

The authors of the article, having taken into consideration, the architectural and iconographic features of the images, have come to a conclusion that these caves were most probably excavated during the reigns of the Traikūṭaka-s who had vaishnavite affiliations. They and their vassals very proudly have mentioned their attributes such as 'parama-vaiṣṇava' and 'bhagavat-pāda-karammakara'. The authors have also taken into consideration the possibility of these caves being excavated during the reigns of Kadambas and Mauryas who are have supposed to have held sway over the Konkan region. One of the authors, viz. Anjay Dhanavade, in his article published in Samshodhaka (2015) earlier has pointed out that the Vakatakas promoted both Śaivism and Vaiṣṇavism.

Without going into the details, at this juncture, of iconography and religious affiliation of the three dynasties viz. The Kadaṃba-s, Maurya-s and the Traikūṭaka-s, and in absence of any epigraphical evidence pointing to any such specific attribution to a given dynasty, we would cast our opinion in favour of the Traikūṭaka-s, who were definitely devotees of Viṣṇu. Another point in favour of them being vaishnavites the name of their capital, which was known by the name Aniruddhapura. The name Aniruddha he refers to one of the four manifestations (vibhavas) of Para-Vāsudēva, the supreme principle in the Sātvata/ Pāñcarātra philosophy.

IV

The above survey of the rock-cut architecture has some significant points to put forth, (i) the relative longer antiquity of the Brāhmaṇical, to be specific the Śaiva, vaiṣṇava and śākta, caves that were excavated in Maharashtra; (ii) affiliation of some of these caves specifically with Pāśupata and Sātvata cults; (iii) and the significance of these in the history of the religious and architectural tradition of Maharashtra. It is very clear now that the rock-cut caves in both the śaiva and vaiṣṇava tradition go back to the Vakataka times. In the case of the vaiṣṇava caves their antiquity can definitely be stretched back to the reins at least of Prabhāvatiguptā (her regency period can be estimated to be circa from 395 to 413CE) and possibly also of Rudrasena II (c. 390 to 395CE), as these two are the royal figures that were responsible for the introduction of Sātavata bhagavatism in Vidarbha area. There are early śaiva caves with inscription in shell characters as at Dēvalane in the vicinity of Bhandak (district Chandrapur), but today we cannot date them precisely on the basis of only the sculptural or the epigraphical evidence noted above. The earliest śaiva images come from Mandhal (district Nagpur). The images of the so-called Sadāśiva, the four-headed, and the eight-headed (interpreted as aṣṭamūrti-Śiva) can definitely be dated to 4th cent. CE on stylistic grounds. At present we cannot attribute them to any predecessor of Rudrasena II (c. 390-395CE), though the māheśvara affiliation of the Vakatakas goes back to Gautamīputra and Rudrasena I who ruled in the earlier half of the fourth cent. CE. We are also aware that the famous śaiva monument at modern Chikkambari (modern chikmara in district Chandrapur) attributed to Rudrasena I, who was the grandson of Pravarsena I (c. 261-330). The first clearly dated śaiva cave can be the twin rock-cut cave at Patur (district Washim) which can be dated roughly to 460CE on stylistic grounds (both architectural and sculptural) and attributed to Dēvasena, father of Hariṣena (c. 460-477CE) of the Vatsagulma branch of the Vakatakas. In the present state of our studies we cannot precisely date the early rock-cut caves at Bhandak (the śākta/ śaiva cave at Gaurala; the Narasimha cave at the back of Vinjhasan hill), the śaiva caves at Dēvalane (district Chandrapur), the Lakulīśa and Uma Maheshvara depiction on the rock face at Salbardi (district Amraoti) the vaiṣṇava and śaiva caves at Bhatala (district Chandrapur); but all these are of Vakataka period (4th-5th cent. CE). What one has to note down in the case of the above mentioned Śaiva, vaiṣṇava, śākta and the Buddhist cave at Vinjhasan is that these are of altogether a different mode and architecturally distinct from the western rock-cut

caves executed in western Maharashtra under the patronage of the Sātavāhana-s, Vakataka-s, and Kalacūri-s. There are also some rock-cut caves in Vidarbha, viz. the caves at Patur and the Buddhist cave at Salbardi (district Amraoti) that are in continuation of the rock-cut tradition of western Maharashtra. It is because of this distinctness as of the Buddhist cave on the Vinjhasan hill and the primitive appearance of the śaiva, vaiṣṇava and śākta caves earlier mentioned that a suggestion has been made by some scholars (e.g. Shri. Chitale who has written on these lesser-known rock-cut caves) that these are definitely earlier than even the Satavahana-Kshatrapa caves of western Maharashtra. These early caves, according to Chitale must have been excavated under the patronage of the early Kshatrapa kings (e.g. Rupiamma of the funerary pillar dated to 1st cent. B.C.E.) and must have inspired the rock-cut activity of western Maharashtra. It is very difficult to accept such an origin of the rock-cut caves of western Maharashtra due to the inspiration of the activity started in the reigns of early Kṣatrapa kings of Vidarbha, though a different explanation can be offered in the case of this early rock-cut activity of Vidarbha. These rock-cut caves are architecturally distinct most probably because the rock-cut caves were excavated by the descendants of those built megaliths of megalithic culture (c. 1000-300 BCE). During the process of urbanisation and in the early centuries of the current era these autochthonous people got converted initially to Buddhism, as is shown by the evidence from the stupa at Pauni (district Bhandara) and the Buddhist caves (1st Cent. BCE) at Chandhala (in the vicinity of Mandhal in district Nagpur). The cave in the Chandhala forest has distinct architectural features in that the ceiling slab on the rock-cut cave is a flat circular stone slab provided structurally to the cave. This flat ceiling slab is in exact imitation of a slab provided in the structure of a megalithic cromlech. Similarly, the śaiva caves at Dēvalane have some similitude with the rock-cut megalithic caves at Bhivkund (in the Chandhala forest of Nagpur district). With the rise of the Śaiva-śākta cults during the Gupta period, as evidenced from the Gupta caves at Udayagiri (district Vidisha, Madhya Pradesh) the contiguous regions of Vidarbha also must have got converted to the puranic and the newly emerging agamic cults in Hinduism. The evidence from the excavation at Pauni very clearly shows that Buddhism was on the wane after the 5th Century in the Vidarbha area.

The evidence from western Maharashtra very clearly shows that there was a sudden rise of an increase in the following of the śaiva cults, as the Rock-cut caves at Jogeshwari, Mandapeshwar, Elephanta, and the Dumar Lena (cave no. 29) at Ellora would show. The evidence from the Buddhist caves at Kanheri and those in the vicinity clearly show that there was a rivalry for patronage during the early Kalacūri period (date of the 6th cent. CE). There are now after the 6th century, only some centres (Nashik, Aurangabad, Shirval, and later at Panhāḷēkājī in Konkan) that are indicative of the patronage received by Buddhism. During the Cālukya, Rāṣṭrakūṭa and the Yādava periods, it is only the Jaina and Brāhmaṇical rock-cut activity that receives active patronage of the ruling royal families.

Bibliography

Fergusson J. & J. Burgess; 1880.*Cave Temples of India*. New Delhi: Motilal Banarsidass

Kramrisch, Stella; 1958.*Ancient India* No. 4, pp.?

Soundarajana K. V.; 1961.*Cave Temples of the Deccan*. New Delhi's.

Spink, Walter; 1967.*From Ajanta to Ellora*. Mumbai: Marg.

Collins, C. D.; 1988.*Iconography and Ritual of Śiva at Elephanta.*, New Delhi: Sri Satguru Publication.

Jamkhedkar, A. P.; 2002.*Mahāraṣṭra Sthāpatya ani Kalā* (in Marathi). Dept. of Gazetteers, Govt. of Maharashtra.

Chitale, S. K.; 2002.*Vidharbhātīl Kōrīv Gumphā* (in Marathi), Nagpur:(Mrs.) S. A. Mule.

Pandit, Suraj A.; 2012.*Age of the Traikūṭakas*. New Delhi: Agama Kala Prakashan.

Pandit, Suraj A. & A. Narayanan; 2013.*Stories in Stone - Historic Caves of Mumbai*. Mumbai: INSTUCEN Trust.

Dhanawade, Anjay; 2015.*Katalgaon, Taluka Lanja, Jilha Ratnagiri Yethil Shaiva ani Vaisnava Leni*. Sanshodhan Patrika; Dhule: Rajwade Sanshodhan Mandal.

Rane-Kothare, Anita; 2016.Research *journal of the CSMVS, Mumbai*.

Joge, Gopal et al.; 2018.*Early Brāhmaṇical Rock Cut Caves at Katalgaon-Javade, District Ratnagiri, Maharashtra, India*. Journal of Royal Asiatic Society of Sri Lanka (NS), Vol. 62 part 2, 65-113, Colombo.

Mahāyāna Buddhism and Esoteric Practices: Kanheri A Case Study

Suraj A Pandit, Sathaye College, Mumbai

Abstract

Kanheri is one of the important Buddhist monastic sites flourished in western India in 1st century BCE. The archaeological evidence suggests that monks continued living here till the early centuries of the 2nd millennium of Common Era. The site evinces three phases of the development of Buddhism from Thēravada or Early to Mahāyāna and then to some esoteric ritual traditions. Kanheri was one of the centres for esoteric Buddhism out of three in western India after the fall of Buddhist Ellora. Panhāḷēkājī evolved independently while Mahākāḷī (Kondivaṭē) survived as a subordinate religious settlement to Kanheri.

Epigraphical and archaeological data of the early period from Kanheri suggests that there were not less than three Buddhist Nikāyas viz. Bhadrāyaniyas, Aparasēlias, and Sarvastivādins, peacefully coexisted at Kanheri from 2nd century CE to 5th century CE. Kanheri evolved as a religious educational centre till 5th century CE with religious satellite settlements in all the directions. Not only the nature of Buddhism as religion was changing but also the nature of monastery had changed in the due course. A new set of religious practices as well as literature came up which is seen reflected in the art and architecture at Kanheri.

This paper aims to understand various sectarian and cultic developments as seen reflected in art and architecture at Kanheri from 5th century CE up to 12th century CE. Another objective of the paper is to understand the role played by the Buddhist monastery at Kanheri in the overall religious landscape in the then Buddhist world. This will shed some light on the catchment as well as spare of influence of Buddhist monastery at Kanheri in the last phase of its development.

Introduction

Fergusson and Burgess in their Book 'Cave Temples of India' (1880) classified the Buddhist caves in two broad categories viz., aniconic Phase representing the worship of the Buddha in the forms of symbols, popularly known as Hinayāna Phase; and iconic phase, represented by image worship popularly known as Mahāyāna. This classification has been followed by scholars till Dhavalikar (1984) wrote a monograph 'Late Hinayāna Caves in Western India'. This is for the first time that change in the material culture in western Indian Buddhist Rock-Cut Architecture has been noticed by archaeologists and some inquiries have been raised. The key question dealt by scholars about the transition from Hinayāna to Mahāyāna is of origin of image worship. A different approach to understand this transition has been taken by scholars like N. Dutta (1978), Cohen R. (1995), Bhalerao M. (2007), Pandit S. A. (2005) with the study of the development of various Nikāyas in Buddhism as seen reflected in Art and inscriptions. Malandra (1993) and Pia Brancaccio (2011) made an attempt to understand the relation between art and literature at Ellora and Aurangabad respectively. This has led to a better understanding of the transitional phase in general as well as Mahāyāna art in specific.

Philosophers have been studying this transition based on the available literary sources. Though there are numerous new sources coming to the light from Chinese and Tibetan studies. It has been generally accepted that the foundation of Mahāyāna Buddhism is formed by Nagarjuna's Madhyamika school of which background was prepared by Sarvastivādins, especially Sautrāntika and Vaibhāṣika. These developments seem to have taken place in the 2nd century CE.

If we accept the classification by Fergusson, then first Mahāyāna Cave appears at Ajanta that is in 5th century CE. This is difficult to believe that the philosophical developments took more than 250 years to leave an impact on material culture.

Kanheri, Nasik, Karla, Junnar, Kuda and Bhaja are the key sites to understand this transition from

Thēravada[85] to Mahāyāna with special reference to the development of various Nikayas in Buddhism. Kanheri is taken here as a case study to understand the Mahāyāna at the site and some rituals associated with it seen reflected in the art and architecture at the site.

I

Transitional Phase, i.e. Early Mahāyāna[86] at Kanheri can be seen in the last quarter of the 2nd century CE at the site. There are fragments of the five images[87] of the Buddha carved in cave 3, i.e. the main caitya. An inscription says that the caitya was given in donation to Bhadrāyaniyas Nikaya. It seems that Bhadrāyaniyas had accepted image worship, transfer of merit and significant position of Acharya in the system by 2nd century CE. (Pandit, 2005: 223-224). There are influences coming from Central Asia via Mathura. (Pandit, 2002: 383-389). Mathura, as well as Central Asia, were the core influence area of Sarvastivāda in the 2nd century CE. Places like Sopara and Padan around Kanheri are mentioned in Purṇāvadāna (Divyāvadāna) in the list of places visited by the Buddha. (Indraji B., 1929) The site was surrounded by Sarvastivāda monasteries while the main caitya given to Bhadrāyaniyas was being excavated in last quarter of 2nd century CE. The evidence suggests the possibility of Bhadrāyaniyas losing their independent identity in the due course and getting merged in Sarvastivāda. (Pandit, 2015: 478) This might have accelerated the development of various cults as seen in inscriptions and art of 5th-6th century CE at Kanheri.

There are cave groups excavated at the site in 2nd-3rd century CE which have a peculiar architectural feature. There is one additional 'L' shaped hall which is seen in one of the caves among these cave groups. The smaller arm of 'L' shaped hall has a small bench. This is most probably to keep the object of worship, maybe an image. (Pandit, 2015: 471-473). It is quite possible that in the beginning the image worship was not widely accepted at site and performed in isolation by a group of people within their Nikaya cave complexes.350 to 450 CE seem to

be the silent era at Kanheri when no excavation of caves has been taken up. Though this is so, the fame of Kanheri had reached out on the trade route. (Pandit, 2002: 389-394)

There are caves at Kanheri which can be stylistically dated to 5th-6th century C.E. They fall into Mahāyāna phase. Most of them have a hall and a shrine. It is interesting to see that no major Vihāra Cave was added to the site. There is only one area at the site which reveals the structural remains of a vihāra complex i.e., at the entrance of the site. Most probably the Thēravada Vihāras were occupied by Mahāyāna monks. This is evident from the epigraphical as well as sculptural data from Caitya Cave 3 that the cave was under worship after some modifications even during Mahāyāna phase.

Image worship was introduced at Kanheri in 2nd century CE itself. These images were placed on pillars in the main caitya though the main caitya had a stupa in the hall as the main object of worship. This was a very simple stupa without much decoration (probably painted). As mentioned earlier there was an addition of an image in the main Caitya placed in front of the stupa in 5th-6th century CE. There is a provision made to install an image in front of the stupa evinced by the small rectangular pits. Unfortunately, due to restored flooring by ASI has minimized the scope of research in this regard. Though this is so, the evidence is available to prove the existence of an added image which was a loose image most probably made of perishable material. Hiuen Tsang makes a reference to such an image in his travelogue on his visit to Kanheri. (Pandit, 2010: 147-157). An additional cell in the courtyard indicates that there are elaborate and extensive rituals performed in the cave and the associated objects and associated material was kept in the cell. This cell does not have any bench or niche indicating the cell was used as Vihāra. It was most probably a storeroom for the caitya to maintain and keep the associated objects of rituals.

There are few other caves at Kanheri, as mentioned above, which have images in the sanctum. It is

---

[85] Word Theravada is used here to indicate early phase in the development of Buddhist Rock-Cut Architecture. This was referred by earlier scholars as Hinayana. Word Hinayana has its own contextual meaning in Vaipulya Sutras of the later period.
[86] This is the same phase which has been referred as 'Late Hinayana' by Dhavalikar. This new term is coined to indicate its affiliation to Mahayana rather than Theravada.
[87] There are two images of the Buddha with attendants and a fragment of the same can be seen on one of the pillars in courtyard of cave 3. There are two fragments which can be seen in hall. Only fragments of attendants are visible. Another pillar in the court yard evinces us the provision made to place an image of the Buddha with attendants. So, there is evidence of total six Buddha images installed in cave 3 in 2nd century CE.

observed that caves like Cave no. 34, 41 and 90 do not have any shrine images, though there is a platform in the sanctum where a small depression is created to fix the knob of the image to install. This is interesting to see that the sculptural imagery and the iconographic features associated at least two of these caves, i.e., Caves 41 and 90, fall into the tradition of the cult of Avalōkitēśvara and Saddharmapuṇḍarīka Sūtra.

Absence of images, or rather the presence of a movable image is significant in these caves. M. G. Dixit has reported a wooden image of Tara from Kanheri. (Sankalia, 1986: 56-59) This suggests the existence of a few more such images at the site. What do such images suggest? Why are they not carved in the shrine panel? All the caves mentioned above are important caves which indicate their cultic affiliations. Cultic imagery is usually associated with specific cult rituals. Though in the absence of images, one cannot talk about their iconographic details, we can reconstruct certain rituals with the help of material remains at the site as well as the study of living traditions.

There are numerous such images seen in Temples in Konkan. They are referred to as "Cala bera" in local tradition, i.e., the "movable body" of the god. The main ritual associated with such images is "sacred procession". Such sacred processions are performed with the chanting of the sacred formulae and singing songs of the cult god or the supreme one. Images are either carried on the shoulder or in chariots. Sacred music, religious songs, the offering of flowers, precious- semiprecious offerings is a part of such ritual processions, 3rd Canto of Saddharmapuṇḍarīka Sūtra gives a reference to such rituals, procession and spiritual merits gained by followers by performing these rituals. (Vaidya, 1960: 21-43) Hiuen Tsang makes mention of a procession of the Buddha image at the time of his visit to Harsha's court. The tradition of ritual processions is quite early and observed even today not only in India but in almost all the religions across the world. Buddhism is also not an exception to this.

.II.

Mahāyāna Buddhism as seen first reflected in inscriptions through various religious sacred formulae and the concept of sharing the merit. Grace merit is one of the characteristic features of Mahāyāna Buddhism where the merit is gained in grace and also can be shared by declaration or vow.

There were numerous ways described and discussed in Mahāyāna literature to gain spiritual merit. One of the ways is chanting of the formulae or the recitation of the text or a section of the text.

The iconographic and epigraphical data at the site suggests that there were two such formulae seen gained popularity, viz. 'ॐमणीपद्मेहम्'and 'येधर्माहेतुप्रभवाहेतुंतेषांतथागतःह्यवदत्तेषांचयोनिरोधएवं वादीमहाश्रमणः' First one is indicated by the sculptural panels of Avalōkitēśvara which suggest that his cult was very popular at the site (Pandit, 2009: 90-100) while the other was mentioned in one of the inscriptions in cave no 3. (Gokhale, 1991: 56) Iconographic study of sculptural panels at Kanheri suggest us that the cult of Tara was popular at site in late 5th and early 6th century CE. (Pandit, 2002 A: 119-125) There are formulae associated with the cult of Tara i.e. 'ॐतारेतुत्तारेतुरेस्वाः' might have gained popularity at the site. This hypothesis needs more scrutiny with reference to the date of appearance of these two formulae in Buddhist literature.

The second formula is the Sanskrit form of a verse in Pali Vinayapīṭaka. This also is treated as the gist of the teachings of the Buddha. This verse was uttered by 'Assāji' in Vinayapīṭaka to describe Buddha's teachings in nut-shell for Sāriputta and Moggalāyāna before their initiation. The verse plays a vital role in Buddhist ritual. There are rituals in which this verse is used as a medium to install dharmakāya of the Buddha in the image.

In Mahāparinibbāṇasutta (Dīgghanikāya, Suttapīṭaka), it is said that Buddha was approached by monks just before his mahāparinirvāṇa. They asked him about 'who will be chief of the Sangha (saṃgha pramukha) after his demise?' The Buddha denied to appoint any 'saṃgha pramukha' and said that his teachings will guide his disciples. (DN, 2.3.216-218) This was the first time when he was equated with his teachings. His teachings here come for the first time as his 'dhammakāya'. In Mahāyāna Buddhism the concept of 'dhammakāya' has evolved in art on the 'opening of the Topes from Kanheri' in 'Journal of Royal Asiatic Society Calcutta' talks about two copper plates. (Bird, 1841: 94-96)

The larger one makes mention to the reign of Traikūṭakas and the stupa being constructed on the bodily remains of Sāriputta. The smaller one has been described just as a famous Buddhist creed'. It is a two-line inscription most probably of the same verse under discussion. In both the cases at Kanheri, inscriptions are found in the context of the stupa. One is monolithic relief stupa and the other is structural stupa made of bricks and stones. This creed is found on numerous sculptures from Nalanda Pala and their associated art schools geographically spread over the region of Ganga- Yamuna Doab and Orissa. Sites of Himalayan Buddhism also give us ample evidence of such sculptures. In both these cases at Kanheri, it is seen that these stupas were worshipped. They were not just the object of worship in the ritual but the 'dhammakāya' of the Buddha. imposing 'dhammakāya' over stone or brick structure through this creed was a part of the ritual. As these stupas are associated with rituals performed at Kanheri, they evince us of certain unique Mahāyāna ritual traditions prevalent at site.

The main stupa, as well as the relief stupa under discussion in cave 3 at Kanheri, are the dhammakāya of the Buddha Shakyamuni as the cave has been referred as the 'Gandhakuṭi' in one of the inscriptions. Acharya who has given the donation of an image of the Buddha carries a title as 'Gandhakuṭivārika'. He seems to be the caretaker of the cave. He most probably was involved in the performing of daily rituals in the caitya. A Nepalese manuscript of 1009 refers to the cave as 'Khaḍga Caitya'. (Leese M., 1983: p. 2 & 10-fn.1) There is a small room provided in the courtyard of the cave 3, as discussed earlier, most probably as a storeroom for 'Paribhōgas' of the 'stupa'. These rituals most probably are associated with the stupa as well as the image installed in front of it. There must be numerous offerings offered to the 'God' in cave 3 daily. Burgess, in his report of Caves of Western India, talks about a fragment of a lady next to the one of the large Buddha statue in Veranda.[88](1994, p. 62) This reminds us of the depiction of two themes, story of Sumēdha Paṇḍita and Story of Rāhula's initiation, at the entrance of cave 19 at Ajanta. This symbolically talks about the acceptance of vow of becoming Bodhisattva by Sumēdha from the predecessor of the Shakyamuni and an appointment of the successor in the form of Rāhula. These are two incidences at the entrance on either side of the door through which the approach is to the 'dhammakāya'

of Shakyamuni completes the circle of mythology which essentially must have played a vital role in the set of rituals performed at the site.

There is a small structural temple at the site which might be of the early Śīlahāra period. The temple has a small water tank adjacent to it. Most probably the stone from the tank was used for the construction of the temple. This must be a small ritual tank associated with the temple at the site, suggests that the image worship and associated rituals as discussed above were popular at the site even in the later period.

.III.

Cave 11, which is popularly known as 'Mahārāja Mahāvihāra' cave, a unique cave at the site. There are only two such caves in India, one is at Kanheri (Cave 11) and other is Cave 5 at Ellora. This was the place most probably used by monks for the group recitation of sutras and sacred formulae. Art historical data and iconographic study of the sculptural panels at the site suggests that Sutras like Saddharmapuṇḍarīka Sūtra, Amitāyurdhyāna Sūtra, Ekādaśamukha Avalōkitēśvara Dhāraṇi, etc were recited at the site. Cave 90 at Kanheri brings out another set of rituals associated with manuscripts at the site. There is a small cell in the veranda of the cave with a provision to fix the wooden door as well as an elaborate niche in the wall. This cell has been interpreted in its context as a subsidiary shrine. The object of worship was a manuscript of Saddharmapuṇḍarīka Sūtra. Elaborate worship of the manuscript is a part of cultic rituals in the cult of Saddharmapuṇḍarīka Sūtra even today. Along with the manuscript, the name of the text is written and worshiped considering that as the form of the teaching of the Buddha.

An inscription from the early Śīlahāra period indicates that a person was appointed to make copies of manuscripts. (Mirashi, 1977: 2-3) It is most probably a part of a ritual in which copies of the manuscript are made and offered to the lord. There are numerous such manuscripts seen in Nepal of the late medieval period where copies of manuscripts are made to gain spiritual merit. In such cases most probably grant was deposited to monastery or temple and the 'authentic' copy of the manuscript

---

[88] While describing Cave 3, Burgess made the following note:
"It ought to be noted also that the pillars at last, and probably the veranda of this cave, have been covered with paintings, as at Ajanta. Little of it is now traceable, but there is a pretty distinct outline of a female in the right end of the veranda by the leg of the large standing figure of Buddha.", (1994 Reprint, 62).

was prepared for the donation. This might have become a popular practice at Kanheri.

The sculpture of Eleven-Headed Avalōkitēśvara is a masterpiece in Buddhist art at Kanheri. This can be stylistically dated to 6th century CE, so proves to be an earliest known image of the deity in the world (Pandit S. A., 2015 A., p. 58-64). There are texts like Sutra, Dharani, and Hṛdayamantra associated with this deity dated back to 4th-6th century CE. They have their own set of rituals associated with them. A ritual text 'Ekādaśamukham' is reported from Gilgit (Dutta, 1984: 35-40). This manuscript is paleographically dated by editors to 6th century CE. This is a ritual guide for the rituals to perform on Bodhisattva Ekādaśamukha Avalōkitēśvara. Most of the rituals are in the form of symbolic acts and chants are in the form of mantras and bījākṣaras. It is difficult to make any meaning out of it without the guidance of the acharya trained in the tradition. There are objects like a ritual bell (Vajraghaṇṭā), flowers, vermilion, turmeric, and many other ritual objects are used in performing the ritual. Specific arrangements are made of the material and the ritual objects which require certain space. It is interesting to see that the image of Eleven-Headed Avalōkitēśvara at the site is placed in an open cell in the courtyard of cave 41, in such a manner that rituals can be performed in front of the image. These rituals must be esoteric in nature. It is really difficult to make out anything without the initiation to the tradition. This again leads us to various questions. Was the entry to masses restricted to these caves?

.IV.

Such restricted access has been pointed out at Ellora in caves 12, 13 and 14 reflected in architecture. (Pandit, 2013: 57). Caves at Kanheri are divided into groups based on their Nikaya affiliation. It has been observed that there is at least one place of worship in each group. These places of worship are associated with their Nikaya traditions. Apart from such places, there is a main caitya which is at the entrance of the site. It is quite possible that in 2nd century CE itself caves were arranged in such manner that the access to main caitya, which might be the public monument, was open for all; while access to other cave was restricted to the followers of Nikaya-s. It has been observed in cave 3 that there are two square pits in front of 6th pillars on either side. That is probably to demarcate the line between sacred and profane. It is seen in all sacred structures where such demarcations are part of the tradition.

The access of laity in the caitya must be restricted up to certain part. We do not know exactly when this has happened. It might have happened in the 5th century CE when images were added in front of Stupa as an object of worship. This suggests that when the image became the central object of worship, there were more restrictions on the access for the laity. It was true for access to the other caves as well. Most of the caves at Kanheri must have remained inaccessible for laity except few exceptions.

There are sculptural panels associated with the cultic developments at the site in 5th and 6th century CE. Those must be the donations by those 'exceptional' donors, who had access to these caves. It is also a noteworthy feature of this period that most of the donations are given by the monks themselves. Either they have gathered the wealth or diverted the funds of their followers towards monastery to give donations. These sculptural panels are the part of another type of ritual.

This new tradition of giving a donation of sculptural panels or paintings can be seen at Ajanta for the first time in western Indian Buddhist rock-cut caves. As mentioned above, it is said in the 3rd canto of Saddharmapuṇḍarīka Sūtra that given the donation of an image of the god is a way to gain spiritual merit. This must be the part of some ritual in which such sculptural panels are given in donation to gain spiritual merit. This also might have helped monastery in 5th-6th century CE to raise funds. (Pandit, 2002: 391-393) These images can be seen in most of the caves occupied by Bhadrāyaniyas and Aparasēlias in the early period with only one exception of cave 56. Sarvastivāda caves give us the evidence of plaster remains but not of sculptural panels with some exceptions as mentioned above. Can it be interpreted as a core and peripheral religious centre! As suggested earlier Bhadrāyaniyas merged in Sarvastivāda. Their caves might have occupied by Sarvastivāda monks. Though this is so, their centre for activity must have remained their own caves. All core rituals probably were performed of the Nikaya in their own set of caves as indicated by caves with 'L' shape hall while all the cult-related rituals were performed in other caves.

In other words, there were three types of caves, one which was accessible for the laity to perform popular rituals on occasions. The second type of caves had restricted accesses to perform cultic rituals of various cults of Buddha, Bodhisattva, and Tara. The third type of caves must have occupied by senior monks who have contributed to the philosophical development of Buddhism through the development of Nikayas. It is believed that Ācārya Acala, Ācārya Dinnāga and Ācārya Atish Dīpāṃkara lived at the site. (Pandit, 2015 B) These caves must be Nikaya specific and might have included some esoteric practices.

Over a period of time, the sectarian caves also have adopted certain esoteric practices, which isolate them. This is one of the reasons why Parsee visitors in 11th century CE could engrave their names in stupa fallen in the courtyard of cave 90 when the monastery was still functioning.

Cave 90 gives us interesting evidence in this regard. There is a panel of 'Sarvaṃdada Avalōkitēśvara' with 10 narrative panels. Unlike other panels of Sarvaṃdada, he is attended by a female deity one in either side. There are two Bodhisattvas, Vajrapāṇi and Maitrēya, shown seated above. The genital organs of female deities are carved with a deep cylindrical hole.[89]This cannot be without any propose. They must have played some role in ritual, maybe some esoteric ritual performed in the cave on a specific occasion.

Bibliography:

Bhalerao Manjiri, 2007, Buddhist Caves at Nasik— An Analytical Study, Unpublished Doctoral Thesis submitted to DCPGRI, Pune.

Bird J., 1841, Opening of the Topes at the Caves of Kanheri, Near Bombay, and the Relics found in them, Journal of Asiatic Society of Bengal, Vol. X, New Series, Calcutta.

Brancaccio Pia,2011, The Buddhist Caves at Aurangabad: Transformations in Art and Religion, BRILL, Leiden.

Burgess J, 1994 (Reprint), Report on the Buddhist Cave Temples and Their Inscriptions, being part of the result of the fourth, fifth and sixth Session's operations of the Archaeological Survey of Western India, 1876-77, 1877-78, 1878-79, Supplementary to the Volume "Cave Temples of India", Archaeological Survey of India, Delhi.

Cohen R.S., 1995, Setting the Three Jewels: The Complex Culture of Buddhism at The Ajanta Caves, Unpublished Doctoral Thesis submitted to University of Michigan, Michigan.

Dhavalikar M. K., 1984, Late Hinayāna Caves of Western India, DCPGRI, Pune.

Dīgghanikāya, Dhammagiri Pali Granthamala, Vipashyana Vishodhan Vinyas, Igatpuri, 1998.

Dutta N., 1978, Buddhist Sects in India, Motilal Banarsidass Publishers Private Ltd., Delhi.

Dutta N. (Ed), 1984 (Second Edition), Gilgit Manuscripts Vol. I, Shri Satguru Publication, Delhi.

Fergusson J. and J. Burgess, 1880, Cave Temple of India, W. H. Allen, London.

Gokhale S., 1991, Kanheri Inscriptions, DCPGRI, Pune.

Indraji B., 1929, Antiquities of Sopara, JBBRAS Vol. 15, Asiatic Society of Mumbai, Mumbai.

Leese M., 1983, The Traikūṭaka Dynasty and Kanheri's Second Phase of Cave Excavation, Unpublished Doctoral Thesis Submitted to University of Michigan, Michigan.

Malandra G, 1993, Unfolding A Mandala: The Buddhist Cave Temples at Ellora, SUNY Press, Albany

Mirashi V. V., 1977, Inscriptions of Shilaharas, CII VOl. VI, ASI, Delhi.

Pandit S. A., 2002, Kanheri: A Study in Its Sustain Patronage, Buddhism in Global Perspective Vol II., Ed. K. Sankarnarayan, Ravindra Pant, Ichijo Ogawa, Somaiya Publication, Mumbai.

Pandit S. A. 2002A, Tara Sculptures from Kanheri, Journal of Anantacharya Indological Research Institute, Vol. IV 2001-2002, Anantacharya Indological Research Institute, Mumbai.

Pandit S. A., 2005, Late Hinayāna Buddhism and the Translation to Mahāyāna: A Study of the Early Buddhist Sangha and the Buddha Figures at Kanheri, Eastern Buddhist, Eastern Buddhist Society, Otani.

Pandit S. A., 2005, Religious Development of

---

[89] In the process of conservation ASI has filled these holes. Those can be seen in all old photographs. See AIIS photo achieves or Huntington photo achieves for details.

Buddhism as Understood through the Art of Kanheri, Unpublished Ph.D. Thesis submitted to the University of Mumbai.

Pandit S. A., 2009, Bodhisattva Images at Kanheri, Journal of Asiatic Society of Mumbai Vol 82 for 2008, Mumbai

Pandit S. A., 2010, Re-Identification of the Monastic Site in 'Mohalach'a' Described by Xuanzang, India on the Silk Route, Ed. Kamal Sheel, Lalji 'Shravak', Charles Willemen, Buddhist World Press, Delhi.

Pandit S. A., 2013, Where Esoteric Buddhism Flourished, Maharashtra Unlimited (Vol II, April June 2013), MTDC, Government of Maharashtra, Mumbai.

Pandit S. A., 2015, Study of Architecture in the Light of Buddhist Nikayas: Kanheri a Case Study, A Bouquet of Indian Heritage Research and Management: Dr. Agam Prasad Felicitation, Agam Kala Prakashan, Delhi.

Pandit S. A., 2015 A, Ekādaśamukha Avalōkitēśvara from Kanheri, Cultural Contours of History and Archaeology, in honour of Snehasiri Prof. P. Chenna Reddy, Vol VII, Buddhism, and Other Religions, Ed. K. Krishna Naik, E. Śiva Nagi Reddy, B. R. Publishing Corporation, Delhi.

Pandit S. A., 2015 B, Kanheri, Three Monks and their Legends, Indian Culture and Art: Continuity and Change: Shri R.C. Tripathi Felicitation Volume, Ed: Prashant Srivastava, Swati Publications, Delhi.

Sankalia H D, "A Unique Wooden Idol of Buddhist Goddess Tara from Kanheri Hills, Jr. of Asiatic, Bombay, Dr. Bhagwanlal Indraji Felicitation Volume, (1986), pp. 56-59.

Vaidya P. L., 1960, Saddharmapundarikasutra, The Mithila Institute of Post Graduate Studies and Research in Sanskrit Learning, Darbhanga.

From Caves to Forts: Transformation witnessed at Daulatabad

Tejas Garge, Director of Archaeology & Museums, Government of Maharashtra

Abstract

The rock-cut monuments of Western India occupy a significant place in Indian history of art and architecture. While in the rest of India the tradition of rock-cut architecture appears sporadically in space and time, it displays a vigorous and continuous activity in Western India for a period of nearly 1500 years, starting sometime in the centuries immediately preceding the Christian era and continuing almost up to the 13th century A.D. In terms of sheer number of rock-cut monuments, this region surpasses the rest of India taken together. The obvious reason for this is the existence of the trap rock or basalt of the Sahyadri hills in Maharashtra, which is suitable for carving, and it's almost vertical cliffs are ideal for chiselling out cave temples.

The monuments in this area are also rich in variety, ranging from cisterns, halls and dwelling units to beautiful temples. This mastery over rock cutting was further reflected in excavations of defences at Daulatabad fort, again a unique example of fort architecture wherein entire experience of 1200 seems to have been utilized. Daulatabad Fort is an impressive monument, dominating the surrounding landscape. Built on a 200-meter-high conical hill, Daulatabad was one of the most powerful forts of the medieval Deccan. The defence system consists of two moats and three encircling fortification walls with lofty gates and bastions at regular intervals. The fort was enlarged and structures were added subsequently as the fort passed on from one dynasty to another. Today the Daulatabad Fort, besides the moat and fortification wall consists of several structures, wells, residential building, mosques, Chand Minar, Aam Khas building (Hall of Public Audience), Royal Hammam, Chini Mahal, Rang Mahal, Baradari, water cisterns, Andheri (the Dark Passage) and 10 unfinished rock-cut caves.

The present paper focuses on the rock-cut moat and dark passage, features which are unique to Daulatabad Fort. The moat is very deep and wide and was excavated out of the living rock and the only entrance to citadel is through a devious tunnel. The long ascending tunnel rises rapidly and tortuously by a flight of steps, which are uneven in width and height, difficult for climbs in the absence of light.

Introduction

The rock-cut monuments of Western India occupy a significant place in Indian history of art and architecture. While in the rest of India the tradition of rock-cut architecture appears sporadically in space and time, it displays a vigorous and continuous activity in Western India for a period of nearly 1500 years, starting sometime in the centuries immediately preceding the Christian era and continuing almost up to the 13th century CE. In terms of the sheer number of rock-cut monuments, this region surpasses the rest of India taken together. Some of them have about 10 to 15 excavations; there are also centres like Kanheri and Junnar which encompass more than a hundred caves each. The monuments in this area are also rich in variety, ranging from cisterns, halls and dwelling units to beautiful temples and belonging to all the major religious faiths- the Buddhism, Hinduism, and Jainism.

These caves not only provide residence to the wondering ascetics during the rainy season (*Vassāvāsa*) but also promote the cause of their faith. They also attracted experts in the field of trade-commerce-agriculture medicine etc. These monastic establishments also served as education centres.

The trap rock or basalt of the Sahyadri hills in Maharashtra is suitable for carving, and it's almost vertical cliffs are ideal for chiselling out cave temples. It is evident that the work was probably executed by carpenters (*vaḍhaki*) in the initial phase as the influence of wooden architecture is clearly visible in the early rock-cut caves; a lot of wooden attachment is to be found in the early caves and the amount of wood-work. As they progressed, the amount of woodwork decreases. The vigorous efforts put forward by artisans in western India are seen in the form of these rock-cut cave temples. The Sahyādri hills also provided ideal locations for construction of fortifications for protection in the later period. Many of the hills selected for excavation of rock-cut caves or construction of a temple encompassed fortification walls of a later date. The sacred spaces of the historical period turned into military garrisons used for defensive purpose. Though forts were often 'constructed' with rubble and well-chiselled stone masonry set in lime or mud mortar, the art of creating 'excavated' features was not forgotten. Rock cut features are often noticed on forts in the form of moats, water cisterns, scarps, gates, steps, etc. The present paper is focused on the rock-cut architecture witnessed at the fort of Daulatabad as it remains a solitary example of extensive application of this technique for defence.

The technique of Rock cutting

As mentioned earlier intention of the designers was to create rectangular or square spaces for dwelling purpose and apsidal caves to accommodate *stupa* at the other end of the cave. Study of a few unfinished caves is vital for understanding the technique of rock-cut excavation.

Cave 29 in Ajanta group of caves is an unfinished *caitya gṛha* (22.8 X 12.84 m) in its first stage of excavation dated to the first half of 6th century CE, and located at the highest level, between Caves 20 and 21.The excavators had finished beam over the façade and work of clearance of rock in front of the arch of *caitya* window was in progress visible by existing chunks of rocks and thin rock walls which were to be removed as excavations would progress. A semi-circular barrel was dug in order to obtain oblong roof of the *caitya* hall. This it is clear that the *caitya gṛha-s* were excavated from top to bottom. Sometimes the height of the façade would exceed up to 40 m. The interiors and the exteriors of this type of cave were probably simultaneously dug (Fig. 1).

Cave 24 is an incomplete monastery (29.3 X 29.3 m) and the second largest excavation at Ajanta dated to the first half of 6th-century CE. On plan, it consists of an open courtyard and veranda flanked by double cell pillared hall with unfinished cell and sanctum sanctorum. The straight marks on the walls of the chamber were the result of hard strokes of a pickaxe or long iron rod, as a result, concave walls were excavated in the hard rock. These concave walls were further straightened with oblique chisel marks created by a pointed chisel. Further, a chisel with a flat tip was used to create a flat surface. Ornamentation of such flat surface could be taken up by decorative

Fig. 1: Unfinished Caityagṛha, Cave 29, Ajanta Caves

Fig.2: Unfinished Vihāra, Cave 24, Ajanta Caves

motifs, sculptures, panels or painted surface. Thus, straight and oblique marks on walls indicate technique as well tools used for excavation. It is most likely that a particular area was excavated by an individual by leaving thin walls in between which were eventually to be removed to create a complete rectangular cavity. The façade and pillars in the veranda of this cave are finished. Thus, this unfinished cave remains important for understanding the technique of cave excavation (Fig. 2).

Such chisel marks were also noticed during clearing the loose rock surface right above the Cave 5 in 2010. After removing loose debris, the hard surface behind it appeared as an unfinished rock-cut cell. This was clear with prominently notable chisel marks, overhanging rock mass and side and back walls carved out of the rock. This excavation appears as two separate cells, but with close observation, it is clear that it was an attempt of carving a facade which is almost 11 m in width. Further, this width is divided into two unfinished chambers due to the presence of a thick rock-cut wall (Fig. 3).

The straight marks on the walls of the chamber were the result of hard strokes of a pickaxe or long iron rod; as a result, concave walls were excavated in the hard rock. These concave walls were further straightened with oblique chisel marks. This was the initial stage of excavation of facade of the cave. This type of cutting technique is already noted at Cave 24 at Ajanta (Fig. 4).

This was probably an attempt of excavation of a *caitya gṛha* as joint top width of the newly discovered cells is 11.3 m which almost corresponds to the width of the facade of Cave 10 and 26 at Ajanta. The height rock mass about 40 m is also good enough to accommodate a *caitya gṛha*. The work was abandoned due to bad quality of rock. The existing surface of the roof of these cells shows that rock is not very compact and homogenous to sustain for a longer duration. For the same reason excavations in this area were abandoned. Thus, it is clear that large scale excavations in rock were taken up by using most primitive tools and implements in iron to create such magnificent rock-cut temples. With the decline in Buddhism and preference given for 'construction' of temples under Yadava patronage, the art of excavating caves was less preferred. However, this mastery over rock cutting was further reflected in excavations of defences at

Daulatabad fort, again a unique example of fort architecture wherein entire experience of 1200 years of rock-cutting seems to have been utilized.

Fortifications and Landscape

Fortifications in Indian Subcontinent are dated back to the 3rd millennium BCE from Harappan sites. These were essentially perimeter walls defining and defending human habitations. The construction material was mud or burnt bricks, stone masonry set with mud mortar and protected with mud plaster. Settlements were close to river banks on flat terrain. These were perfect rectangles, squares or parallelograms. A semi-circular citadel was also attempted in rectangular lower town as seen in Banawali. An outer fortification enclosed other components in the city like a citadel, middle and lower town.Some times they were placed by each other (Kalibangan, Mohenjodaro) some in some cases in concentric fashion like Dholavira. These were often constructions and only the site of Dholavira has revealed evidence of rock-cut reservoirs surrounding the city. (Fig. 5)

In historical period building material was mud walls as noted at Adam, mud and burnt bricks, e.g. Ahhichatra and stone as noted at Rajgir. The outer shape of the fortifications was essentially dependent on terrain and organic growth of the settlement. Systematic and well laid out settlements were also seen at Shisupalgarh and Taxila. These were again essentially fortifications to habitation areas. (Fig. 6)

In medieval India, a separate category of military garrison evolved apart from fortifications to habitations. Many of the settlements including Daulatabad fort continued as fortified habitats and many of them especially hill forts evolved as military bases devoid of civilians. Evidence of fortified ports and sea forts was also other common phenomena witnessed during this period. Evidence of such fortifications is seen from Bahamani period onwards in the Deccan. The existence of such examples is often credited to the geographical settings for the purpose of defensive warfare. As observed by Jadunath Sarkar (1920: 5)

> This country unlike Gangetic plain, could not be conquered and annexed by one cavalry dash or one year's campaigning, for here natives had a chance of making a long struggle against the superior number.

Fig. 3: Unfinished attempt of cave excavation, Ajanta Caves

Fig. 4: Close up of unfinished wall showing chisel marks, Ajanta Caves

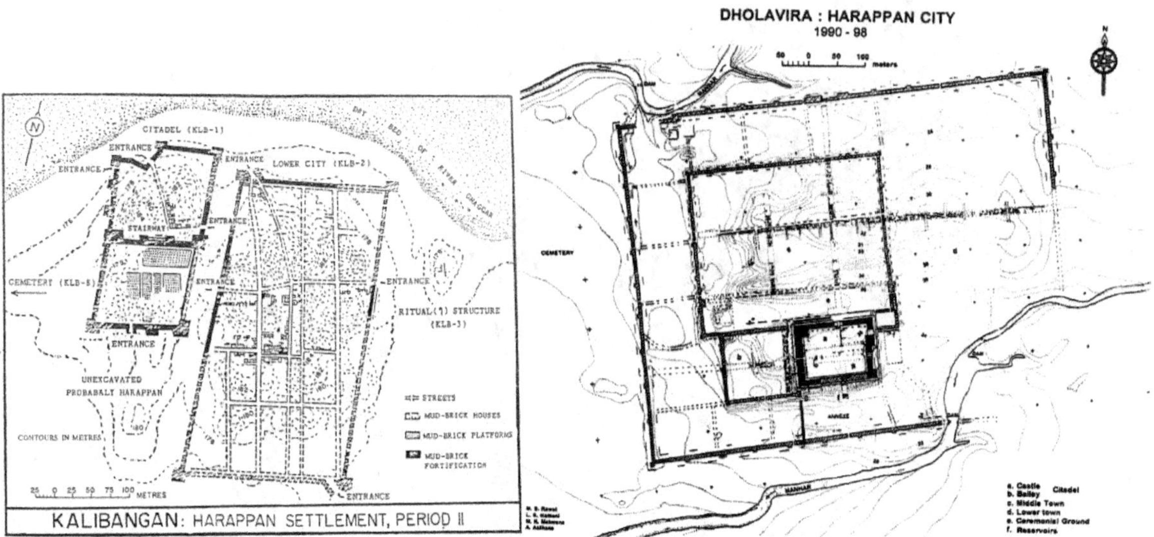

Fig. 5: Layout of the Protohistoric forts in the Indian Subcontinent

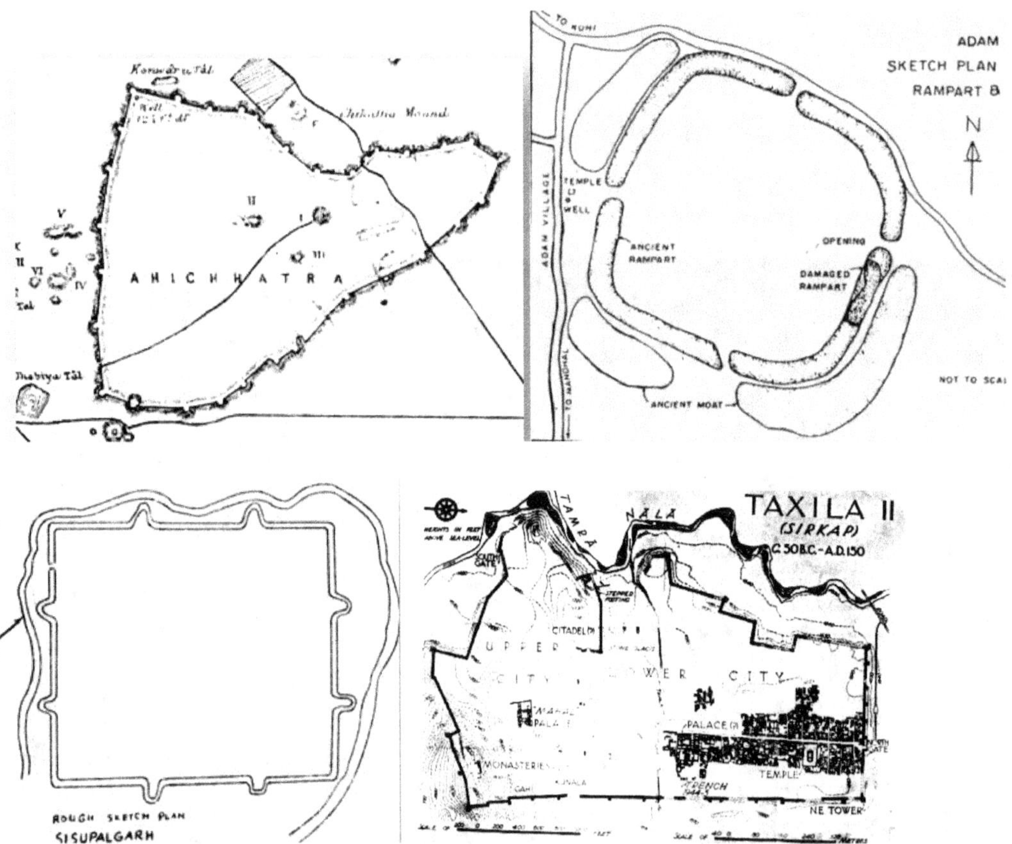

Fig. 6: Layout of the fortifications in the historical period in the Indian Subcontinent

The medieval fortifications occur on plain, hills and sometimes it was a combination of hill and land fort, e.g. Daulatabad Fort. This era was also marked with the invention of gunpowder and firearms, so the height of the fortifications was raised, bastions, battlements and entry points were designed in a more complex fashion. Most common material was random rubble and chiselled stone masonry set in mud and lime mortar. Many of the land forts especially in north India were constructed in burnt bricks. Many forts in the Deccan are noted with continuity of rock-cut features in a limited way. At many places digging a moat in the rock was also stone quarry supplying material for the construction

Fig. 7: Rock cut moat and rock base for fortifications, Diu, Gujarat

of the fort. Some of the forts constructed during the Maratha period have such features, for example, rock-cut gateways are noticed on many such forts such as Ramshej, Harihargad has narrow steps entering into a tunnel-like gateway. The rock base on which the fortifications of Diu were erected were excavated in order to create a rock-cut moat. However, the fort of Daulatabad surpasses all other forts in the application of rock-cut architecture in terms of scale and ingenuity. (Fig. 7)

Daulatabad Fort: A Historical Perspective

Daulatabad Fort is an impressive monument, dominating the surrounding landscape when driving on the road from Aurangabad to Ellora. The fort rises dramatically from the plain and has as its citadel a volcanic hill, which has been sculpted to give a sheer drop into an encircling, moat which has itself been cut into the bedrock with a vertical outer side. Outside of this inner core, there is an outer zone encircled by substantial defences with strongly defended gateways. The route to the citadel is through a darkened passage (*andheri*) through which one has to pass before reaching the citadel, carrying burning charcoal sticks. Medieval defenders were able to attack intruders from concealed vantage points, and there are also traps that precipitated the unwary intruders into the moat. Within the outer

zone, there are buildings for officials, the royal baths and sundry other buildings. Below the level of the moat, there are a few cave temples of a similar style to those at Ellora. The lower town, also within the outer zone, contains an extensive settlement with further temples, houses, and workshops. Beyond the outer zone, there is a further defensive wall that encircles farmland and the village.

Daulatabad Fort is situated on an isolated hilltop about 600 feet high and on the rocky slopes of the hills (Fig. 8). The small stream locally known as river Manpuri River drains the area, bounded on the north and east by the Balaghat range of Sahyadri Hills. The fort looks down the plains on the south and west. Daulatabad was founded by the Yadavas of Deogiri (The Hill of Gods) in 11th-century CE. under king *Bhillama V*, who led victorious campaigns against the Hoysalas, Paramaras and Cālukyas of Kalyāṇa. Subsequently, Yadava rulers retained their capital at Deogiri until CE 1296 when Ala-ud-din Khilji defeated Rāmacandradēva, son of Krishna and held sway over it by forcibly reducing Rāmacandradēva as his vassal. Later, Malik Kafur led his armies in CE 1306-07 and 1312 against the recalcitrant Rāmacandradēva and his son Śankaradēva successively, subdued them and killed the latter. Malik Kafur placed Harapāladēva on the throne who later declared his independence.

Fig. 8: Conical hill of Daulatabad Fort, Aurangabad

Qutb-ud-din Mubarak Shah Khilji made a successful campaign against Deogiri and annexed the same to the Delhi Sultanate. *Muhammad-bin-Tughluq*, who succeeded the Khiljis at Delhi renamed Deogiri as Daulatabad ("Abode of Wealth") and got the capital shifted from Delhi to Daulatabad in CE 1328. But for various reasons he re-transferred his capital back to Delhi.

By a quick succession of political events, the area was wrestled from the Imperial authority and the Bahmani rulers under *Hasan Gangu* extended his control over Daulatabad as well. By 1499 the Nizam Shahi of Ahmednagar not only captured but also made Daulatabad as their capital in CE 1607.The subsequent period witnessed a series of wars between the Deccan Sultans and the Mughals under Akbar and Shah Jahan. In 1633 CE Daulatabad was finally captured after a prolonged siege of four months. It was during this time *Aurangzeb* was placed as viceroy of Deccan who led his campaigns against Bijapur and Golconda from Daulatabad. For a short period, Daulatabad was under the control of the *Marathas* before the *Nizams* of Hyderabad took control of it in 1724 CE.

Built on a 200-meter-high conical hill, Daulatabad was one of the most powerful forts of the medieval Deccan. The defence system consists of two moats and three encircling fortification walls with lofty gates and bastions at regular intervals. The entire fort complex together with all the fortification walls consists of an area measuring approximately 94.83 hectares. The fort was enlarged and structures were added subsequently as the fort passed on from one hand to the other and from one dynasty to another. Today the Daulatabad Fort, besides the moat and fortification wall consists of structures like stepped wells (*baolis*), *kacheri* (court) building, *Bharat Mata* Temple (temple dedicated to Mother India), *Hathi* (Elephant) tank, *Chand Minar*, *Aam Khas* building (Hall of Public Audience), Royal *Hammam*, *Chini Mahal*, *Rang Mahal*, *Baradari* on the hilltop, water cisterns, rock-cut structure and *Andheri* (the Dark Passage).The 10 unfinished rock-cut caves formed to the south of Rang Mahal belong to the Yadava period. The vestiges unearthed from time to time in the fort complex revealed the existence of a multi-cultural religious activity at Daulatabad. These consist of various sculptures of gods and goddesses of Brāhmaṇical pantheon, the Jaina *Tīrthaṃkara-s*, architectural members of secular and non-secular character, canons, utensils of copper, etc. The excavations carried out within the fort complex between 2003 and 2007 have laid bare the lower city complex consisting of main lanes and by-lanes bordered by remnants of various structures of different dimensions.

Daulatabad Fort is one among the impressive and large forts of medieval India. In general terms, it can be divisible into the Outer and the Inner Fort. The citadel of the fort is about 300 feet high, built on a solid rock mass, and stands as an important landmark in its surroundings. Among the remarkable features of the fort are a long moat cut into the bedrock, the precipitous escarpment, the intriguing devices, for example, the spiral passageway at the inner entrance, with dark tunnels and false entry points leading the enemies to fatal destination. All intriguing device points carved out of solid mother rock are quite impressive. Other main buildings of interest are Chand Minar, Chini palace and the Nizam Shahi Palaces. The plan of the fort and its architecture, both rock-cut, and structural, combined with the selection of site and novel features of defines place the monument in an exclusive category of rock-cut forts and deserves to be declared as a World Heritage Site.

Ambar Kot

The exterior most wall surrounding the fort is popularly known as Ambar Kot. It is believed that Malik Ambar, the Abyssinian Commander of Nizam Shah of Ahmednagar constructed it to protect from the onslaughts of Mughals. This fortification wall, enclosing an irregular oval area is about 14 km long. The outermost wall of the fort consists of 45 bastions built massively with their connecting curtain wall and nine principal gates with flanking bastions and towers. The walls have been built with stone and mortar locked up with a good breadth of rammed earth between the outer and inner casings. The height of the wall varies from 9 to 12 meters and has battlements with circular towers at the angles. The bastions at irregular intervals are generally semi-circular or octagonal in shape. Wall walks are a regular feature and are constructed from bastion to bastions, over gates and this is protected by high battlements. The town wall is extremely strong, being built of huge blocks of stones. The buildings in the Ambar Kot area that have withstood the ravages of time are Hammam and a couple of mosques.

Mahakot

The next unit of defence inside Ambar Kot is Mahakot. The defence management in Mahakot at every step creates obstacles for the enemy making it impossible for him to enter. The Mahakot defences were made complicated by the construction of four distinct lines of enclosure walls with innumerable silently brooding bastions and ramparts which would have to be scrambled before the main entrance could be reached. The fortification walls were either built or added at different periods by Yadavas, Khiljis, Tughlaqs, Bahamanis and the Nizamshahis. The outer wall of the fort is 5 km in circumference consists of 54 small and big bastions

of single, double and triple storied. The average height of this wall is between 6 to 9 m and 2 to 3 m in thickness. These walls, however, end on reaching the moat on the north and south side of the fortress. The interior fortification wall is followed by a succession of walls and gateways and courtyards. The inner defensive wall was probably rebuilt during the Tughlaq period encircling the expanded town. At the inner side, there are strong chambers that serve both as guardrooms as well as stores for grain and ammunition. The thick timber gates with iron studs and long spiked nails protect the entrances, which have beautifully carved designs. Every single space between the outermost and innermost gates is covered by gunfire from all sides. The guns were well entrenched and protected by battlements, made the encroacher completely defenceless. Guardrooms in the courtyard display canons belonging to different periods and dynasties. The area consists of noteworthy monuments like the Hathi Tank, Bharat Mata Mandir, Chand Minar and ruins of an extensive palace built by Mughal rulers.

Kalakot

The Kalakot is situated immediately at the foot of the hill. It encompasses a rectangular area and encompasses within itself a huge palace complex built by the Ahmednagar rulers. Different kinds of techniques were used keeping in view the need for defence. The peculiarity of this complex is the provision of deep rock cut moat, strong thick fortifications having bastions, zigzag gateways, wide wall walked with battlements and the strategic position of gun-turrets. On the western side lies the deep rock-cut moat that encircles the conical hill while the rest of the three sides are protected by a double line of fortification fronted with a broad dry moat and a glacis. The entire walls and bastions provide the best example of military engineering skills. There are at least 5-6 zigzag gateways within a short distance with recesses for storage of ammunition making access to this area quite difficult. The gateways are so powerful that all the strength and military strategy fails to break open the gates. On the curtain walls of Daulatabad, there is a wide walkway, which runs all around from bastion to bastion. The walkways are 1 to 1.50 m wide and served as a sound defence strategy to shoot arrows through crenels between the merlons, through the loopholes and also machicolations. Gun-turrets strategically located at important places are large and great in height with provision for mounting big guns which cover not only the Mahakot but also

Fig. 9: Rock-cut moat, Daulatabad Fort

Ambar Kot and the area much beyond. (Fig. 9)

Moat

The Moat is very deep and wide and was excavated out of the living rock. It is so steep that it is almost impossible to cross it not only for human beings but also for the reptiles. The moat was also inaccessible through wading because of aquatic animals and the cross wall within the ditch, which works as a barricade for a swimmer. A very plain plateau surrounds the moat, so it is impossible for the enemy to hide and reach the base of the fort without being noticed. Originally the moat was crossed by a drawbridge, which was taken up at night. Later in 1874, a masonry bridge was constructed during Nizam of Hyderabad on the orders of Sir Salar Jung. This bridge was the only entrance to the main fort. The height of water in the moat was under control and in time of the siege, the portion of the moat included the bridge could be flooded and to render the bridge impassable. The present iron bridge is newly constructed in 1952 for the convenience of tourists. (Fig. 10)

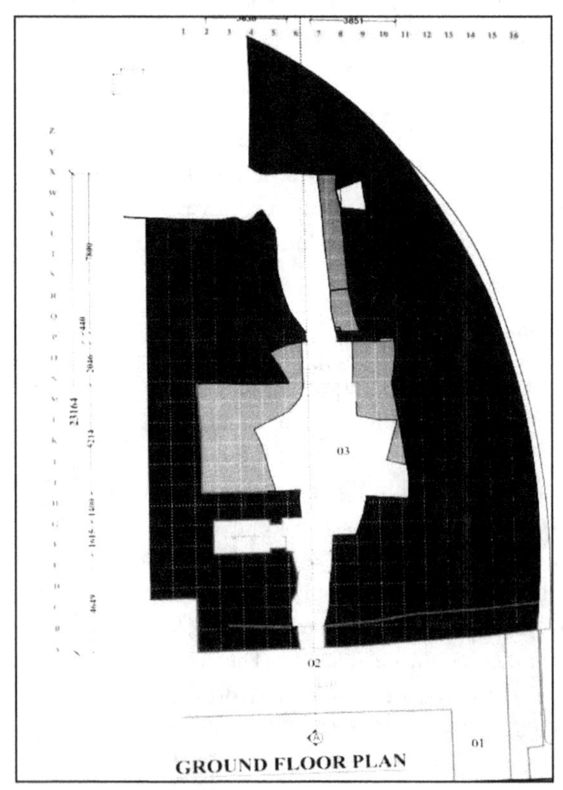

Fig. 10: Rock-cut dark passage (Andheri), Daulatabad Fort

Dark Passage (Andheri)

The only entrance to citadel is through a devious tunnel, which in times of siege was rendered impassable. This sub-terrain passage is a long ascending tunnel rises rapidly and tortuously by a flight of steps, which are uneven in width and height, difficult for climbs in the absence of light. The labyrinth arrangements and the darkness allow the enemy army to kill themselves. A long tunnel containing numerous chambers cut out of the solid rock was used in the olden times as guardrooms and storehouses. The turns and twists open out on a rough window, now covered with grills, originally was a trap set for enemy intruders, which ended in the ditch. The tunnel was impassable when the great obstacles come in the form of darkness, inlaid iron spins, barrier of smokes and splash of hot oil and water from above, it was a trap set for enemy intruders. This tunnel is the only access to the top, that is, the citadel which is totally inaccessible (Fig. 11).

This passage is provided with a lofty courtyard open to the sky and on one side the wall has been carved so as to give it the appearance of a temple of the Yadava period. While rest of the rock-cut walls have small rock-cut chambers and hideouts on uneven levels probably meant for soldiers defending the opening of the passage. The entry door is adorned with the pilasters, diamond-shaped flowers and mouldings on the outside typical to the Yadava idiom. The doorframe is similar to structural temples of the Yadava period however here applied as an opening to the tunnel. After entrance a wide rectangular space is provided having massive rock-cut pillars. Some of the brackets have the typical cobra-hoods common to that style. A small door opposite the main entrance opens on a dark passage. Steps are cut in the rock so as to form a rough and ready staircase to go up, but these are of uneven width and height, and the passage has to be tackled with the help of artificial light. This sub-terrain passage turns and twists, opens out on a rough window, next comes a landing or stage which leads to another and smaller passage. At a place midway between the two there are holes, now covered with grills, eventually opened out into the ditch (Fig. 12).

According to Dr. Mate (1989: 214):

…pillared hall is very similar in appearance to the *mandapas* of temples. There again the complete absence of figure-sculpture on the pillars, beams, and the ceiling, the traditional places for carving figures, is noteworthy.

There are no figure-sculptures on the frame. There is an overdoor, the band above the lintel proper. In early temples, the Yadava temples included, the overdoor had a number of niches or *dēvakulikas* that housed images of various deities. In the present case, there are *dēvakulikas* or miniature replicas of temples, but there are no images in them. Their place is taken by diamond-shaped lozenges.

The pillared hall is very similar in appearance to the *mandapas* of temples. There again the complete absence of figure-sculpture on the pillars, beams, and the ceiling, the traditional places for carving figures, is noteworthy. This absence unmistakably points to a post-Yadava date. The significance of this fact for the chronology of the evolution of Daulatabad is immense. Since the caves could be placed on stylistic grounds to the 12th-13th centuries or the Yadava period, the scarp and its associated ditch become a post-Yadava or Bahmani creation.

Clearance of Moat by ASI in 2004-05

The Archaeological Survey of India carried out clearance work of rock-cut moat before entering the dark passage (*Andheri*) during 2004-05. This was carried out under the supervision of Dr. S. K. Mitra, then the Superintending Archaeologist of the Aurangabad Circle. The moat was filled with debris consisting of random rubble of stone, silt, sand, bones of animals mostly monkeys, etc. A structure constructed with well-chiselled stone masonry is reported right over the rock-cut bed of the moat. "It appears like small shrine having a small flight of steps dedicated probably immediately after completion of the moat (Mitra:2012). "Few architectural members of a structural temple are also reported from this clearance work. (Fig. 13, 14 and 15)

Summary

Absence of inscription raises serious doubts about moat and tunnel being excavated during the Islamic period. On stylistic grounds, the rock-cut tunnel can be ascribed to Yadava period. Report of the shrine (?) built right above the rock-cut surface of moat also indicate its pre -Islamic origin. The original rock-cut

moat was

Fig. 11: Aerial view of the courtyard in front of the dark tunnel, Daulatabad Fort (Photo Courtesy: Prasad Pawar)

Fig. 12: Entrance of the rock-cut dark tunnel, Daulatabad Fort

Fig. 13 and 14: General views of clearance work of moat, Daulatabad Fort (Courtesy- Archaeological Survey of India)

Fig. 15: Structure (shrine) reported in debris clearance work of moat (Courtesy- Archaeological Survey of India)

reworked with construction activity at scraps on either side. Rock cut architecture continued in post Rāṣṭrakūṭa period commonly seen in the form of religious cave architecture. Rock cut moat and tunnel at Daulatabad was a bold attempt to utilize expertise on rock cutting acquired over about 1400 years of experience. It was for the first time that rock cut activity was being utilized for purposes other than the religious on a large scale.

Yadavas of Deogiri were in war with Kakatiya's of Warangal from south and Khiljis from North. Deogiri initially flourishing religious town was

modified according to imperial needs even sacrificing access to a cave on the rock scrap in order to excavate rock-cut moat. Absence of figures/sculptures in *Andheri* may not be due to its authorship by the Islamic rulers but due to a fact that the sole purpose of the excavation was different. Excavators had created feature related to defence works which practically had nothing to do with religious architecture. In the Dark Passage provision of a barrier of smokes was one of the most ingenious and effective defence strategies in this tunnel. A somewhat similar device described by Polybius was adopted during the siege of Ambracia in 190 BCE to expel the Romans from the mine they had driven towards the city. Sulphur was burnt over a grating fixed to the opening on the top to create smoke, which was sucked into the tunnel below. Enemy soldiers desperate to escape the toxic fumes invariably headed for the fresh air tunnel, which had only three or four steps and then tumbled down into the deep moat. This passage is not found anywhere else on any of the forts of medieval India making this fort unique in the history of architecture. Its outer wall is surrounded by a moat and glacis in much the same manner as medieval fortress of Europe. Its basic design and character are Hindu as its originators are the Yadavas who laid its foundation. The smooth and deep excavation around the base of the fort relates to earlier period as it is in the tradition of the skilled labourer who has scooped out a whole temple at Ellora from a sloping hill, only a few kilometres away. The trenching technique which isolated the great Kailāśa Temple of Ellora from rest of the rock mass, similarly entire hillock is isolated from the surrounding land mass by excavating deep rock cut moat.

Daulatabad fort represents an imaginative plan which was never attempted before and the finest specimen of Military engineering. The Dark Passage (*andheri*) is certainly a creation of an intelligent human mind, who has thought in several possibilities of attempts of ways to enter the fort and a type of architecture that can restrict the intenders from entering the citadel.

Daulatabad fort also represents the unique remain of rock-cut architecture of the Yadavas of Dēvagiri. The rock-cut caves at Daulatabad are dateable to the 11th and 12th centuries and can be placed contemporary of the Jaina caves at Ellora. These caves, among other extant remains of the Yadava phase at Daulatabad, showcases the architectural and artistic development in this region during the 11th and 12th centuries CE. The andheri (dark passage) hewn into the solid rock of the main hill is a masterpiece and one of its kind in India, if not in the world. The andheri enabled the occupants of the fort to defend with utmost confidence as it could not be captured through a direct attack. The next line of defence is a huge rock-cut moat surrounding the entire hill which housed the royal household during the initial years of occupation. A draw bridge could have served as the only entrance into the main fort

and event of the moat is scaled, the invaders face the biggest challenge i.e. the andheri. Hence putting together, the rock-cut moat and andheri they serve a unique defence system and represent the ingenuity in deserving such an impenetrable defence mechanism. The rock-cut architecture and art in South Asia are unique in the history of world architecture. The rock-cut architecture in India, emerged during the rule of the Imperial Mauryas in 3rd century BCE reached to its zenith in western India under Sātavāhanas, Vakatakas, Cālukya, and Rāṣṭrakūṭas further experienced a new dimension in form of the rock-cut fort of Deogiri fort (Daulatabad) under the Yadavas.

References

Kamalapur J.N.; 1961. *The Deccan Forts.* Bombay: Popular Book Depot. Pp. 17, 101 & 106-110.

Maharashtra State Gazetteers (Government of Maharashtra)—AURANGABAD District (1977 revised edition). Bombay: Government of Maharashtra Gazetteers Department. Pp 964-969.

Mate, M.S. and T.V. Pathy (Ed); 1992. *Daulatabad— A Report on the Archaeological Investigation.* Pune: Deccan College & Aurangabad: Marathwada University.

Mitra S.K.; 2013. *Daulatabad Fort: History, Archaeology, and Conservation.* Lecture delivered during Structural Camp of Institute of Archaeology, Aurangabad.

Naravane, M. S.; 1995. *Forts of Maharashtra.* Delhi: APH Publishing Corporation. P. 236.

Qureshi, Dulari; 2004. *Fort of Daulatabad.* New Delhi: Bharatiya Kala Prakashan.

Sarkar, Jadunath; 1920. Śivaji and His Times, London: Longmans, Green & Co.

Ritti, Shrinivas; 1973. *TheSeunas (The Yadavas of Dēvagiri).* Dharwar: Karnatak University.

Toy, Sidney; 1957. *The Strongholds of India.* London: William Heinemann Ltd.Pp.33-39.

Verma, Onkar Prasad; 1970. *TheYadavas and their Times.*, Nagpur: Vidarbha Saṃśōdhan Maṇḍaḷ.

Valedictory Address

The "*Ajantacarita*": The Legacy and Future of Walter Spink

Geri Malandra, Malandra Consulting LLC, Durango

Introduction

It has been my great honour and privilege to reflect on Dr. Walter Spink's legacy and future as reflected in the stimulating papers presented during the course of this unique and important seminar. So, it is my pleasure to begin with a few words of thanks.

First, I must express my admiration and gratitude to Dr. Rajan Welukar, Vice Chancellor of the University of Mumbai, for his genuine support of the seminar and of the Centre for Archaeology. Dr. Welukar described his vision for the Centre's success—exhibiting a scope and vibrancy that will attract South Asian and international students, scholars and community members from diverse fields. By this measure, the seminar has well embodied the Centre's vision, scope, and success!

To Dr. Arvind Jamkhedkar, I owe deep thanks for his mentorship, leadership as a scholar and administrator—and for remembering and inviting me to this singular event. It has been a very great honour and personally moving to participate in the 2012 and the 2015 seminars on Maharashtra's great cave temples of Ellora and Ajanta. More personally, as a New Yorker originally, Mumbai has always felt like my second home; Dr. Jamkhedkar's warmth and friendship make to seem even more so. In his opening remarks, he grounded our discussions in the respect and understanding due to Maharashtra's great local tradition of artistic expertise in rock-cutting.

To the INSTUCEN Trustees, my admiration and respect for your vision and support which have illuminated this seminar.

To the Centre for Extra-Mural Studies leaders, Ms. Mugdha Karnik and Dr. Kurush Dalal, only you two know how often I sent questions and requests in advance of the seminar. I hope you both know how grateful I am for your kind and personal attention—not just to me, but for every detail that has gone into making this seminar such a success. And, in her opening remarks, Ms. Karnik established the ecumenical, tolerant, broad-visioned tone for the seminar.

To the many University of Mumbai professors, staff, and others who contributed such great efforts on behalf of this gathering.

To each the learned speakers, our eminent senior scholars, and the younger generation, whose work is so inspiring and will definitely sustain the legacy of Dr. Spink into the future. In my view, you have well demonstrated the "vibrancy" that Dr. Welukar called for as a measure of success for the Centre!

To the attentive audience—of students, scholars, community members—whose support, energy, good questions, and discussion made the seminar come alive during our sessions and in the informal conversations over meals and tea breaks.

Finally, to my guru, my friend, our great honouree, dear Walter Spink, for his six decades of relentless, creative, thought-provoking, joyful scholarship and teaching. Through his "*Ajantacarita*," he has inspired all of us to "look, look, look," "work, work, work," and "think, think, think." Through his writing, his seminars, and occasions like this seminar, Dr. Spink has entranced the world and helped us all question, understand, and appreciate Maharashtra's magnificent, unduplicated rock-cut caves.

*****

For my own remarks, I would like to address two perspectives on the development and future of the "*Ajantacarita*":

I will reflect briefly on one aspect of the meaning of Ajanta, Ellora, and the cave temples generally— within the context of Maharashtrian sectarian traditions.

Then, as a conclusion to the seminar, I will draw together the key connecting themes from the presentations that could carry our work forward through the coming century of Ajanta and cave studies.

*****

The place of Ajanta, and the rock-cut caves generally, within the context of Maharashtrian sectarian traditions

The *Ajantacarita* impact. Dr. Spink—despite or, perhaps, thanks to his critics—has made Ajanta central to our vision and our experience of South Asian art, history, and culture. Hariśēna and Varāhadēva may have the credit for creating the site. But, Dr. Spink's labours are the true *Ajantacarita.* Without his work, our understanding of Ajanta and the rock-cut caves more broadly would be far dimmer. With the publication in the *New York Review of Books* of a review article about his multi-volume *magnum opus*, we might even say he has gained "rock-star status" among art historians![90]

He has been patient and persistent, if not outright relentless, in developing and refining his story. He asserts that the debate and disagreements keep him going. Yet, his sense of urgency together with the unique richness of Ajanta draw us all to continue to wonder and to learn more. I would go so far as to state that Professor Spink's *Ajantacarita* has in its own way put the cave temples of Maharashtra on the world map as no other site or type of study could.

Dr. Spink first drew our attention to key themes in the "talking points" he sent in advance of the seminar. He distilled, in three brief pages, the essence not just of his "short chronology" argument. Beyond this, he demonstrated evidence and raised questions about Hariśēna's position as the "greatest of all" Indian emperors and he made the case to re-label this phase of history as "post-Vākāṭaka" rather than "post-Gupta. Crucial elements of his

methodological practices were also clear: using traditional sources like Daṇḍin's *Daśakumāracarita* blended with epigraphic evidence to tease out the personal and specific detail that brings history to life; and his appreciation for the role of craftsmen and technological innovation that carried forward into succeeding generations— "the sons and grandsons (and grandnephews) of Ajanta's earliest workers."

It may be frustrating that not everyone has accepted the *Ajantacarita* "short chronology;" or that the achievements of the Vākāṭakas were not even mentioned in classic histories like Romila Thapar's.[91]

We face preconceptions that are very difficult to shift:

Text vs. material evidence: First, I'll note the privilege given to written texts over all other sorts of evidence. This is typical of most historians and historians of religion, as contrasted with those of us trained in archaeology, art history, or other disciplines that focus on tangible objects.

Richard Cohen, himself a Spink student and scholar of South Asian Buddhist literature, characterized this attitude well in discussing (in order to counter) the seeming contradiction and prevailing belief that Buddhism is "a priori antisocial—a discursive, not a social construction." From that point of view, and I quote here,

"That which is properly Buddhist is universal, never local; it is preserved in texts, not archaeological sites (except insofar as they reproduce textual paradigms); it is realized in mental cultivation not bodily gesture."[92] [my

---

[90] William Dalrymple, "The Greatest Ancient Picture Gallery," *The New York Review of Books*, Oct. 23, 2014, http://www.nybooks.com/articles/archives/2014/oct/23/greatest-ancient-picture-gallery/?pagination=false&printpage=true.

[91] A lesser slight, but one underscoring this point, occurs in R. M. Davidson's social history of the tantric movement. He retells the political and military history as linked with and influencing social and religious developments in the Deccan, and discusses the Rāṣṭrakūṭas at length, but does not even acknowledge their patronage of the temples of Ellora, citing examples form elsewhere in medieval India of royal patronage of new divinities in new temple complexes. He emphasizes the new, medieval "political and military ideology of the universal conqueror…evident in the use, appropriation, and dissemination of culture through the agency of the royal courts… [and] also the rise of elaborate temple building and the development of regional schools of art." See R M. Davidson, *Indian Esoteric Buddhism: A Social History of the Tantric Movement*, 2002, pp. 30-57, 89-90).

[92] Richard S. Cohen, "Nāga, Yakṣiṇī, Buddha: Local Deities and Local Buddhism at Ajanta," *History of Religions*, Vol. 37, No. 4 (May, 1998), p. 364. In this article, Cohen takes exception to the claims of scholars like the anthropologist Sherry B.

emphasis]

For those of us who deal with actual, built or excavated structures, that preconception is hard to align with the material evidence we can see with our own eyes. We can, and should, look for evidence, not theory, about both the spiritual and human at our sites.

<u>Ganges-centrism and the importance of "location, location, location."</u>: Secondly, an equally stubborn preconception in our field is what, with respect, I would call the "Ganges-centric" view of Indian history. Dr. Spink has certainly called our attention to this phenomenon, in terms of history's ignorance of the great Hariśēna! At certain periods, Maharashtrian individuals (Śivājī, certainly) and events might penetrate this barrier, but not as a rule!

There is no question that the issue of "location" is paramount in understanding our sites. For example, Cohen explicates the Buddhism of Ajanta as a religion of the place.[93]It may be obvious to us, but well worth re-emphasizing, that

"Our knowledge of Ajanta's Buddhism is tied to gifts of monasteries, the wellsprings of Buddhist culture, society, and civilization. The institutionalization of a Buddhist community at Ajanta through the establishment of a monastic "village" sets this *sangha* in a <u>network of relationships that circulated obligation </u>as a currency in <u>the local socio-political economy</u>." [my emphasis]

The larger point is that we must understand and utilize texts and knowledge of the broader traditions. But we must equally study the local contexts—as our speakers well demonstrated—if we are to completely understand and explain the rock-cut monuments.

<u>Translocality and salience of rock-cut monuments:</u> A balance, if not tension, exists between the ideal

translocality of religious precepts and figures, and the reality that they are observed and worshipped at specific, concrete, real localities.[94]

As Dr. Spink sees matters through Ajanta, my perspective is inevitably coloured by my studies of Ellora. So, I offer one example from Ellora in later times as it may apply more generally to our rock-cut caves.

Unlike Ajanta, the rock-cut Buddhist caves at Ellora neither offer nor directly connect to written hints about patronage or sectarian affiliation. Yet, Ellora was nothing if not cosmopolitan, housing Brāhmaṇical, Buddhist, and Jaina communities. Like Ajanta, Ellora is located near a mountain pass that had military (and probably economic) value. Unlike Ajanta, Ellora's caves were abandoned but not forgotten. History shows that it attracted visitors from distant lands, long after its religious communities and political patronage faded.

Most critical in this context, unlike Ajanta, Ellora did claim a place in the pan-Indian sacred space of more than one religious tradition, within the system of tīrthas and the tradition of pilgrimage, *tathagata*, to them. Ellora was the site of Gṛṣṇeśvara *tīrtha*, one of the twelve pan-Indian *jyōtirliṅgas* (*liṅgas* of light).In the village, a temple resides to this day, just a mile west of the rock-cut temples.[95]As we know, the first reference to Ellora as a *tīrtha* comes much earlier, in the 742 C.E. copper plate inscription of Dantidurga which associates Elāpura with *guheśvaratīrtha*.[96]Later, Elāpura was included in a list added to the *Matsya Purāṇa*.[97]And it is listed as one of the fifty Śākta *pīṭhas* in a 16th- or 17th-century text.[98]

The phenomenon of spatial transposition or regional substitution has often been noted in the context of Indian pilgrimage to sacred sites. The substitution can work in both directions. Thus, it has been said

---

Ortner who, in her study of Sherpa rituals, asserts that "It seems fairly safe to say that orthodox, canonical Buddhism was… a religion of antisocial individualism… There is, then, an a priori logic to the argument that Buddhism, given its premises, will be antagonistic to social life." Quoted in Cohen, Ibid, p. 363 and note 8.

[93]Ibid, p. 365.

[94] Cohen argues that "as a social phenomenon, Buddhism cannot be understood apart from its local manifestations nor solely through its local manifestations." Ibid., p. 369

[95]Geri H. Malandra, *Unfolding a Maṇḍala: The Buddhist Cave Temples at Ellora*, 1993, pp. 11-14 and notes 54, 55, 56.

[96] Ibid, p. 12 and note.63.

[97] In a list of holy places where *śrāddha* should be performed. Ibid. notes 66, 67.

[98] In the *Jñānārvaṇa Tantra*. Ibid. p. 12 and note 68.

"all the tīrthas on earth are… in Kashi";[99] worship at Kashi is equivalent to worshipping at all sacred sites on earth.

Pilgrimage to these places is the ideal. Extending Cohen's arguments about Ajanta, I would propose that Ellora embodies that exact balance or tension between translocal ideal beliefs and local expression and practice.[100]

This issue of translocality presents a noteworthy overlapping of ideal, reality, and location of ascetic practice. Anne Feldhaus quotes a tenth-century Vīraśaiva saint:

"To the utterly at-one with Śiva… his front yard is the true Benaras."[101]

So, on the one hand, every holy place is encompassed by Kashi. On the other hand, with the right practice, any place can be a true Kashi!

Feldhaus points out that Cakradhar, the 13th-century founder of the Mahanubhavas, encouraged his followers to "shun holy places…and to avoid attachment to any place at all;" in other words, "to stay at the foot of a tree at the end of the land."[102]But, he also commanded, "stay in Maharashtra."[103]Subsequently, his followers elaborated on the command, advising: "stay in Maharashtra because every place worth going to is there. Maharashtra is a microcosm of India"[104]Its holy places may be simultaneously local AND universal.

Ellora certainly exemplifies such transformations and translocations, effected by the interaction of geography, politics, and religion. I would argue, further, that its architecture, sculpture, and implicit religious practices referred to that context as a regional *tīrtha*.

Extending this argument, we may infer that the Kailāsa temple (cave 16) implicitly refers to Śiva's abode in the Himalayas; a Mount Kailāsa in Maharashtra. When the Buddhist caves of the previous century were excavated, just following the initial Brāhmaṇical phase at Ellora, we may also infer that a regional transposition was intended. Particularly in the latest Buddhist caves, 11 and 12, the focus is on the Buddha in *bhūmisparśamudrā*, the mudrā symbolizing the event of his enlightenment which took place at Bodhgaya. Small images of Bhūdēvī and Aparājitā at the base of many of these shrine images underscore their meaning.[105]The visual evidence appears explicit: worship at Ellora could be tantamount to worship at Bodhgaya.

At the end of Ellora's history as an active religious centre, its nature as a *tīrtha*—now for Jaina worship—persisted, as Dr. Shah also discussed. On an image of the Tīrthaṃkara Pārśvanātha the dedicatory inscription, dated 1234-35, says of the donor Cakrēśvara:

He made "…many huge images of the lordly Jinas…and converted the Cāraṇādri thereby into a holy *tīrtha*, just as Bharata [made] Mount Kailāśa [a *tīrtha*]."[106]

Here, again and finally, the regional substitution or translocation is explicit: Ellora for Cāraṇādri or Kailāśa or Bodhgaya. This recognition continued beyond the life of the rock-cut caves. The contemporary practice continues to affirm Ellora's place in living systems of pilgrimage, as tourists and pilgrims, alike, travel to the temple and to the caves. Ochre-robed monks worship Buddha images while devout Hindus make offerings to images in the caves and at the temple… continuing the translocations and transpositions that go back at least to the 7th century. And, in this, Ellora exemplifies the magnetic, eclectic, multi-sectarian character of Maharashtra's rock-cut caves that our speakers

---

[99] Diana L. Eck, *Banaras, City of Light*, 1982, p. 283.

[100] This is not just a South Asian phenomenon. In the Christian tradition, too, travel to regional sites "can be regarded as a complex surrogate for the journey to the source and heartland of the faith," where "reduplicative shrines" may imitate major pilgrimage centres. Malandra, p. 11 and note 57.

[101] Anne Feldhaus, "Maharashtra as a Holy Land: A Sectarian Tradition," *Bulletin of the School of Oriental and African Studies*, Vol. 49, No. 3 (1986), p. 533.

[102] Ibid.

[103] Ibid. p. 535

[104] Ibid. p. 546.

[105] Malandra, p. 13 and notes 75, 76, 77.

[106] Ibid. note 79.

highlighted during the seminar.

Legacy and Future of "Ajanta Studies": "2ⁿᵈ Archaeology of Maharashtra International Conference—Rock-Cut Caves of Maharashtra

Turning now to our common themes and future:

Dr. Jamkhedkar observed, in the Concept Note for this conference, that "Professor Spink's work…has been a subject of debate, but it has also simultaneously inspired a number of young scholars to take up afresh work on a number of other individual sites." The presentations at this conference certainly demonstrated that inspiration and give one confidence that the current and future generations of scholars will carry forward the Spink legacy with enthusiasm and fresh perspectives! In his introductory address, Dr. Jamkhedkar further "excavated" the predecessors, sources, and evolution of methodology that culminated in and highlight the uniqueness of the Spinkian approach to Ajanta studies.

Dr. Spink's keynote address demonstrated his grand vision of Ajanta, based on a very close reading of even small, seemingly minor features of the caves, including missing clues like the absence of grime from oil lamps that were not lit in undedicated caves. One of his key insights, that revolutionized Ajanta studies and is perhaps still subject to debate, is that the mixed styles observed at Ajanta were the result of simultaneous, not sequential work. He perceives the hands of "local and city artists' families." From these deductions and so much more, Dr. Spink emphasizes the pre-eminence of Hariśēna and his ministers: Varāhadēva, the "staid, solid bureaucrat," and Upēndragupta, the "local king and lavish donor" to Ajanta. Even after his decades of research and writing about this remarkable 14-year period of intensive work at Ajanta, Dr. Spink observed, "It is staggering what we don't know—there is MORE thinking and working to do!"

And in our *tête-á-tête* Dr. Spink so graciously helped us to understand on a more personal level how he developed his unique, humanistic style of scholarship. We explored the questions: "Who is Walter Spink?" What IS Spink's Ajanta? How can we all best transmit his legacy into the future? We learned about his scientific leanings and predilection for detail; about his advice to "keep looking;" and that if he were to do more, he would work on Ajanta's paintings.

Throughout these discussions and in the learned papers presented, important themes emerged as chapters in a new *Ajantacarita*, ranging from the megalithic antecedents to cave architecture to Maharashtra's distinctive and historic hill forts. Across these seemingly diverse topics, our seminar scholars highlighted the crucial importance of:

- Chronologies
- Cross-region relationships
- Characteristics of early and later monuments, from the long-standing tradition of rock-cutting in the Deccan to unusual, unique iconographic schemes
- Religious sectarian traditions: Buddhist, Brāhmaṇical, Jaina
- Genres of sculpture and painting
- Patronage, socio-political, and socio-economic contexts beyond the Indian subcontinent.

Across the presentations, among these themes, common methodological threads were woven that will carry the *Ajantacarita* into the future:

Cross-disciplinary depth. Spink, Dr. Jamkhedkar, Professor Sundara, and Dr. Pandit demonstrated how crucial it is to combine deep knowledge and analysis of inscriptions, sectarian texts and traditions, architectural features, evidence of craftsmen's ateliers, sculpture, and painting—scholarship of Maharashtra's rock-cut caves depends on expertise in all of these areas.

Chronological depth. Mane, Dr. Daylen, Dr. Shah, Dr. Jamkhedkar, and Dr. Garge made it clear that to understand the unique, broad, and deep context of the caves, we must go back into Megalithic times, look forward into medieval times, and extend our point of view beyond Maharashtra.

Questioning chronologies: Dr. Welankar, Dr. Dhavalikar, and Dr. Bhalerao demonstrated that, based on the expertise of multiple disciplines and points of view, we must have a willingness to question commonly accepted, linear chronologies. As Dr. Dhavalikar pointed out, even the distinction between Hinayāna and Mahāyāna caves is not linear at some sites.

Expanding the ancient: Dr. Ganvir showed us how important it is to continually explore more recently discovered sites; new discoveries of "old" caves continue.

Questioning authorities: Dr. Alone, Mr. Pradhan, Dr.

Manatunga, Dr. Dandekar, and Ms. Haldar exhibited a willingness to question authority and complementarity of sources, standard comparisons, patterns of power, and relative chronologies.

There IS, indeed, so much more to do!

Concluding remarks

Finally, with respect, I must conclude by slightly modifying Cakradhar and his followers' injunctions to stay in Maharashtra. We can be deeply grateful that Walter Spink did choose to "stay in Maharashtra"—so much, if not EVERYTHING, worth going to IS indeed here!

I would like to express my deepest personal gratitude for the chance to witness and participate in this conference.

My admiration, congratulations, and felicitations to the organizers and presenters for bringing to life the importance, beauty, and future of Maharashtra's rock-cut caves.

Clearly, Dr. Spink's legacy and the future of rock-cut cave studies are in good hands!

References

Cohen, Richard S.;1998. "Nāga, Yakṣiṇī, Buddha: Local Deities and Local Buddhism at Ajanta," *History of Religions*, 37(4): 360-400 (p364).

Dalrymple, William;23 October 2014. "The Greatest Ancient Picture Gallery," *The New York Review of Books*, 61(16). Accessed online 26 June 2019: http://www.nybooks.com/articles/archives/2014/oct/23/greatest-ancient-picture-gallery/?pagination=false&printpage=true.

Davidson, R. M.; 2002.Indian *Esoteric Buddhism: A Social History of the Tantric Movement*. New York: Columbia University Press.

Eck, Diana L.; 1982. *Banaras, City of Light*. Princeton: Princeton University Press.

Feldhaus, Anne; 1986. "Maharashtra as a Holy Land: A Sectarian Tradition," *Bulletin of the School of Oriental and African Studies*, 49(3): 532-548.

Malandra, Geri H.; 1993. *Unfolding a Maṇḍala: The Buddhist Cave Temples at Ellora*. Albany: State University of New York Press.

Rees, Gethin;2010."A Hiatus in the Cutting of Buddhist Caves in the Western Deccan," *Ancient Asia* 2:119-134.DOI: http://dx.doi.org/10.5334/aa.10209

INSTUCEN Trust – A Profile

The INSTUCEN Trust (http://instucen.org), ever since its founding in April 2010, has made waves in the field of archaeology education and outreach in Mumbai and beyond. The Trust, helmed by Ms. Mugdha Karnik (former director of the Centre for Extra-Mural Studies, University of Mumbai) is not affiliated to any university, although it has collaborated closely with the University of Mumbai, the Sanjeevan Trust and the Deccan College Post-Graduate and Research Institute, Pune.

INSTUCEN Trust is well known for sponsoring:

1. The ***Annual Explorations in Maharashtra Workshop*** (2014-2019) wherein professional and amateur archaeologists alike have presented their findings (Proceedings available);

2. ***The Annual Archaeology of Maharashtra (International) Conferences*** (2013-2018) where many renowned speakers like Prof. Arvind P. Jamkhedkar (Chairman, ICHR & Chancellor, Deccan College), late Prof. M. K. Dhavalikar, Prof. Walter Spink, Prof. Geri Malandra, Prof. Vasant Shinde (Vice-Chancellor, Deccan College), Dr. Tejas Garge (Director of Archaeology & Museums, Govt. of Maharashtra), Dr. Kurush Dalal, late Dr. Shridhar Andhare, Dr. Abhijit Dandekar, Dr. Pushkar Sohoni and many others have participated and presented papers (Proceedings ofAoM 1,3, 4& 5 in preparation);

3. The annual ***Geology and Archaeology Mega-Exhibition***, single-handedly organised by Dr. Mugdha Karnik, which has been attended by over 20,000 people and widely covered in the press and electronic media;

4. The annual ***Kanheri Site Seminars*** (2014-2019) led by renowned Buddhist studies expert Dr. Suraj Pāṇḍit;

5. Many other workshops in Stone tools, Heritage Walks, Arabic Epigraphy & Calligraphy, Ancient Indian Games, Site Seminars on the Caves of Mumbai and other subjects;

6. ***ArchaeoBroma***, the first-ever conference on the archaeology, history, ethnography and sociology of food organised in May 2018 by Dr. Kurush Dalal;

7. *T*he 2012-2015 ***Excavations at Chandore***, Raigad District, Maharashtra, directed by Dr. Kurush Dalal, several aspects of which have been published in peer-reviewed journals;

8. The 2015 & 2016 seasons of the ***Salsette Explorations Project***, a much-regarded project on explorative urban archaeology, also well-covered in the media;

9. A much-appreciated multi-disciplinary course in ***Forts & Fortifications*** at the Maharashtra Seva Sangh, Mumbai.

10. ***Playing with the Past***, the first ever national conference on ancient and medieval Indian board games which brough scholars, manufacturers and players together

11. ***Glory of September***, nature trails in the Sanjay Gandhi National Park to highlight the biodiversity of the northern Konkan

12. The newly begun ***Archaeological Excavations at Mandad*** in Raigad District, with a view to understanding ancient and medieval marine trade with Rome and the Middle East.

13. Talks by eminent scholars such as Shailendra Bhandare and Renate Syed

14. A unique ***Tree Walk for Women*** at Jijamata Udyan on the occasion of Women's Day 2020

INSTUCEN Trust has also sponsored and otherwise supported many young researchers, who have done exciting work in mapping Gadhegals in Maharashtra and Goa, the ethnoarchaeology of the Bene Israel and exploring and reviving Ancient Indian Games.